D1256936

MULTI-STOREY LIVING

The British Working-Class Experience

MULTI-STOREY LIVING

The British Working-Class Experience

EDITED BY ANTHONY SUTCLIFFE

CROOM HELM LONDON

BARNES & NOBLE BOOKS NEW YORK
(a division of Harper & Row Publishers, Inc.)

First published 1974

© 1974 by Anthony Sutcliffe

Croom Helm
2—10 St. Johns Road, London SW11

ISBN 0 85664 036 0

Published in the USA 1974 by
Harper & Row Publishers Inc.
Barnes & Noble Import Division

ISBN 06-496615-1

Printed in Great Britain by
Biddles of Guildford
Bound by James Burn, Esher

Contents

PLATES

TABLES

FIGURES

APPENDICES

'Les appartements ne sont pas faits pour jouer.'

Guy de Maupassant, *Bel-Ami*

Preface

This book is about an oddity. Currently flats account for only about one dwelling in ten in England and Wales and even this low proportion would not have been reached without an exceptional post-war boom in municipal flat building whose wisdom is now seriously questioned. In 1911 only one dwelling in thirty was a flat in England and Wales and a century before the proportion was almost certainly lower still. This lack of a vernacular flat tradition makes England the clear odd-man-out in the context of European housing patterns. Yet if we are deviants from the norm in this respect, our own minority of flats constitutes a deviant form of housing in a society which is rooted in a tradition of small, separate houses. Throughout most of Britain flats have usually been, and still are, associated with low standards of accommodation and undesirable socio-cultural phenomena. Scotland, it is true, is an exception, but in this as in so many other aspects, Hibernian practice scarcely impinges on British customs and attitudes except insofar as it reinforces them.

Why then a book about the development of a deviant, arguably inferior, dwelling-type? And, with the study of the social history of housing in industrial Britain still in its infancy, is it not premature to devote a whole volume to a single type of accommodation? We would make three responses to such a challenge. First, even as a minority dwelling-type flats have their own intrinsic interest. For some, indeed, they have a compelling fascination, best expressed perhaps by the illustrations in this volume. Part of this fascination stems from the potentially horrific concept of the vertical stacking of families and from the spectacular contributions to the townscape which it can produce. Intriguing, too, is the very minority status of the flat, which confers on it a curious distinction as the gamely-struggling underdog of British housing except when, as the predominant dwelling-type in the more fashionable areas of London, it earns an equally distinct cachet of superiority. Second, an understanding of the development and varying fortunes of the British flat is essential to any appreciation of the tenacity and significance of our predominant small-house tradition. The great flat debate, whose almost uninterrupted course through well over a hundred years of rapid urban growth is one of the themes of this volume, illuminates a wide range of housing and other social questions.

The vision, or nightmare, of an alternative form of housing often effectively concentrated the minds of those who perceived it. Finally, and perhaps most important of all, we need to know more about the development of the flat because, notwithstanding its current minority status, it has tended since the nineteenth century to house a growing proportion of the population. This trend will almost certainly continue, though perhaps more slowly than in the 1960s. Moreover, the low national-average figure disguises extremely high proportions of flats in the central areas of our larger cities and particularly in London. Here, the flat has become the norm.

But why attack this problem in the form of a symposium, inevitably patchy in its coverage? Much of the explanation for this strategy is to be found in the current immature condition of housing history. Like S.D. Chapman, whose symposium *The History of Working-class Housing* (David and Charles, 1971) may fairly be said to have put housing history on the map, we believe that there is still much to be gained from a team approach in which nuances of individual interest and varying techniques are allowed freedom to establish the bounds of a new area of study. However, our concentration on a single type of dwelling produces a unity of theme and a continuity which should permit comfortable end-to-end reading.

Three of the studies here consider certain aspects of the contemporary progress of the flat. As historians, we have no positive guidance to offer for the future. We can dare to hope, however, that our attempts to out-line and explain the long saga of a much-maligned type of dwelling will at least provide some perspective for those who will determine the future role of the flat in these islands. Perhaps, too, we can help those who, with varying degrees of volition, inhabit flats, to understand the pheno-menon which cannot help but have a certain influence on their lives. But if such objectives are too ambitious, we can at least hope that we have shed a little light on an unjustly neglected aspect of housing history.

Detailed acknowledgements of help and advice received have been made by the contributors in their chapters. As editor I am indebted to Mrs Rita Riddle for typing part of the manuscript with unfailing patience and accuracy, and to my wife Moyra for her sustained interest and for putting up with me towards the end. As my companion during the last year in a cottage flat she has played a crucial part in isolating the advantages and disadvantages of flat living.

Sheffield,
July 1973.   Anthony Sutcliffe

Chapter 1 Introduction   *Anthony Sutcliffe*

It is a striking feature of housing history that the essential characteristics of basic dwelling-types change very little over time. This continuity, a product of the virtually unchanging determinants of housing needs and of the apparently universal conservatism of the construction industry, is reflected in the development of the particular house-type which concerns this volume. The characteristics of the flat, both in absolute terms and in relation to other types of dwelling which themselves have changed little, have remained virtually constant in Britain since its first appearance in Scotland some four centuries ago. The constant currency of the word 'flat', during the last two centuries at least, has reflected this continuity. The term originated, in the form of 'flat' or 'flett', in fifteenth-century Scotland where it referred to the interior accommodation of a house. During the eighteenth century, now usually modified to the spelling 'flat', it came to refer to a floor or storey of a house and this sense of the word penetrated into English usage from the beginning of the nineteenth century. The Scots had long referred to apartments or suites of rooms within multi-dwelling buildings as 'houses', but in the early decades of the nineteenth century the English began to extend their use of the word 'flat' to embrace this meaning. This secondary usage of the word found such favour in England and America that by the end of the nineteenth century it had virtually stifled the now ambiguous meaning of 'floor' or 'storey'. In twentieth-century England the word 'flat', now referring exclusively to a type of dwelling rather than to an element in its construction, has gone from strength to strength. Its big Victorian rivals 'tenement' and 'apartment', which referred to working-class and middle-class flats respectively, have all but disappeared from popular usage in England since the 1920s, though 'tenement' is still used by Englishmen in respect of older Scottish working-class flats, while 'apartment' has a currency and significance in the United States very similar to that of 'flat' on this side of the Atlantic.

The linguistic and semantic stability of 'flat' is a boon, for it allows us to define 'flat' in terms which have commanded general assent in England since the early 1800s as *a structurally distinct dwelling whose habitable areas occupy one floor, or part of one floor, in a building*

1

containing two or more floors. In other words, the distinctiveness of
the flat as a dwelling is that an occupying household is accustomed to
another household or households living vertically above it, or below it,
or both. Alternatively, in buildings which are not entirely residential in
use, a household occupying a flat will be aware of accommodation
above it, or below it, or both, being used for non-residential purposes.
It is unfortunate that, for the sake of clarity, this definition excludes
dwellings whose habitable areas occupy *two* floors, or parts of two
floors, in buildings containing three or more floors. This variant, now
usually called a 'maisonette', was extremely rare in England until the
1950s, but it is normally considered to have more in common with the
flat than with the traditional house and we shall not therefore exclude
it from consideration. On the other hand, the definition's exclusion of a
type of accommodation to which the name 'flat' or 'flatlet' has recently
been applied, being a room or rooms inhabited by one family in a
multi-occupied house to which no relevant structural alterations have
been made, is deliberate. The phenomenon of house-sharing has been
with us for a long time; it has certain similarities to flat living and may
have contributed to its genesis, and we shall be referring to it from time
to time, but we shall maintain a clear distinction between this and the
subject of this volume, the *structurally* separate flat.

There can be no doubt that the standard of accommodation offered
by the English flat has always been markedly inferior to the separate
cottage or villa. Its major drawbacks have generally been in the
increased dangers of fire and collapse, from falling objects and to
anyone falling from a window, and the inconveniences of noise, stairs
or lifts, lack of storage space, drying clothes, disposing of refuse,
inclement weather at higher levels, restrictions on hobbies, pets and
other spare-time activities and (in tall blocks) isolation from neighbours. Its compensating advantages are few; it is generally easier to run
than a separate house, it can be warmer, there are usually no stairs to
climb inside the dwelling so that rooms can be more intensively used, it
can sometimes offer attractive views out and certain communal
facilities, and the householder is not normally directly responsible for
external maintenance and the upkeep of the immediate surroundings.
Even some of these meagre virtues need qualification. Part of the flat's
reputation in contemporary Britain as an easy-to-run dwelling stems not
so much from its arrangement on a single floor as from its relatively
small floor area. Its communal facilities and upkeep are often associated
with an unwelcome degree of supervision or, in its absence, with
vandalism. Admittedly, growing experience in flat design and construc-

tion and certain technical innovations since the mid-nineteenth century have allowed some defects to be minimised but they have not eradicated the flat's basic inferiority as a dwelling, which remains compounded in England by construction costs which have always exceeded those of traditional houses with equivalent accommodation.

Although the flat's obvious defects prevent its appealing to the mass of the population, its particular combination of virtues may stimulate a *positive* preference among certain groups. In particular, it may attract childless households in either early or late adulthood. Such people may well appreciate the flat's relative ease of internal and external upkeep; it may also appeal to those who are prosperous enough to maintain two homes. Demand from these sources is currently stimulating the construction of numerous apartments in the United States and Canada and it is not insignificant in Britain. It is, however, difficult to envisage how this demand in any society, however 'advanced', could come to constitute more than a minor pressure on the housing supply mechanism. Moreover, these groups will certainly be influenced by much more than the flat's *internal* comfort and convenience.

So far I have deliberately discussed the pros and cons of flats on the implied premise that a potential occupier chooses between a flat and a house solely on the basis of the standard of accommodation offered. In reality, of course, such simple decisions are very rare indeed. The choice of a dwelling in the open market is normally substantially influenced by its location, both in its relation to place of work and other frequently visited places, and to the type of area in which it stands. This location's attractiveness is normally reflected in the market value of the dwelling's site, which in certain circumstances may be high enough to bring into the reckoning the flat's major virtue — that of allowing more dwellings to be erected on a given area of land than would be possible using villa or cottage types. In the English private sector this factor, in combination with the flat's other virtues, has produced extensive flat-construction only in such attractive middle- and upper-middle-class residential districts as have survived close to the centres of the larger cities, in particular in London. In addition, it is a growing feature of the more desirable suburban areas and of certain seaside resorts, again especially in the south-east. In the public housing sector rather different considerations apply, to which we shall return, but here too the attractiveness of a flat, if it has any, lies in its location rather than in its qualities as accommodation. Generally speaking, the bigger the urban area the more attractive the flat will be, owing to higher land values and transport difficulties. In densely-populated urbanised countries like

England the relative overall shortage of land, perhaps accentuated by official countryside protection measures, may increase the range of locations in which flats find takers. However, it is a matter of simple observation that these factors have not yet produced a general predominance of flats outside inner London and certain parts of the central areas of other major cities. In this respect English urban areas contrast strongly with those in most of continental Europe.

Up to now I have discussed the flat's advantages and drawbacks in the context of England's experience since the nineteenth century. Essentially, however, they can be attributed to flat housing whenever and wherever in the world it has appeared. From its first recorded beginnings in republican Rome, through its revival in early modern Europe, its generalisation as a form of mass housing in the nineteenth century, to its recent apotheosis in the tower block, the flat has always been a rather inferior dwelling with locational compensations. Some of its worst defects, it is true, have been limited since the mid-nineteenth century, thanks in particular to four crucial innovations – high-pressure water supplies, water-borne sewerage, the passenger lift, and the turntable ladder – but these improvements do not appear to have modified substantially the flat's position in the urban housing conjuncture. Thus it is possible to speak of an international, eternal flat. In consequence, the flat's relative rarity in England while it has swept the board over most of the Continent needs some explanation.

I have already suggested that very few urban households would choose to live in a flat if they had the alternative of a house in a suitable location and that before the mid-nineteenth century there was even more to discourage such a choice than there has been since. Thus the accommodation of more than a small minority in flats can result only from population pressure on available residential land within an urban area, which forces some or all of its inhabitants to choose between living at high densities in flats and leaving the urban area altogether. Such pressure may result from socio-economic differentiation within the town's population, which may force certain groups to compete for restricted areas of land while more fortunate groups enjoy a generous allotment of space. This situation may well force a high proportion of a town's population into flats but it cannot produce universal flat-dwelling. Alternatively, the pressure on land may be the product of some external restriction on a growing town's outward extension, whether natural like a ravine or moutain range, or man-made like a defensive wall. This pressure, if accentuated, may well ultimately force the whole of a town's population into flats.

These two types of pressure are to a large degree mutually exclusive. The first type is germane to the city in industrial society, where the rich live on the outskirts and the poor inhabit restricted inner areas where much land is taken up by the institutions which give them employment. In the towns of pre-industrial Europe, however, the rich usually concentrated in the centre and forced many of the poor to the outskirts. As such towns rarely grew large enough to stop the poor walking to their work, this residential arrangement could not alone have produced flat-generating pressure on residential land. However, in contrast to the towns of industrialised Europe, most pre-industrial towns were surrounded by a wall and in certain circumstances this restriction could produce pressure of the second type.

Now although industrial urban growth certainly often produces high inner-area densities. especially in its early stages, there are reasons for supposing that these densities will not *necessarily* produce flat living. The industrial towns of England, Belgium and much of northern France escaped this fate in the nineteenth century, with the small, terraced cottage constituting the typical accommodation of their working people. Possible explanations of this pattern are complex, and I shall return to them in respect of England, so suffice it to say here that walking to work remained relatively easy in the early industrial towns and that when the size of some of them began to create difficulties it was not difficult to apply to internal urban transport those innovations in inter-urban transport without which such huge agglomerations could not have emerged. Moreover, the middle classes of these towns chose for various reasons to reside in certain segments of the periphery, so allowing working-class areas to expand elsewhere. Finally, the change from living in small houses to living in flats required such a radical modification of organisation and attitudes among occupants, builders, investors and administrators that it was generally regarded as a last resort and non-flat solutions to high pressures on land were exploited to the utmost.

Now this argument, if valid, suggests that the origins of the flat cannot be sought in the process of industrial urbanisation alone, and that its multiplication throughout the urban areas of most of Europe during the nineteenth century represents the extension of a pre-existing flat tradition. There is indeed much evidence to show that multi-occupation of large town houses was common in pre-industrial Europe and that purpose-built flats were erected in many of the larger towns. In some cases, such as Paris and Edinburgh, this deliberate construction of flats began as early as the sixteenth century or the late middle ages.

By the eighteenth century the majority even of the middle classes in Paris lived in flats and this high-density pattern was to be found, though in a less spectacular degree, in many other large towns. However, it still has to be explained how this flat tradition came to be extended into the very different circumstances of nineteenth-century urban growth.

To understand this phenomenon it is necessary to go back to its origins. I have already argued that in the pre-industrial town pressure on land sufficient to force people into flats can be caused only by some external restriction on the general outward growth of the built-up area. One does not, of course, have to look far for such a restriction and in pointing to the fortification of most continental towns from the high middle ages until, in many cases, the nineteenth century I am merely following in the footsteps of that great urban scholar, Steen Eiler Rasmussen. Admittedly, early medieval towns were small, their walls often enclosed large areas of open land and small houses predominated. Moreover, the walls were often extended as population grew. But the greater the fortified area, the higher was the cost of extending it and the weaker the overall defensive system became. As the long-term trend of urban population during the fortification period was upwards, there was a natural tendency, especially in the bigger towns, to raise residential densities rather than extend the walls. Defence was not, however, the only influential factor. The towns were fortified from an early stage of their growth because their wealth was coveted and no extra-urban organisation could undertake their defence. Thus their survival required a measure of political independence. This political independence reached its zenith in the Italian city-state, but throughout most of medieval Europe the absence of that strong central government which typifies the nation-state allowed most towns to maintain a political and legal status distinct from the surrounding rural areas which were more easily controlled by lords or princes. Some towns were strong enough to control their rural hinterlands, but they usually preserved the dominant status of those who lived within the walls. Thus the walls were often a legal as well as a military boundary, surrounding exclusive, privileged enclaves. Competition to reside within the walls could be intense and those who failed to gain admittance were often reduced to the status of squatters, living in impoverished settlements outside the gates. Thus wall extensions were not only costly, they also often enfranchised those inferior beings who would not otherwise have been allowed into the town, to the annoyance of established citizens.

This restriction on total area tended to intensify the competition for central locations which was such a marked feature of pre-industrial urban life. Even within the walls, peripheral locations were often inferior. Because the pre-industrial town drew its wealth principally from commercial exchange and/or administrative functions, central locations near to docks, market places or palaces were particularly valuable. Because such activities created little smoke or noise, and did not require the presence of a mass proletariat, the directing classes of such towns could reside in the central areas close to their work. Although poorer people could be forced to live further out, their need to live *somewhere* within the restricted area enclosed by the wall meant that the rich could often achieve the residential space which their wealth could command only by building upwards. The result was the big medieval town house of three or more storeys, or even, on chronicly restricted sites like Edinburgh's, the purpose-built block of flats for rich people. Building high also made the houses of the rich easier to defend against popular riot or attacks by rival families and from the thirteenth century onwards it conformed to developing architectural fashions of Italian origin. Subsequently, shifts in the location of the most desirable central districts, caused by structural changes within the town or building obsolescence, might well lead to the multi-occupation of the older town houses by poorer people. This multi-occupation could eventually be reflected in structural alterations which would convert a mansion into a block of flats.

High building presented a challenge to pre-industrial techniques of domestic construction. Roman *insulae* were notorious for their frequent collapses; in this as in other respects Ancient Rome over-reached itself. Medieval towns which had no convenient access to building-stone developed timber-frame construction for buildings of more than one floor, but stone was always the best guarantee of safety and durability in tall buildings. This put Europe south of the Loire at a considerable advantage, for good building-stone was more readily available there than in the north. True, it was more expensive than timber construction, but its use was thus a further incentive to build high, for if one was going to use stone, one might at least take full advantage of its good structural properties. This southern European tendency towards height was accentuated by a recognition that tall buildings kept the sun out of streets, courtyards and rooms.

Yet above all, it was the over-riding restriction of the walls which pushed towns in most of Europe, north and south, towards high building. At first the multi-occupation of these buildings was probably rare, except insofar as rich households included families of relatives and servants who might be lodged within the same house, and masters had apprentices who lived in, but gradually the division into separate suites of rooms began to occur. I am tempted to select the sixteenth century as the crucial early stage in this development. Some of the bigger cities may well have been approaching it before the Black Death of 1348; Paris, for instance, with over 200,000 inhabitants, was already building high and I suspect that sharing was frequent. But then came a period of stagnation and decline from which most towns did not begin to recover until the later fifteenth century. The sixteenth century, on the other hand, saw sustained urban population growth, particularly in the bigger cities. It was precisely at this time that the tall, timber house became the typical residential building form in the northern towns, as did the heavy, stone house in the south. On the whole, fortifications were not extended in proportion. Growth slowed in the seventeenth century, but the new high-density living pattern was not undermined before a new wave of population growth reinforced it in the eighteenth century. By this time, the division of large, old houses was no longer enough to satisfy the need for small dwellings and purpose-built flat blocks were to be found in many of the bigger towns.

By this time, the eve of industrialisation, most continental towns had thus developed an experience of multi-storey living which went back two or three centuries. This was time enough for the self-perpetuating mechanism, in part social and in part economic, which was to maintain the flat through industrialisation, to establish itself. At first, I have argued, citizens will regard multi-storey housing as a necessary evil, but once it begins to predominate among certain classes or among the whole population, patterns of family and social life will adapt to it. The result is an inertia difficult to upset; flat-dwellers probably know of, and wish for, nothing better and the rich social life outside the home, which high densities frequently stimulate, compensates them for a difficult domestic existence. Rural immigrants will of course be accustomed to a different type of accommodation, but their difficult economic circumstances during their early years of town residence will prevent their generating effective demand for low-density housing, even if the restricting fortifications have been removed. Builders' and investors' habitual conservatism will lead them to erect established housing types even in the very rare situations where the pressure of demand does not force them to do so. This conservatism will be reinforced as long experience of flat building produces building techniques and public regulations which favour flats as against separate houses and make them actually cheaper to construct. It is probable, too, that the housing example of larger cities, and especially of capital cities, will spread to smaller towns via social, financial and legal diffusion processes. This example is especially important in that the middle classes are more likely to be flat-dwellers in the bigger cities than in smaller towns and it may well therefore produce middle-class flats in towns where such accommodation might otherwise have been used only by the poor. Certainly, once the middle classes become confirmed flat-dwellers in any town, there is very little chance of escaping from the 'flat-trap' thus created, even if external restrictions on growth are removed.

So pernicious was this pre-industrial urban flat and multi-occupation tradition that industrially-induced urban population growth did little to undermine it; in many respects it was even accentuated. By the time the walls were removed and the emergence of a European pattern of nation-states which made that removal possible had devalued the cities' privileged status, inflated land values, entrepreneurial short-sightedness and popular apathy virtually precluded low-density suburban developments. With building land in continental Europe universally obtainable in fee simple, the town's dynamic population growth made suburban land a ripe target for speculation. In towns where the existence of a flat tradition ensured that new multi-storey building could easily find tenants, the value of a peripheral building site was determined on the basis of its development with flats. This inflation set a premium on low-density housing which only the more prosperous could afford to pay. Even they, however, took little advantage of this opportunity, either because, as in Paris, they were by now so attached to the social cachet of central residence that they did not wish to move to the suburbs, or because, having done so, their established willingness to live in flats simply produced a further inflation of land values in those peripheral areas favoured by the middle classes. Municipal governments, especially in Germany from the 1870s, tried to intervene by drawing up official extension plans, but these merely encouraged speculation by creating an implicit programme of development for suburban land. It was even suggested by English critics that Berlin's extension plan was actually *designed* by dominant property interests in the Council to produce high land values and flats in the suburbs.

It used to be thought that the mass urban public transport which began to develop around the middle of the century had the power to break down this high-density pattern but in reality it very rarely did so, at least during the greater part of the nineteenth century when most urban transport systems remained in private hands. The owners were loth to extend their transport lines beyond the existing built-up area unless, as frequently in the United States, they were engaged in or associated with land speculation ventures. Consequently even the development in America of the world's most advanced and extensive urban transport systems often did little to counteract the development of extremely high residential densities not only in the inner areas of cities but also in their suburbs. In fact, the unique combination of rapid population growth, unbridled land speculation and teeming central slums of aspiring European immigrants, came surprisingly close to producing a flat tradition in the big eastern cities. A minority got away early, it is true, to low-density suburbs, but less wealthy people who tried to follow their example found themselves competing for land on the inner fringes of a low-density belt which the absence or unsuitability of transport services prevented them from leapfrogging. Now although the outer low-density belt tended to move further from the city centre as the élite demanded even more residential space and modern dwellings, it did not move fast enough in a situation of frenetic population growth to permit those who followed to live at equally low densities. This gradual raising of inner suburban densities is a common feature of industrial towns, but in America it was accentuated by the serious overcrowding and high densities in the central areas where successive waves of foreign immigrants were forced to live during their early years of adaptation and depressed incomes. To such people a suburban flat could offer a considerable improvement in accommodation. That some of the biggest eastern cities were sea or lake ports, and so could expand only in certain directions, did not help matters. In New York some fringe suburban areas were developed with flats from the start, and the Federal Census of 1900 shows a mere 17.5 per cent of the 735,000 households in an enlarged city living in separate, single-family houses. In the boroughs of Manhattan and the Bronx, which had constituted New York City until two years earlier, the proportion was as low as 10.4 per cent.

The tenement block in which so many New Yorkers had come to live was less common elsewhere, but the two-storey, two-flat houses and the 'three-deckers' which endowed flat-living with a modicum of gentility were to be found in most eastern cities. These types, in combination with the sharing of older houses in the city centres, were largely responsible for the proportions of households living in single-family buildings in 1900 being as low as 29.0 per cent in Chicago, 32.2 per cent in Boston and 41.4 per cent in St Louis. The other cities with more than half a million people were much better off; Philadelphia had 84.5 per cent of its households in separate houses and Baltimore, whose two-storey row housing often stimulated comparisons with English towns, 72.6 per cent. On the other hand, a number of smaller towns had extremely high proportions of multi-family buildings, especially those New England centres which had started out as industrial colonies in which employers had put up cheap, 'barracks' housing. Thus the proportion of households living in single-family buildings was 27.1 per cent in Paterson, New Jersey, 25.3 per cent in Worcester, Massachusetts, and a mere 16.6 per cent in Fall River, Massachusetts. At the other end of the scale lay the newer western and mid-western cities, yet even Los Angeles had no more than 83.5 per cent of its households in single-family buildings and San Francisco, another port, had only 58.9 per cent. Admittedly, the trend in most towns in the 1890s, the only decade for which the necessary census figures are available, was towards single-family buildings, but clearly the pressures which had caused such densities to build up could not be eradicated overnight. In fact, flat-building was again to spurt ahead in the 1920s.

The above discussion of the development of flat housing in some of its major strongholds, if valid, goes a long way towards suggesting an explanation of the comparative rarity of flats in English towns. Above all, it suggests that the absence of external restrictions on the physical growth of most English towns from the early sixteenth century onwards was crucial to the non-emergence of a flat tradition in pre-industrial England. The walls of most towns, except in the northern areas still subject to Scottish incursions, began to be removed or ignored as early as the end of the fifteenth century. Thus nearly all were open towns when population growth accelerated in the sixteenth century. What made the walls superfluous was the relative security from foreign attack which sea frontiers provided and a strong, unified royal government which from the end of the fifteenth century hardly ever had difficulty in maintaining civil order. But this strong rule, whose origins dated back to the eleventh century and even earlier, meant that English towns never developed the distinct privileges of their continental counterparts. For instance, unlike many towns on the continent and in Scotland, English towns were usually unable to prevent industry moving to the countryside and their liability to royal taxation was a permanent grievance. Consequently there was less competition to reside within the towns' official boundaries and differences between town and countryside were much less pronounced than on the continent; a forerunner, this, of later suburban traditions.

The towns' diminished attraction may even have limited their populations; apart from London, English towns certainly remained small by continental standards until the eighteenth century. Even in London, relative ease of expansion avoided the need for purpose-built flats, though royal concern here from the later sixteenth century about families sharing houses suggests that the pressures common in the big continental cities were far from unknown. There was indeed a danger that London's rich landed and trading population might control sufficient peripheral land to restrict the expansion of poorer residential areas and living in lodgings in multi-occupied houses had certainly become common among the working classes and probably part of the middle classes, too, by the eighteenth century. But the leasehold tenure system under which so much of suburban London was developed greatly discouraged purpose-built flats. A landlord who sells a site in fee simple (or who, in Scotland, feus it) can have little or no control over its development and by selling to the highest bidder he realises a speculation whose end product may well be high-density housing or flats. Under the leasehold system, however, the ground landlord has an interest in maintaining the value of the site and the buildings on it during the period of the lease. He also has powers to control the building development undertaken by the leaseholder. In London the demand for suburban housing from the rich was so strong from the seventeenth century that landlords decided that their site values could best be maintained by low-density, high-class housing. The builder, for his part, did not have to bear the burden of the capital cost of the land and was usually willing to co-operate with the landlord.

So London's growth took the shape of small, middle-class houses and no flat tradition developed in the capital which could be exported to provincial towns. On the contrary, statute and case law, and local regulations, rarely referred to flats, which further discouraged their development. English law, in contrast to Scotland's, did not permit the separate ownership of individual floors of a house. The post-fire building regulations, though not specifically prohibiting flats, were tailored for individual houses and so tended to discourage the erection of multi-dwelling buildings. The same was true of later London building acts and the building regulations which began to govern provincial towns from the early decades of industrialisation. The poor, it is true, frequently lived in rooms, but as they could not command new housing, this practice was never reflected in new building. On the contrary, the association of multi-dwelling buildings with poverty, poor facilities and structural obsolescence added to the unattractiveness of flats among more prosperous groups.

Thus England proceeded into industrialisation without having developed its own flat tradition. It is the lack of such a tradition which largely explains why industrial urbanisation produced virtually no private flat-building in English towns. Only massive speculation in suburban land could conceivably have produced a different result. Now much speculation certainly occurred, but in many towns the leasehold land system kept it in check and in freehold towns the inertia of centuries was the major contrary force, in that landowners hesitated to put off small-house development because they could not be confident that they could thus create a demand for flats later on. Nor did the sharp cyclical depressions which struck England during the spectacular urban growth of the first half of the nineteenth century encourage such a long-term strategy. So that same conservatism which kept continental builders erecting flats even when they *could* have changed to small houses led their English counterparts to multiply terraces of small houses even when flats might have found takers. Even the totally exceptional restriction of Coventry and Nottingham by jealously guarded common fields until the mid-nineteenth century failed to produce flat-building in either.

Now although the English industrial town avoided the flat, it did not thereby avoid high-density working-class housing. In Liverpool, for instance, as Iain C. Taylor demonstrates in Chapter III, the combination of mass casual employment and restricted growth possibilities produced gross densities as high as 700 persons per acre by the middle of the nineteenth century. That the pressures which created these densities failed to force working people into flats was partly due to the extent of overcrowding which was tolerated both by the poor and the authorities in early Victorian Britain. But overcrowding was only part of the picture; essentially, the flat did not appear because it was not needed. Even without overcrowding, extremely high densities could be achieved in that distinctive product of English industrial urbanisation, the back-to-back house. Perhaps a hypothetical example will illustrate the point most clearly. A block of twenty back-to-back houses, each covering an area thirteen feet square in external measurements, and surrounded on all sides by ten feet of clear open space for access, privies, drying etc. will achieve a density per net residential acre of 630 people, if each house is occupied by five persons. If these back-to-backs are of the three-storey, three-room type so common in Birmingham, Sheffield and other towns, a household of five persons will be well below the overcrowding threshold fixed in the late nineteenth century. So 630 per acre is not really trying! Add an inhabited cellar under each house, overcrowd the whole, and you are into four figures. With houses like these, who needed flats?

This high-density pattern grew up in the central working-class areas of most industrial towns between the late 1700s and the middle of the nineteenth century, when there was little public regulation of buildings or indeed of the environment in general. From the 1840s, however, high death rates and the generally unpleasant character of urban working-class existence were increasingly associated by the middle classes with back-to-back housing and the multi-occupation of older houses which had become the equivalent high-density mode in London and the major towns of pre-industrial England such as Bristol. It was the subsequent discouragement and eventual outlawing of back-to-back housing, and the measures taken to eradicate both it and multi-occupation, which were largely responsible for bringing the purpose-built flat into English towns. Some pressure was relieved as time went on by better and cheaper transport, higher real wages and shorter hours, but decentralisation could never be more than a partial solution. The bigger the town, the less of a solution it was, and consequently the model housing organisations and the local authorities, who normally tried to tackle the problem of housing provision in the areas of worst pressure, built far more flats than separate houses.

It was not, however, until the 1930s that a concerted public effort was made to replace the dense central masses of working-class housing. Until this time hopes could still be entertained that decentralisation might yet be the answer. So even as late as 1911 when, significantly enough, the rise of the purpose-built flat prodded the census authorities into enumerating flats for the first time as distinct from separate houses, it was still very much in a minority. Over England and Wales as a whole structurally distinct flats accounted for 3.4 per cent of the total stock of dwellings, but this bald average conceals the fact that the great majority of flats were to be found in two parts of the country, the London area and Tyneside. The predominance of flats in the latter area was the result of the proliferation during the later nineteenth century of that fascinating phenomenon, the terrace of two-storey 'Tyneside' (or 'Newcastle') flats. In the city of Newcastle itself, 55.67 per cent of dwellings were flats and South Shields scored even higher, with 72.00 per cent. Many smaller towns also had very high proportions of flats and a total of sixteen local authority areas in Durham and twenty-one in Northumberland exceeded the national average. I suspect that the emergence of this type in the Newcastle area is the product of that city's relatively late fortification and certain natural obstacles to its outward expansion, combined perhaps with the proximity of the Scottish example, but this is pure guesswork.

In the London area the flat phenomenon is easier to understand, as the product of massive size which squeezed a lot of people, including the middle classes and rich in some cases, between high land values and inconveniently long journeys to work. Within the LCC area 17.83 per cent of all dwellings were flats; among the boroughs the proportions ranged from 2.31 per cent in Woolwich to 60.80 per cent in Holborn. These figures reflect the numerous purpose-built and converted flats created in the central area by private investors as well as by model housing companies and the London authorities; in the prosperous borough of Kensington, for instance, as many as 17.41 per cent of dwellings were in flats. More interesting still are the high proportions of flats to be found in some outer boroughs and suburban areas. Leyton, for instance, had 12.13 per cent flats and Walthamstow, 11.67 per cent; even Richmond had as many as 8.28 per cent flats. Most of these suburban flats were in two-storey terraces of the 'Newcastle' type, which were a natural development of the sharing of traditional houses by two families which high rents had made very frequent in the London area. In fact, the census evidence suggests that up to 40 per cent of households in early twentieth-century London did not enjoy exclusive occupation of a separate house. Even though the majority of these occupied rooms rather than structurally distinct flats, it is clear that London's sheer size had driven it against the national trend to produce extensive flat living, with the rich taking the lead for the first time in English urban history. Elsewhere, however, the flat still had not become generally necessary by 1911 and even in the biggest provincial towns (outside the north east) flats as a rule accounted for less than 1 per cent of all dwellings. In Liverpool they made up only 1.76 per cent.

After 1921 the census authorities gave up trying to distinguish individual flats. The experiment was not repeated until 1961 and 1966, when it again reflected a wave of flat building. The contrast with 1911 is considerable. In 1966 one dwelling in ten in England and Wales was a flat and flats were to be found in large numbers in all cities and most of the larger towns. Much of the increase since 1911 was due to the multiplication of the local authority flat, yet only half the total of occupied flats enumerated in 1966 were in this category. Over one-third were private rented, most of them unfurnished, and nearly one-tenth were owner-occupied. About two-thirds of the owner-occupied flats were to be found in the south-east region, but the private-rented flats were more evenly distributed, only half of them being located in the south-east region.

Thus the new century of higher living standards, town planning, better public transport and the motor car had by no means reversed the trend towards flat living which is discernible before 1914. Indeed, the trend had almost certainly accelerated. Partly responsible was the fall in average household sizes, which created a demand for the adaptation of the existing housing stock. This demand is reflected in the large number of converted flats enumerated in 1966: 340,360, over one-fifth of the total of flats in England and Wales. In London and the south east, however, the progress of flat living seems to reflect further pressure on land. In 1966 nearly two flats out of three in England and Wales were to be found in the south-east region and 29.5 per cent of dwellings in Greater London were flats. Thus London's size has tended to bring its housing structure closer to the big continental capitals whose predominance of flats is the product of a long-established tradition. But the most spectacular advance, both in terms of aggregate numbers and in country-wide distribution, is to be found in the category of the local authority flat, of which 772,270 were enumerated as occupied in 1966.

We have already seen that flats were the most common type of housing erected to replace publicly-demolished high-density slum housing before 1914. It was not, however, inevitable that they should continue to play this role after the Great War. Growing working-class participation in suburbanisation from the 1880s and the general unpopularity of model and municipal flat dwellings had contributed in the early 1900s to the construction of the first municipal working-class suburban housing. This tendency was accentuated after the war by a spate of town-planned, low-density suburban housing under the early post-war Housing Acts, and for a time it could be hoped that the higher central densities might be dispersed. But the necessary conjuncture was never established. The continuing shortage of low-rent housing, low earnings and unemployment, the relatively high cost of public transport, the slowness of antiquated and stagnant industries to disperse to the suburbs and the strength of working-class slum culture all combined to maintain a strong demand for cheap, central housing. By the 1930s it was considered no longer tolerable that this demand should be met by crumbling, pre-bye-law housing. This was the crunch. Demolition meant either dispersal to the suburbs, where many slum-dwellers had neither the desire nor the ability to live and where middle-class and even working-class suburbanites resented their presence, or rehousing on the spot, which under contemporary building standards could only be in flats.

This was a quandary, but for the first time in English housing history continental experience seemed to indicate a solution. Like Britain, most continental countries had been forced to plunge into public housing after 1918 but, in conformity to their traditions, their suburban developments had mostly been in the form of flats. This effort had given leading architects of the so-called Modern Movement the chance to put into effect those ideas on the social obligations of architecture which they had begun to evolve before 1914. The result was a new type of 'luxury' flat which could appeal to middle-class as well as working-class people. Indeed, its first appearances in England in the 1920s were in the form of middle-class rented blocks which, in contrast to their nineteenth-century predecessors, were not limited to London and the south coast resorts. The advent of this new type of flat, described by Alison Ravetz in Chapter V, removed some of the stigma of the older working-class tenement and made multi-storey living fashionable at precisely the time when suburban sprawl was taking some of the shine off the suburban ideal and reinforcing demands for preservation of the countryside. With many influential architects making extravagant and untested claims for the value of flat housing as a way of life, and everywhere else in the world, including the United States, building them in great numbers, England took the plunge into large-scale flat building which has never since been rescinded.

From this time onwards we enter the realm of contemporary history. Although England is still far from developing a flat tradition in the continental or Scottish sense of the term, many of the self-perpetuating mechanisms observed abroad after the initial acceptance of the flat as a necessary evil have been in operation. Flats have become cheaper to build. Building regulations, together with legal and financial practices, have gradually adapted to them. Flat design, construction and equipment have improved with experience and more people have grown accustomed to living in them. The middle classes have increasingly set an example. More important though, and perhaps more ominous, has been the emergence of artificial restrictions on the outward growth of many towns. Just as effectively as any medieval wall, the definition of green belts has held in our cities and has been associated with a rise in land values and planned densities. So increasingly municipal flats have come to house those who are without a home, in addition to those who have previously lived in slums, and like middle-class flats they have increasingly been sited in the suburbs.

This process has not always been an easy one, reflecting the degree to which flats have been foisted on people owing to what is in many respects an artificial land shortage. In particular, the extraordinary high flat episode, described by E.W. Cooney in Chapter VI, put the flat under a cloud and brought about a period of questioning and reappraisal. But without a much more effective dispersal of population from the big cities and from the south east in particular, the need for a high proportion of flat building cannot be superseded. Thus the latest figures indicate that, despite the virtual demise of the high flat, flats still account for about half the dwellings built by local authorities and in the pressure areas this proportion is considerably higher. Private builders have not adopted the flat to the same extent and flats at present account for no more than one-tenth of dwellings built in the private sector. Here again, however, the pressure areas record much higher proportions.

So this lengthy process, which began in the 1840s, has now secured a firm place for the flat in English urban life, bringing the country, in this respect at least, closer to a Scottish neighbour which, as Roger Smith indicates in Chapter VIII, has been endeavouring since 1918 to escape from its much older high-density trap. What then of the future? The flat will not necessarily go on to represent a still higher proportion of the housing stock; it may be that the post-1950 flat boom has done enough to adjust the housing stock to meet the need for urban homes and the special requirements of non-family groups, especially in the case of municipal flats. But my suspicion is that unless land planning policies are radically altered the proportion of flats will continue to rise, though more slowly than it has over the last twenty years. In any case, higher living standards will probably increase the demand for flats as the proportions of childless and two-home households increase. So the flat is here to stay; we hope that this volume will contribute to an understanding of how so un-English a state of affairs has come to pass in this pleasant land.

Chapter 2 French Flats for the English in Nineteenth-century London

J.N. Tarn

Flats do not seem to be the ideal British concept of home. The working class has been obliged to inhabit them in increasing numbers since about the middle of the last century, but there is no evidence that they enjoyed them then any more than they do today. Sometimes they were conveniently near to sources of work which was, I suspect, their only merit. The rich on the other hand have accepted the concept of flat-life, particularly this century, and the luxury flat is today a recognised part of the urban scene but is by no means the regular habitat of the wealthy and it is often not the only home in the family. It is probably also the only kind of high-rise domestic building which is built entirely to satisfy an existing demand. The middle classes have for long been banished to suburbia with its semi's and detached houses in pocket-handkerchief gardens, because they cannot afford to live anywhere else, although one suspects that they would not choose to live elsewhere if they had more choice. The flat is still not an accepted integral part of British life, as it is in Paris or even in Edinburgh; its history in this country is very much a reflection upon English insularity and conservatism, or, as others might argue, upon our common sense and Freudian urge to be connected with the ground.

Tenements, as working class flats were always called, were introduced by the model housing agencies in the 1840s.[1] They were an emergency measure, even at that time, an attempt to house artisans decently and in some numbers in central London. The need for cheap housing was explicit, but the economics of providing it in the right places were to tax everyone for the rest of the country. Piling up houses as flats and packing the people carefully, like sardines, into the centre of the city seemed to be the only answer, at least until the transport revolution of the 1880s. Then it became possible to think of expanding the city and with the advent of the garden suburb early this century the working man merged his housing ideals with those of the middle class. Before that he had looked upon a tenement in a block of model dwellings as one of the few ways of living near to his work in some degree of decency, in the provinces, and in London, too. As he grew slightly better off, he aspired to a mean ill-built terraced house in the endless bye-law street as an alternative to tenement accommodation in the centre of the city. But neither model dwellings or speculative terraces were attactive places visually and, although the model housing movement did much to show that it was possible to live healthily at high density, they left the working man with a latent desire to move into a house of his own when he could.

To those who were able to make a choice, the house was as much a part of English life as beer; the narrow urban plot, the lease, the party wall, all were essential ingredients of their existence. The English were accustomed to climbing stairs and they had their homes so arranged that, until the eighteenth century at least, it was usual to find the servants living under the same roof – usually literally – and cooking and working in the basement, while the family lived on the three or four floors in between rather like the jam in a sandwich. In this way a large part of the working population was dispersed thinly throughout the residential parts of the central area of a city. This pattern of existence continued at least until the rich were driven out of the centres of towns by industrial development and pollution.

'The actual town residence is a vertical slip of comparatively tall building, and it consists, above the street pavement, of perhaps four or five storeys and a low roof. The Londoner cooks underground, dines on the ground level, receives visitors on the first floor, sleeps on the second floor, lodges his children and guests on the third floor, and his servants in the roof. From the bottom to the top of this house is an open shaft, called the staircase, which is a complete conductor of smell, noise and draught, an intolerable evil to old people, children and invalids.'[2]

This was how the English house appeared to a critical observer as late as 1876 and the same writers point out that a dinner party could be a fatiguing experience:

'First from the street-door to the curb-stone of the pavement a strip of carpet is spread, and over this the guests are conducted, often under an umbrella, to the threshold. Having passed a long narrow passage, they are made to climb two flights of stairs. The ceremony of reception over, they then descend to the street level, only, however, to scale, after dinner, the same two flights of stairs, and ultimately to be conducted down them again to their carriages – this process of climbing having to be renewed before they reach their own bedrooms.'[3]

The élite were, then, rather like a breed of mountain goats and prejudiced into the bargain, sticking rigidly to their routine, obviously in the teeth of common sense. The English argued, of course, that to climb four or five flights of stairs before reaching your own front door was equally debilitating, even though once there you could be entirely on one level. They objected to the French flat because it had 'dark, close, stuffy passages, with kitchen, bedrooms and living rooms, all huddled together, and the majority are reached, only after a fatiguing climb'.[4] The writers of this paper obviously thought that the English were prejudiced, and certainly they displayed conservative attitudes towards urban and domestic change. They disliked, too, the radical new planning which Haussmann had carried out in Paris since 1850, with its grandiose architectonic layout cutting through the old pattern of medieval streets more for political reasons than those of aesthetic design or for domestic comfort. They clung tenaciously to the intimacy of the square and the terrace.[5]

The gulf which exists between the French and English way of life is a historic fact quite unrelated to the ebb and flow of political relationships. It was as great in the last century as it is now and although there was plenty of knowledge of how day-to-day life was conducted across the channel it seems to have been rejected by the English with customary insular and benign incredulity.

'The English man's nose is a highly sensitive organ, and he expects his house to be fresh and pure without keeping the windows and doors perpetually open. He will not reside in a house in which the staircase is guarded by a a man and wife with the chance of an additional incumbrance every ten months and a half. He will not mount more than four flights of stairs — say forty-five steps — at a time, although he will do this without grumbling several times a day. He will not live continuously in any boundary that resembles an hotel. The noise of any instrument of insular music, either of human or mechanical contrivance, which he will tolerate through a party-wall, he strenuously condemns if under his feet or above his head. In fact, to make horizontal dwellings really successful in central London, where tall houses are inevitably necessary, the floors must be as thick as party-walls, and sound-resisting; and both the Parisian door-porter and the London staircase must be superseded, if not altogether abolished.'[6]

To the problem of the party wall, as well as that of the party floor, we shall shortly return. It was not, however, just the juxtaposition of rooms in the 'French Flats' which caused concern, but also the whole ethos of their way of life. Some twenty years earlier than this last comment another journal had also remarked upon the flatted way of life:

> 'A Frenchman cares less for comfort at home than for amusement abroad: he is content to dine even with his wife, and perhaps family also, at a restaurant and his idea of a house scarcely extends beyond a *salon* and *salle à manger*, and, provided they be showily fitted up, he himself puts up with much that an Englishman would think intolerably annoying.'[7]

It is difficult at times to see how the English had become so deeply convinced of the rightness of their way of life. The Scots had adopted — and still do — the pattern of multi-cellular buildings and like the French they did not observe a social barrier between house types; there were tenements for the working man and the middle classes as well as flats or apartments for the rich. Much of the New Town at Edinburgh was developed on this pattern and the result was a social and architectural entity.[8] There were, of course, plenty of tenemented slums in Scotland although that is not the point I want to stress here. The adoption of a basic housing unit had architectural advantages because the larger-scale units of buildings which it permitted enabled a much more cohesive urban character to be achieved which minimised, although it did not do away with, the monotony so typical of the bye-law street. Yet, despite the fact that Nash had created this same scale of development around Regent's Park in London early in the nineteenth century, there is little evidence that Londoners really accepted it. Cubitt's terraces, like so much of Bloomsbury, are linear rather than axial compositions. Cumberland Terrace is unique in its imperial orchestration of architectural elements, while the long, tired, stretches of Bayswater exhaust the scale of the London street and stretch and tax to the limits one's credulity in the efficacy of the single house as an element of the new industrial city. Yet afterwards, in the hey-day of the garden suburb, which was heralded quite early on by Norman Shaw at Bedford Park in 1877, and even in the weary acres of humble speculative housing for the artisan and the middle classes at fashionable low densities this century, the emphasis remains on the house as a family entity, slowly changing in form as the social structure of our society has altered but essentially the same unit, at least conceptually, as it had been during the development of the terrace during the Georgian age.

To say that the English have had any real doubts about the way they lived during the last century would certainly be an overstatement; all the evidence suggests that the ideal was a nation of house-dwellers and that ideal has triumphed. But during the nineteenth century they did have qualms — it would be wrong to call them more than this — which were based on a number of factors which were at that period quite novel. First, there was unparalleled urban expansion and thus eventually the problem of commuting in and out of the larger cities, which was most acute in London because of its size and its traffic congestion. In most provincial towns during the last century distance was no real obstacle for the rich although it most certainly was for the poor, because of their need to live particularly near to their source of employment for economic reasons. The central areas, therefore, tended to become working class ghettos. Secondly the town was dirty because it was heavily industrialised and that was an argument for population dispersal rather than for central area redevelopment in the eyes of those who were able to move home at will.

The new suburbia was clearly monotonous and, except for the villas of the rich, the cheap and endless terraces of the bourgeoisie lacked the elegance previously associated with the residential areas of Bloomsbury and the western and northern parts of central London. Suburbia was also the province of the new unscrupulous speculative builders and the general standard of building declined although the traditional ways of selling land through a system of leases still continued, as did the practice amongst small-scale building tradesmen of constructing a few houses at the same time as a joint financial venture. This was because of the lack of capital investment in building as a whole in all except the rare cases of a firm like Cubitt. The examples of houses which collapsed during construction, because of sharp practices and skimping amongst tradesmen, were frequently reported in *The Builder*, particularly amongst the cheaper house-builders. Suburban housing had a bad name for much of the Victorian period but the public was often so desperately in need of simple accommodation that it had little alternative but to accept whatever was available. There were also occasional sanitary scandals about housing in suburban areas, particularly where the building regulations — such as they were — were not enforceable, or where, for other reasons, the builder had managed to build where adequate drainage was impossible.[9]

For these reasons amongst others, a flat in a large block was seen by some to have real advantages. There appeared to be a possibility of better control over its construction and drainage because it was a more ambitious building venture and, of course, there were precedents for this belief in the success of the exemplary buildings for the working classes in central London. There the complexity of the problem had often necessitated the employment of architects and usually involved respectable builders, resulting in a tighter standard of building and bringing healthier living conditions. So the climate, particularly later in the century, was right for the flat question to be brought up periodically as a possible way of alleviating the keen frustration which was felt over housing conditions, even though the basic idea of high-rise flats remained foreign to English minds.

Flats were introduced first to this country for the artisan in the late 1840s; then the idea of living in a flat in the middle of London attracted the rich, perhaps because they could usually regard it as a second home rather than a sentence to live all the year around in the urban desert. Only later did they attract the middle classes who were one-house families:

> 'Dwellings in flats, however, are no longer built exclusively for the lower classes. They are being adopted by the other extreme of society, and the success of those in Victoria-street has led to the building of others in the aristocratic Grosvenor mansions at Pimlico. Having thus been partially adopted by both extremes of English Society, we hope before long to see them adopted by the middle strata, and when they shall have had experience of their comforts, privacy and convenience, they will wonder that they have themselves been such "flats" as for so many years to dwell in lodgings.'[10]

There is an elementary economic argument here, too; household expenses on cleaning and servants were also cited as good reason for welcoming flat life. A correspondent who signed himself 'Solomon Set-Square' wrote to the *Building News* in 1869 in praise of flats for all classes:

> 'As to Westminster and Pimlico "mansions", let any one who can doubt their superiority to the town dwelling of, say £100 a year, walk into Victoria-street, Westminster, and judge for himself, or better still, listen to the praise of the "oldest inhabitant". They are incomparably superior to the £100 house in everything that makes a building perfect; cheaper to live in, safer to sleep in, more healthy,

more comfortable, and certainly more architectural, both externally and internally . . . To the middle class tenant they are a saving in many respects. A lady who requires three servants to do the work of a five-storey house, will easily "work" a one-storey house with two, or even one, of these "greatest plagues of life"; and, what is of even greater consequence, she can herself, without effort, personally look into all that is going on in her household.'[11]

The suburban house was also reorganised onto basically two or three floors for exactly the same social and economic reasons; it was adaptable and flexible enough to remain a viable house type for a wide section of the community, so the middle classes remained very much against the flat because it involved a more radical change of attitude perhaps associated with status. The rich obviously chose to live in them for convenience and perhaps because they were less conscious of the status conferred by an individual house. What is interesting, however, is that the rich were prepared to live in central London despite the environmental problem. It is clear that in addition to the practical convenience there was a fashionable aspect to flat life — after all it was novel, otherwise why should rich people, according to Solomon Set-Square's assertions, accept homes which were quite as ugly as the ubiquitous tenement blocks of the model housing societies? This means that the 'flat set' were a special group, but their homes did appear ugly to many people and doubtless this was still another factor which militated against the flat in the eyes of the great majority of middle-class people who were so keen to get away from urban areas as the century drew to a close. It is a strange paradox that blocks of flats, whether for poor or rich, were visually depressive because their architects did not know how to handle the physical mass of building which was necessary to create an economically viable project.

The place where the new housing type was born in London is Victoria Street, which was cut through a notorious slum district between 1852 and 1870. The first of the novel blocks of upper-class flats went up in 1853. They were built by a Mr Mackenzie as his 'own speculation, and the idea we believe, originated with him'.[12] *The Builder* contained an illustration of the design for buildings which were to be eighty-two feet high.[13] Each staircase led to two flats on every floor, with a drawing room, dining room, four bedrooms, a kitchen and servants' quarters at the rear and a separate service stair. In fact a very adequate 'French flat'. Gradually thereafter the street came to be associated with upper-class residential development, although for a while it attracted very little attention. Behind Victoria Street working-class flats were built on cleared sites by the Peabody Trustees in their plain semi-classical style and architecturally they are probably to our eyes at the least no less attractive than what remains of the original Victoria Street itself. Peabody built plain, rather dull and basically vernacular blocks. The private developers erected even larger buildings, equally dull but more ornate and eclectic, and as befitted their origins there were occasional French overtones.

If Victoria Street became the focus of attention for the new, slightly eccentric branch of the housing movement, it also suffered the same fate as much of the work of the exemplary housing societies. Flats attracted mild interest but there was no wave of building in the next decade and there seems to have been even less interest on the part of the middle classes than of the rich. A decade after the construction of the earliest aristocratic flats in Victoria Street the whole subject was still being discussed in a very general way, although it is possible to detect some frustration that nothing had come of the earlier experiments. There is here, of course, a direct parallel with the slow progress of the model housing movement itself, although in the 1860s there was much more activity at working-class level.

'Will you allow me, through your paper, to call the attention of builders and owners of house property, to what is considered by many a great want in our metropolis, more especially at the west end? I allude to what are called flats, such as those in Victoria-street, Westminster, and of which many exist in Paris, to the great convenience of many persons who do not wish, or cannot afford, the trouble and expense of a large establishment . . . Now, people who have been long accustomed to the comforts of their own houses, find lodgings a very poor substitute, whereas by taking a flat, they would have all the advantages of their own house, and would certainly not require more than two servants, thus saving very considerably in wages, etc. Victoria-street, Westminster, is not exactly the place one would choose for a dwelling in, but on the outside of the park, in Tyburnia, I believe, flats would be eagerly sought after.'[14]

If such buildings were rare and traditional attachment to the house still a strong enemy of the flat, it is noticeable that occasionally an experimental building was constructed during the 1870s, a decade which, on the whole, was probably the most active period at every level

for the housing movement during the century.

Palatinate Buildings, New Kent Road, quite near the Elephant and Castle, were built in 1875. The blocks were eighty feet high, with shops on the ground floor of the block facing the New Kent Road and the roof was designed as a playground and drying area as in the working-class buildings of the previous twenty years:

> 'Each dwelling is entirely complete within itself, including as regards apartments, convenience for every domestic and social requirement. There are parlours or day rooms, and bedrooms, together with kitchens, completely fitted with modern ranges, and other requisites for general culinary purposes, and the windows of all the dwellings are fitted throughout with Venetian blinds,'[15]

Queen Anne Mansions, perhaps the most famous and horrifying of all nineteenth century apartment blocks, was begun in 1877.[16]

The previous year the Architects' Conference had visited some flats in Stoke Newington built by Matthew Allen.[17] George Godwin, writing in *The Builder* at this time, when interest in the subject was increasing, called his leading article 'Houses in Flats for London'.[18] He noted the usual English prejudice against flats and then touched upon a practical problem which appears to have worried many people: that of fire and the adequate construction of floors which, as he pointed out, are rightly considered as 'party walls', in a horizontal plane, so far as flats are concerned. It is difficult to see exactly why this particular problem kept bothering people when working-class flats had been constructed successfully for many years and forms of fireproofing had been found for them which apparently worked. Mackenzie, in his Victoria Street flats of 1853, had used cast-iron girders and brick arches with a timber ceiling below and a joisted floor above and although this was not a perfectly fireproof method of construction it had none of the hazards of completely exposed metal skeletons in mills and factories. There is no evidence to suggest that flats were in fact a fire hazard at this time and one can only assume that it was yet again a case of prejudice, although perhaps a more understandable one than many of the others. Godwin admits the possible construction problems and the additional costs involved in making the floor incombustible.

He goes on to discuss the positive assets of the system and the factors which advantageously affect cost, starting with the important issue of availability of land and the savings which could result from a greater intensity of land use. The construction of flats of course would also allow more people to live in better residential areas, so there were considerable social as well as economic arguments in their favour. Some people clearly thought of a boom in flat building as a means of stabilising certain residential areas and of practising an embryonic version of modern urban renewal ideas. Then there were the constructional advantages of these major building undertakings. Because of their size there was no alternative but to build well and professionally since the collapse of a block of flats would have resounding consequences, whether it was under construction or actually completed. Unlike a small house built in the suburbs, in an apartment block the tenant would be much more certain of a really well-designed home free of builders' mal-practices. No doubt Godwin was basing his argument here on the similar advantages which had accrued over the years to the working man in his model dwelling, although it should be remembered that these were the work of philanthropic trusts and companies and not of the speculative builders – however responsible – who would have to take the initiative in building the blocks of flats.

Finally there were the potential architectural advantages which could be gained from the construction of fine, impressive ranges of domestic buildings in city streets. There had, of course, been criticism of the appearance of the new buildings in Victoria Street, just as many people thought that the model dwellings were ugly, decribing them all too often as 'barracky' – not without some justification. *The Saturday Review*[19] had had some harsh things to say about the appearance of flats and Godwin was at pains to refute their allegation:

> 'No two sets of apartments (in a block of "flat" houses) should be exactly alike, and the architect should not be allowed to settle where the windows are to go till he has designed the inside of the rooms. Uniformity ought to be a matter of no account, and it should not be deemed indispensable for a room to have four corners, each a right angle . . . But we may venture to say that the British architect, should a demand arise for flats, with his usual disregard as to who is to live in the places he designs, will make them exactly alike.'[20]

A plea such as this for functionalism in the design of flats was, of course, usually ignored and the dull repetitive blocks were to continue despite criticism of this kind. Godwin believed that an architect was necessary – as indeed he should as he was one himself – and that, even at their most banal, architect-designed flats were preferable to speculatively built houses. It is interesting that he also made adverse comment about the tall buildings which were increasingly popular in America; he did not want those in London either.

There were other comments along these lines at this time, mainly in the correspondence columns, which reinforce the main points of the discussion. Descriptions of the French and the Scottish way of life in flats were given to illustrate its novelty and advantage; practical economic points were discussed and so, too, were those of building appearance and repeatedly the point was made that no provision was ever considered for the middle classes in flats.[21]

The growing volume of discussion at this time was no doubt part of the wider interest in housing and public health matters which led to the passing during 1875 of the Cross Act, dealing with slum clearance, and the second great Public Health Act. But while there is a great volume of literature on health and housing issues, because these were relevant to the problems of the working classes, there was hardly any about the housing problems of the remainder of the population and of course there was no real grasp of the wider and more general problem of urban expansion. The only real exception were the group of articulate anti-urbanists centred around William Morris. They supported the utopian idea of breaking down the whole physical mass of the city as an urban organism — a concept that was to gain support at the end of the century with the birth of the garden city movement and the inspired visions of Ebenezer Howard.

If the literature on flats was scanty by comparison with the publications on model dwellings, at least one major paper was given at the Society of Arts in 1876. It was simply called *Model Dwellings for the Rich* and its authors were T. Roger Smith and W.H. White.[22] They were able to refer to only one previous attempt to deal with the subject; this was Arthur Ashpitel and John Whichcord's pamphlet, *Town Dwellings*, published in 1855, which at that time had fallen on stony ground.[23] Perhaps the reason why the times were more propitious in 1876 is contained in the authors' opening remark:

'At the present day when the custom has become all but universal for Londoners to live out of London — to regard town in fact as a place of probation through which men must pass daily before hoping to enjoy their lives elsewhere — it may seem quixotic to suggest a contrary procedure; yet to dwell within reach of the heart of London is almost a necessity for that increasing class whose mental activity is of importance to the community in general.'[24]

London was a very large city by the mid 1870s. The 1881 Census gives a total population of 3,844,000 but it is not only the sheer size of the metropolitan area but its rate of growth which is important. By this time the population of central London had already reached its peak and was to decline continuously until the present day; but the inner ring of suburbs, as Pevsner points out, had been doubling in population about every twenty years since the beginning of the century.[25] After the 1870s the growth eases off, but the pace slackens less quickly in the outer ring, in places like Camberwell, Fulham, Hammersmith, Hampstead and Wandsworth, which taken as a group had increased from 542,000 to 1,093,000 between 1861 and 1881 and then went on to 1,601,000 in 1901. The total population of London in 1881 had increased by nearly one million people, that is by about one-third of its size in 1861. When put into terms like this, it is easier to understand why a whole series of new issues seem to become important in the late 1870s. The journey to work and the problems of transport in a city where it was no longer possible for many to walk to work altered the popular view of life in the central areas. The great fleets of omnibuses were now joined by the new trams which, although still debarred from central London, were cheap and popular and spread their tentacles in just this outer ring of suburbs.[26] The growth of suburban trains, workmen's cheap fares and the development of the central underground railways were other facets of a movement during these years to relieve the pressure on a busy city. They were a direct result of symptoms suggesting that the city then, as now, was in danger of seizing up.

Smith and White shared the commonly-held view that the house as a unit survived because of the leasehold pattern which prevailed in London, so that the increasing height of buildings did not necesarily change the basic housing pattern unit or its method of construction:

'Northumberland Avenue, from Charing-cross to the Embankment, is ninety feet wide, planted with trees and paved with wood. It may be lined with houses eighty or ninety feet high from pavement to cornice; and according to the London system the builders of these new houses will devote their skill and energies to the distribution of the ground and first stories alone, and leave the upper ones to take care of themselves, confident in the fact that in the neighbourhood of Charing-cross sets of rooms are so urgently required and diligently sought, that anything of the kind however primitive will let at an almost fancy price.'[27]

The authors also shared the usual English view of the basic differences between our way of life and that of the French, although they summed it up rather picturesquely:

> 'One important difference, for example, is that Englishmen often pass the day in their dining rooms, and only sleep in their bedrooms: whereas a Frenchman lives in his bedroom and only eats in his dining room.'[28]

This may sound naive or an over-simplification of the facts particularly when one considers how much time the French spend eating and preparing their meals! But it does illustrate yet again the popular middle-class idea that the two ways of life were so different as to be irrelevant to one another; perhaps it also is a fundamental reason for the middle-class rejection of the 'French flat' as a viable way of life.

Smith and White go on, of course, to make their proposal for a block of flats in the inevitable manner of the day. Their insular view of social habits does not extend to architectural and planning matters, so perhaps it is worth quoting their proposal in detail because of the contemporary picture it gives of the problems which a flat should attempt to overcome:

> ' . . . each residence would be divided into three distinct sections, each served by its own corridor. That in the service section would communicate by a special passage with the dining room, and in this passage a small tramway might be laid down for the conveyance of dishes and similar articles. The section containing the living room would comprise a large hall, a dining room, a library, a drawing room and sometimes a gentleman's smoking-room as well as a ladies' boudoir. The sleeping room section would consist of a sufficient number of bed, dressing and bathrooms, with a fireplace in each room. In the service section there would be placed a butler's pantry, a servants' hall, in addition to the kitchen, scullery, and stores, and bed-rooms for the female servants; but all the men-servants would be lodged in separate rooms in the roof. Each section would communicate with the others by means of swing folding-doors, without locks. In all the rooms of the sleeping-section water would be laid on, and a means of exit for it provided . . . We propose to face the external walls, both towards the street and towards the quadrangle with hard impervious substances such as glazed bricks, relieved by majolica ware and a little polished granite – in fact to use externally only

those materials that will "wash" . . . To sum up: a building planned upon the principle of which we have given an outline, a principle which we have worked out upon paper, and which applies equally to a square, an oblong, or a triangular site, combines internal economy and constructional strength — economy in the kitchen and domestic arrangements, extra comforts in the dressing-rooms, and a set of sitting-rooms, not en-suite, but on the same level, and entered from the same corridor. It divides the three sections of a house, so that the foul air generated in each may pass away naturally without rising, as in our actual houses, from one section through the others. All our living-rooms, both of day and night occupation, would face a public street, only the corridors and service-sections being lighted from the back of the house or the courtyard. The tenant need not mount a single stair from one year's end to another. The members of each family would be as privately located as if they inhabited a vertical strip of building, in which the various rooms are connected by the usual staircase ladder; but, instead of climbing, they would walk from room to room. By the horizontal system of residence families desirous of living in the heart of London can be agreeably lodged, and at comparatively reasonable cost. House-rent would rise, but household expenses and household annoyances would diminish. The character of London house-building would be raised. Bad neighbourhoods could thereby, perhaps, be redeemed, and good neighbourhoods undoubtedly guaranteed from deterioration. Such buildings as our Model Dwellings for the Rich would "pay", we are confident, all those concerned in their erection. When the upper classes have set an example by inhabiting them, the insular prejudices against such residences will surely disappear; and the middle classes, who must require a reform in the London system, will soon follow in the steps of their more fortunate brethren.'[29]

This apologia for the flat is important as much for what it omits as for what it actually says. The flat is conceived as a horizontal house with all the articulated parts still segregated; kitchens, living rooms, bedrooms, are still there as separate entities, separated now by a system of corridors. The British way of life is preserved, or at least an attempt is made to preserve it. The building is conceived as a block, probably with a central courtyard which would be more like a light-well than a courtyard, one suspects. The mention of glazed bricks conjures up the frequent London habit of using white glazed bricks to enhance the dim natural light of internal areas. Admittedly only the secondary service rooms look out into the court, as the authors are at pains to point out, and all the main rooms will face the streets. None the less, the building which we can conjure up is still rather 'barracky' and although it will have a modern elevator to bring the tenant to his flat that, one suspects, would in practice merely be a licence to build as high as possible. Much of their argument about what we today would call planning blight and the possibility of arresting decay in selected neighbourhoods by the introduction of flats was doubtless wishful thinking without far wider powers of development control than then existed, but their proposals would at least have brought the same level of professional competence and standard of building as was to be found in working-class model dwellings to a wider section of the public.

The report of the discussion which followed the paper suggests that these ideas had some support — Chadwick, for example, who was not present, sent a letter praising the idea of flats on health grounds — but Professor Robert Kerr, who was himself a man full of ideas for working-class housing which he had expanded in a similar kind of paper at the RIBA in 1866,[30] suggested that the Londoner would not readily give up his house; and this conservative view is clearly the dominant one amongst the audience. The middle classes probably had no one to blame but themselves if nobody risked building flats in an effort to tempt them away from their houses.

White lectured the following year at the RIBA on the same subject, with the title 'Middle-Class Houses in Paris and London'.[31] His point of view remained essentially the same, but there was more emphasis in this paper upon the French way of life and in the discussion which followed it was clear that English architects did not simply look upon housing in a different light; they saw a clear distinction between the London of the late 1870s, with its meagre collection of new streets, and the modern, replanned capital of France. In addition to Victoria Street there were few other streets recently built or in the course of construction. Shaftesbury Avenue, the Victoria Embankment, and Holborn Viaduct were complete; Charing Cross Road was only started in 1887 and Kingsway was not completed until 1905. By comparison Paris had been transformed, with great, tree-lined boulevards laid out by Haussmann and it presented quite different opportunities for the siting of fine blocks of apartments. In some ways the London architects seem to have felt slightly inferior to their French contemporaries and one speaker railed against

'the delusion which had become almost a portion of the Londoner's creed – that health could be secured most certainly by sleeping nightly in what he called the country – in what was in fact, a small, ill-built, ill-ventilated, and ill-drained box, but which he called his "suburban villa", planted upon ill-drained land, and surrounded by remnants of decaying vegetation. In order to pass to and fro between his suburban villa and business, he underwent the toil and anxiety of rushing to a railway station more or less distant from his house or his office, twice daily and in the course of transit probably shut himself up in the foul atmosphere of a smoking carriage.'[32]

The President of the RIBA, concluding the discussion from the chair, rather testily and perhaps rather churlishly summed up White's paper, at the same time displaying the full force of English conservatism: 'Mr. White not only wanted to revolutionalise our houses, but our instructs and habits and modes of life'[33] and clearly that would be unacceptable.

The upper-class flat movement did not produce specialist architectural experts in the same way as the model dwellings movement of the 1840s. Perhaps because the main development came much later in the century and also because building flats became a matter of professional interest to architects, a number of firms were involved. I have only found one reference to a firm which actually gave a paper about their work as flat-builders; this was by F.E. Eales of Charles Eales and Son, at the Architectural Association.[34] The firm's most important works in the field were Oxford and Cambridge Mansions, built in 1882–3, and their extension, known as Hyde Park Mansions.[35]

So much for the theoretical view of housing. What it demonstrates quite clearly is the discrepancy between the ideas about what might be built to overcome many of the contemporary urban problems and the impact it might have, as opposed to what actually was built and its lack of impact upon the face of cities except in certain Edwardian London suburbs. As an instrument of house policy it remained a beautiful dream because clearly the middle classes were on the whole sceptical and upper-class needs were modest.

There were, however, practical problems as well as ideological and conceptual ones. Matthew Allen, in a letter to *The Builder* in 1879, pointed some of them out.[36] His views should be listened to, because he knew what he was talking about, having built nearly all the blocks of flats erected by the Improved Industrial Dwellings Company over the previous seventeen years.[37] He said that land was the main problem; it was difficult to obtain usable plots in suitable places and at the right price for flatted developments, which of course was also the cry of the model agencies. He went on to discuss the problems of building at this sort of scale, rather than the normal housing scale which, as we have already noted, appeared to have been much less daunting for the builder and speculator. Mortgages were notoriously difficult to obtain for flats – indeed Allen says they were almost unobtainable – so it was hard to sell them once they were built and of course there were a host of other problems concerned with the communual facilities if the flats were sold. There is evidence, nevertheless, that there was a demand for flats, particularly the really central ones. Although flats were a better capital investment in the long run for the speculating builder, they also required a much larger initial financial outlay and the risks involved for the typical small builder were obviously greater than he could take. It is clear that the traditional methods of building led to small-scale investment, particularly at the cheaper end of the market, and many English builders were simply not so organised that they could run the risk of building a block of flats, the equivalent of perhaps a whole street of small houses, which would often take several years to complete. Allen himself had tried the experiment, since he could hardly be classed as a small-time builder with his large-scale operation for The Improved Industrial Dwellings Company, which must have secured him a substantial and steady income as well as accruing resources. He had built ten blocks of flats during the last seven years in Manor Road, Stoke Newington, specifically for the middle classes. Each block contained forty-four flats, their size ranging from five to twelve rooms and the basic rent was from £25 to £60 per annum. He gives the impression that they were successful both as an investment and as social entities; but his experience in working-class housing probably ensured that he understood the fundamental planning problems of flats and also all the short-cuts in constructional economy which, without resorting to malpractices, tipped the balance between financial success and bankruptcy. In fact Allen was an expert and as an experienced, reliable builder was a rare person. He was also not an architect and he did not believe in employing one either.

During the 1880s there is considerably more evidence of flat construction, although usually for the upper classes, or else on a miniature scale. Kensington was a favoured area, but it was by no means exclusive. Prince Teck Buildings, Earls Court, a small block of flats, was built in 1881;[38] Oxford and Cambridge Mansions and Hyde Park Mansions have already been mentioned. They tended to be upper-class flats, in pretentious blocks of no aesthetic merit whatsoever, but for a relatively short space of time there appeared to be a possibility that London might become a town of 'French flats'. More were built at this period than it is possible to draw attention to. As the social structure of the country gradually changed and the mid-century gaps between the classes became blurred so the idea of flats spread a little more into middle-class life. The main impetus, however, still came from the rich and a number of quite well-known architects were now involved in this sort of work: for example Bassett Keeling, who built Prince's Mansions, Victoria Street,[39] Ernest George and Peto who produced a very flamboyant French building in Grosvenor Place[40] and Leonard Stokes, Kensington Court in the Bayswater Road.[41] Others were done by men of much less reputation and it is generally true that blocks of flats such as these brought out the worst in most architects. The problem was too pretentious architecturally, the buildings too large to be handled in design terms, and the clients too lacking in taste. So the resultant designs were less than usually memorable either from the point of view of the *fin du siècle* era itself or of their architects' reputations.

During 1882 *The Builder* again carried comment on the problem under the heading 'The Town Buildings of the Future'.

'... there can be no question that a flat should be a cheaper habitation than a single house. The ground-rent should be proportionately less; there are possibilities for economy both in heating and lighting, and the cost of building a flat should also be proportionately less than that of erecting an ordinary house, and there must be many feasible improvements to be made such as automatic lifts and so forth.'[42]

The one significant factor which aided the development of flats seems to have been related to the growing acceptance of the elevator. Needless to say, a lift of any sort was at first unpopular in this country and this effectively limited domestic building to four or five floors in height. Gradually the lift was recognised as safe and convenient and as a result the potential height of residential buildings increased. But the lifts were not only still regarded with some suspicion, even in the 1880s, they also added appreciably to the cost of building. A figure of £400 to £500 was quoted in 1884 for the installation of a lift ascending six stories to which could be added the water rate for the hydraulic system and the wages of an attendant, perhaps amounting to a further £800 a year.[43] The same writer (this was F.E. Eales) notes that it was possible to obtain identical rents, with or without lift access, up to about five floors, so great was the demand in central areas of London. He also mentions the constructional problems of building higher than this in load-bearing brickwork; the real American framed constructional system had not reached England yet.

Technical problems like these were a cautionary factor, but the tendency was to exploit the possibilities of the elevator and before the London Building Act of 1894 prohibited buildings, with the exception of churches and chapels, having a main elevational height to the eaves level of more than eighty feet (although two floors were allowed within the roof), there was a spate of exceptionally tall buildings in London. Henry Alers Hankey had built Queen Anne Mansions before this restriction. He started as early as 1873, designing the first part himself, and he completed it in 1889, with the assistance of E.R. Robson as architect.[44] Although it has now been demolished its site is still the subject of major building and environmental debate today, which is in some ways a fitting continuation of a story which has always aroused passion. The building rose to fourteen floors at one point and, of course, had hydraulic lifts to make this a practical proposition. There was not even the pretence of attractive design; no concession appears to have been made to appearance and the Peabody estate south of Victoria Street, in Abbey Orchard Street, which was built to far more stringent economic standards, always appeared attractive and spacious by comparison! The building obviously answered a real need at that time, but in many ways it also condemned itself and any successors which it might have had because of its physical brutishness; it can hardly have been a home at any time during its existence to any but the most hardened urbanist.

One other development deserves to be singled out, although for rather different reasons. This is the Albert Hall Mansions:

'Of the design the less we say the better, suffice it, that an Athenian would not have understood it, a Roman would have called it barbarous, a Goth would have shuddered at it.'[45]

Yet, as *The Builder* concluded, the block was not the work of some unknown hack but of a 'distinguished architect'; none other in fact than Richard Norman Shaw, who was an established 'modern' architect when in 1878 he designed it to stand next to his Queen Anne style Lowther Lodge, built five years previously as a private house. The Albert Hall Mansions were also in his Queen Anne manner and this should have ensured their success as well as their popularity as a style which could be imitated for modern flats. It certainly did the latter but to modern eyes it is vastly disappointing. The volume of building was too great to support the delicacy inherent in the reticent precedents for Shaw's early style and, sadly, the flats are unconvincing and in reality a failure architecturally. They are dull and monotonous, the detail stretched to breaking point across the massive facades. Little wonder that Shaw later took refuge in the full-blown classicism of the Piccadilly Hotel when called upon to build in another major street many years later.

It is sad that Shaw failed, but it was probably inevitable that he should do so, because the free style was quite unsuited to this purpose and, although it provided a model for various other blocks of flats it was not a style destined to appeal to those whose sense of urban scale gravitated towards the Edwardian Baroque. If they were not the majority they were certainly the most influential. It was a style probably best handled by the young LCC architects on their working-class housing estates in relative urban backwaters at Millbank and Boundary Street for example. It would never have done in Victoria Street.

In fact the dice were heavily loaded against the success of high-rise flats by the last decade of the century despite their apparent ascendancy. Except as a pied-à-terre for the rich or the residence of bachelors, the middle classes increasingly rejected the flat as a way of life in favour of the garden suburb and the much more appealing versions of Shaw's architecture developed by himself and by other free-style architects as the style of suburbia. By the end of the century the Englishman was more firmly wedded than ever to the concept of his house with its patch of garden and he appears to have gritted his teeth against the growing problem of commuting, recognising it as a necessary evil. The situation is little different today; the flat is still regarded as an aberration if not actually as frankly evil. Moreover, far more of the nation realised that a house of their own was within their grasp and they were not likely to give up the vision of the promised land for a flat. The English remained a nation of house-dwellers.

The saga of the flat during the nineteenth century, then, remains a passing fascination with a foreign way of life. The conservatism of the Englishman was as deep-rooted as the ancient pattern of leasehold development and his faith in the party wall was matched only by his fear of the party floor. But perhaps the most cogent reason for the ultimate failure of the flat as a way of life lies in the growing desire on the part of every class to get away from the town because it was ugly and suspected of being unhealthy. It was possible to show by 1890 that urban dwellings could be made quite healthy, but strangely the stamp of ugliness, inhumanity and lost hope for the future which characterised flats in the minds of all classes was probably in the end the factor which turned the English to their suburban house and garden.

The story of this short-lived romance with 'French flats' is a useful comment on English social insularity and the architecture which resulted is a curious comment on the tastes of the rich and a sober reminder that affluence does not necessarily create great building, nor a better sense of urbanism than that nurtured by the organisers of 5 per cent philanthropy.

Notes

1. See my own account of these in *Working Class Housing in Nineteenth Century Britain*, Lund Humphries, London, 1972. p.4 *et seq.*
2. T. Roger Smith and W.H. White, 'Model Dwellings for the Rich', *Journal of the Society of Arts*, XXIV, 31 March 1876, p.456 *et seq.*
3. *Ibid.*
4. *Ibid.*
5. The way eighteenth-century concepts of housing continued to be accepted well beyond the middle of the nineteenth century by Cubitt in North London illustrates this; see Hermione Hobhouse, *Thomas Cubitt, Master Builder*, Macmillan, London, 1971, p.345 *et seq.*
6. *The Builder*, XXXIV, 2 March 1876, p.291; this is from a letter from W.H. White. *The Builder* also reprints much of the Society of Arts paper later the same month, bringing it to a wider audience and also showing its intrinsic importance at this time.
7. *Building News*, III, 20 Feb. 1857, p.181.
8. See A.J. Youngson, *The Making of Classical Edinburgh*, Edinburgh U.P., Edinburgh, 1966.
9. *The Builder* is again the chief source of incidental information about this problem. By the 1880s the speculative builder was almost a music-hall joke; see articles on the subject in XLVIII, 27 June 1885, p.898 and LVII, 28 Dec. 1889, p.460, 'The Art of Jerry Building'.
10. *Building News*, XV, 15 May 1868, p.323.
11. *op.cit.* XVII, 17 Dec. 1869, p.464 and XVIII, 14 Jan. 1870, p.22.
12. *The Builder*, XI, 3 Dec. 1853, p.721.
13. *Ibid*, p.722.
14. *The Builder*, XXVI, 7 March 1868, p.182.
15. *op.cit.* XXXIV, 1 Jan. 1876, p.8.
16. *op.cit.* XXXV, 8 Sept. 1877, p.917.
17. *op.cit.* XXXIV, 24 June 1876, p.612. They were sited in Manor Road and Bethune Road, three storeys high with from five to thirteen rooms. Other middle-class flats are mentioned in St John's Wood (*op.cit.* XXXVI, 23 Feb. 1878, p.187) and Kennington Road (*op.cit.* XXXVI, 23 March 1878, p.292). Enough indication, I think, to show that the idea was spreading.
18. *The Builder*, XXXIV, 8 Jan. 1876, p.25.
19. *The Saturday Review*, 23 October 1875.
20. *The Builder*, XXXIV, 8 Jan. 1875, p.25.
21. see for example *op.cit.*, 1875, pp.83, 270, 291.

22. *Journal of the Society of Arts*, XXIV, 31 March 1876, p.456.
23. A. Ashpitel and J. Whichcord, *Town Dwellings: An Essay on the Erection of Fireproof Houses in Flats: A Modification of the Scottish and Continental Systems*, 1855.
24. *Journal of the Society of Arts, loc.cit.*
25. N. Pevsner, *London, Except the Cities of London and Westminster*, Penguin Books, Harmondsworth, 1952, p.37.
26. T.C. Barker and M. Robbins, *A History of London Transport, I: The Nineteenth Century*, Allen & Unwin, London, 1963, p.185 *et seq.*
27. *Journal of the Society of Arts, loc.cit.* p.458.
28. *Ibid.*
29. *Ibid.*
30. *RIBA Transactions*, 1866–7, p.37.
31. Reported in *The Builder*, XXXV, 24 Nov. 1877, p.1166.
32. *op.cit.*, 8 Dec. 1877, p.1219.
33. *Ibid.*
34. And fully reported in *The Builder*, XLVI, 8 Mar 1884, p.351.
35. Oxford and Cambridge Mansions were illustrated in *The Builder*, XLIV, 3 Feb. 1883, pp.144–5; Hyde Park Mansions *op.cit.*, 4 Aug. 1883, p.144, and further work there *op.cit.* XLIX, 17 Oct. 1885, p.532.
36. *The Builder*, XXXVII, 29 Nov. 1879, p.1327.
37. A full account of his work is in my own paper 'The Improved Industrial Dwellings Company', *Transactions of the London and Middlesex Archaeological Society*, XXII Pt.1, 1968, p.43.
38. *The Builder*, XL, 21 May 1881, p.647.
39. *op.cit.* XLVI, 21 June 1884 p.912 and LI, 14 Aug. 1886, p.232.
40. *op.cit.* L, 15 May 1886, p.708.
41. *op.cit.* LVI, 16 Feb. 1889, p.129 and 1 June 1889, p.411.
42. *op.cit.* XLII, 17 June 1882, p.730.
43. *op.cit.* XLVI, 8 March 1884, p.351.
44. *op.cit.* LIV, 18 Feb. 1888, p.128, Curiously, this development attracted little attention at the time.
45. *op.cit.* XXXVI, 12 Jan. 1878, p.37.

Chapter 3 The Insanitary Housing Question and Tenement Dwellings in Nineteenth-century Liverpool

Iain C. Taylor

*This paper will not attempt a definitive history of early multi-storeyed housing in Liverpool. For this, more detailed work on private papers, debates in council and committee records would be necessary. Rather, it is hoped to provide here the context for an understanding of the decisions which were to produce some of the country's earliest examples of tenement dwellings. The period covered by the paper will extend from the earliest regulation of the housing market in the 1840s as far as, but not beyond, the time when the subsidised council flat becomes an acceptable municipal enterprise in Liverpool. This dwelling will be viewed as a socio-political phenomenon, whose roots lie in fifty years of increasing public involvement in the regulation and ameliora-tion of the urban environment. It will be argued that the reasons for the increasing interference in the free operation of the housing market, with the council flat as the ultimate outcome, are to be found in the context of Liverpool's debate on public health and insanitary housing. It was the annual roll-call of 'unnecessary' deaths, proclaimed nationally each year, which pricked the sensitive palms of municipal pride, and provided the stimulus to corporate action. Sometimes such action was progressive, led by conviction, but more often it was hesitant, forced by the momentum of events to provide too little, too late. Liverpool's reputation for pace-setting action in the field of public health and housing, it will be argued, needs a more balanced assessment by social historians. The list of Liverpool 'firsts' has diverted too much attention from later, less incontrovertibly beneficial, developments.

Pre-Regulation Health and Housing

For virtually all of the half century following the publication of the first Registrar General's reports, Liverpool was the unchallenged champion at the head of the nation's least sought-after league table — that of average mortality. This, the unhealthiest example of the

*This paper was written while with the Department of Geography, University of Liverpool and financed by a fellowship from the Canada Council.

Victorian town, 'the black spot on the Mersey',[1] had its rude awakening in the early years of 'the sanitary decade' of the 1840s. The veil of ignorance was then rudely ripped aside by a small group of local reformers with William Duncan (later to become the town's and the country's first medical officer of health) at its head. Their revelations proved all the more shocking for their unexpectedness.[2] The town's exposure to sea gales had been given credit for its assumed healthiness,[3] but medical statistics were to prove otherwise. Duncan used his records from the South Liverpool Dispensary and the growing evidence from the Registrar General's annual returns to launch one of the most formidable propaganda campaigns of the sanitary crusade. He constructed a brilliant argument which had as its basis the existence of a geographic co-variation between the rates of mortality and environmental pathology.[4] The presence and importance of inhabited cellars and court dwellings, the density with which houses were crowded together, the availability of adequate water supplies and the diet and social habits of the people were assessed in spatial terms. That Duncan was, like many medical men of the time, mistaken in his identification of the causal links between life-conditions and disease did not, paradoxically, affect the accuracy of his conclusions, namely that dirt and insanitary, overcrowded dwellings assisted the propagation of disease organisms.

By the time Duncan reported to the Sanitary Inquiry, Liverpool's insanitary housing problem was already immense. It was this legacy, soon to grow even larger through the town's greatest building boom (see Fig.3.1), that was to provide the context for the insanitary housing

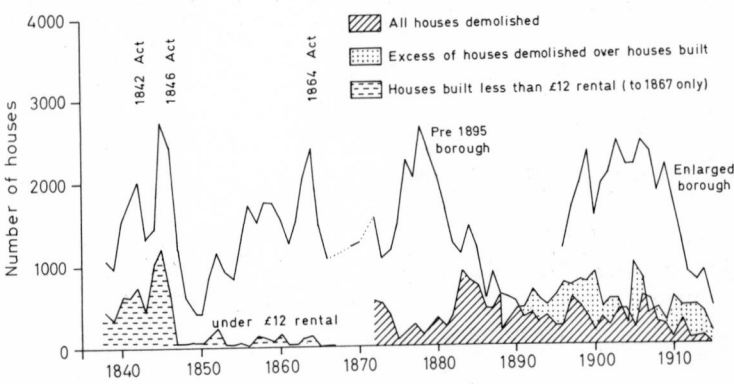

3.1 House building and demolition in Liverpool, 1835–1914.

debate over the following century. The amount of court housing, cellar dwellings and multiple occupation were seen as the major enemies of health. Some indication of the scale and extent of these conditions at mid-century is essential to an understanding of the municipal action that was set in motion.

Overcrowded and insanitary conditions were not of course peculiar to the nineteenth century. In Liverpool their origins lay in the quickening economic life of the 1780s. By 1790 cellars provided accommodation for 6,780 persons and court houses for a further 7,955, in total over a third of the town's population.[5] These numbers had grown to a cellar population of over 20,000 and a court population of over 40,000 by 1833.[6] Later estimates vary according to which of three surveys is utilised (see Table 3.1).[7]

Table 3.1   Court and Cellar Dwellings in Liverpool 1835 − 1841

Investigation	Number of Courts	Court Inhabitants	Number of Cellars	Cellar Inhabitants
Manchester Statistical Society, 1835 − 6	2,271	40,000 (est.)	7,493	31 − 37,000
Mr. Whitty, Head Constable, 1837	−	−	7,862	39,310
Corporation Surveyors, 1841	2,398	55,534	6,719	28,454

Sources: See Note 7.

This is not the place to investigate the differences between these various estimates and to assess the relative merits of each. Suffice it to say that there are good reasons for suspecting an under-estimation of ·the numbers of cellars by the Corporation and some over-estimation of the cellar population by the other surveys. It is likely that approximately 32,000 people resided in cellars in the early 1840s and that this figure probably increased up to the period of the cellar clearances later in the decade. In terms of overcrowding, both of houses on the ground and of the people within them, Liverpool was the most densely populated town in the kingdom. For the parish as a whole Duncan calculated 138,224 persons per square mile compared with approximately 100,000 for Manchester, 87,000 for Leeds and 50,000 for London. Indeed one area of six enumeration districts bounded by

Table 3.2   Overcrowded Districts in the Borough of Liverpool 1851

Ward	Total Number Enumeration Districts	Average Population	Number of Enumeration Districts by Density Class (Persons per Residential Acre)			
			More than 900	600–899	300–599	Less than 300
Scotland	47	1,274	3	5	25	14
Vauxhall	25	1,025	4	6	13	2
Exchange	14	1,230	2	3	6	3
St Pauls	15	914	—	1	8	6
Castle Street	7	1,222	—	—	5	2
St Peters	9	1,031	—	—	1	8
Pitt Street	9	1,349	1	1	4	4
Great George	15	1,248	—	2	5	7
Rodney Street	17	1,164	—	1	2	15
Abercromby	20	966	—	1	1	18
Lime Street	16	1,082	—	1	3	12
St Annes	19	1,187	—	1	8	10
Parish Total	**213**	**1,212**	**10**	**21**	**81**	**101**
North Toxteth	44	632	3	4	14	23
South Toxteth	48	662	2	11	24	11
Everton (Twp.)	23	1,073	—	1	5	17
Kirkdale (Twp.)	8	1,040	—	—	—	8
West Derby	21	1,036	—	—	4	17
Borough Total	**357**	**1,004**	**15**	**37**	**128**	**177**

Source: Author's computer output from 1851 Census enumeration summary data.

Marybone, Addison, Byron and Great Crosshall Streets enumerated 7,938 inhabitants on about 49,000 square yards, giving over 700 persons to the acre or, if expressed in terms of a square mile, slightly in excess of half a million![8] These figures of Duncan's have been recently checked (and verified) and densities for the whole of the borough calculated.[9] While it is clear that Duncan selected some of the most overcrowded districts to make his point, he by no means painted a false picture. Table 3.2 indicates that in 1851 over fifty enumeration districts in the borough were grossly overcrowded, having in excess of 600 persons to the residential acre, and a further 128 were moderately overcrowded. Over half of all the districts in the borough had nett population densities of over 300 persons to the acre.

Table 3.4 illustrates that the high population densities were due in part to the high numbers of occupants per dwelling. Yet as in most English towns outside London, this occupancy was intensive rather than extensive. In Liverpool the common building height for most pre-bye-law houses was three stories plus the cellar. Three-roomed dwellings were general and the rooms most frequently contained less than 1,000 cubic feet each. The average dimensions of rooms in 636 houses surveyed in the overcrowded quarter mentioned above was 822 cubic feet.[10] In Liverpool, therefore, seven persons per dwelling is clearly in excess of the two-persons-per-room measure usually accepted in the nineteenth century as the lower limit of overcrowding. 42.7 per cent of the parish and 33.8 per cent of the borough population (110,000 and 127,000 respectively) lived in districts which exceeded this overcrowding yardstick.

Health of the Town Legislation

It would be useful to consider briefly the town's response to the health and housing question after public attention began to be focused on it. The Corporation's actions indicate, in particular, the motivation, manner and scope of politically acceptable public regulation of private property, which once established was to set the broad guidelines for public policies for the rest of the century.

The events which led up to the adoption by Liverpool of the country's first legislation designed to improve the healthfulness of working-class dwellings are complex and involve a fascinating interplay between local and national pressures. A brief outline will suffice here. On the one hand there were the activities of a small group of dedicated local sanitary reformers and their sympathisers. On the other, the work of national reformers such as Slaney and Chadwick with their investigative enquiries appeared to be leading towards prohibitive legislation which was bound to affect Liverpool's freedom of action. It was this threat, more than any other, that was responsible for the haste with which the Council moved. Duncan appeared before Slaney's committee on the Health of Towns in April, 1840; in July, Slaney's bill (Small Tenements Bill) was introduced; in August Duncan again gave evidence, this time to Chadwick's Sanitary Enquiry.

This parliamentary activity appeared to have galvanised the Council, for in November the Health of the Town Committee was established and within four days had ordered the Corporation's survey into court and cellar dwellings. While awaiting this report the committee began to look closely at the implications for Liverpool of Slaney's bill. It was unimpressed; the ban on back-to-back houses, increased space requirements and open areas in front of cellars would all push up building costs. Liverpool therefore determined to oppose Slaney's bill and the later bills introduced by Lord Normanby. As a counterblow to the possibility of national legislation (which was in fact delayed five years) and to secure exemption from it, the Council framed its own local bill.[11] Dr Duncan, who was largely responsible for the new climate of opinion, was apparently left entirely unconsulted and felt the bill contained severe 'defects and omissions'.[12] Nevertheless it enabled the Council to petition against Normanby's bill, stating that the local act 'would effect *all* the purposes proposed by the Buildings Regulation Bill.' (my italics)[13] (See Table 3.3) The tactic certainly worked for when re-introduced in 1842, Clause 36 of the bill to regulate buildings in large towns specifically exempted Liverpool.

In fact, Liverpool had produced a modest substitute for Normanby's proposals and Liverpool's later enactment brought it only slightly closer. Aside from showing how quickly the Council could move when it felt London threatening its autonomy, this early sanitary activity provides the first revelation of the all-important economics of house building. Normanby's bills were opposed by Liverpool because they were felt to be particularly extravagant with land. They would have added from £34 to £41 10s to house costs whereas Liverpool's bill was only to add £6 to £9 10s to the average cottage (built for between £80 and £110).[14] Not surprisingly therefore, faced with an increase of 10 per cent as opposed to 30—40 per cent, the owners and occupiers of land felt willing to agree to the Corporation's 1842 bill.[15] Nevertheless the importance of this first interference in the housing market should

Table 3.3 Regulations contained in Lord Normanby's Bill (Regulation of Buildings in Large Towns), 1841 and the Liverpool Acts of 1842 and 1846.

Subject	Lord Normanby's Bill	Liverpool Act 1842	Liverpool Act 1846
1. Courts: Entrance width Main width	Open, 20 feet 30 feet	Open, 6 feet if narrowed by privy, otherwise 15 feet 15 feet	Full width 15 feet to 8 houses then 1 foot extra per additional house
2. Cellar dwellings	Banned unless fronted by open area 3 feet wide	Banned in courts after 1 July 1844. Allowed elsewhere if fronted by open area 2 feet wide. Banned if cellar heights less than 7 feet or if ceiling less than 2 feet above ground level	As 1844. Occupation banned unless 7 feet in height or ceilings less than 4 feet above ground (cellars built under the 1842 act exempted)
3. Structure	Back to backs banned, 20 feet between rear walls	No provisions	No court house higher than 30 feet
4. Sanitary provisions	Separate yard and privy per house. No provision	Privies and ashpits to be provided per court. Owner to flag courts and provide privies	Privies and ashpits shared with Health Committee agreement. Courts to be flagged
5. Street width	30 feet	24 feet	30 feet
6. Others	— — — Building notice to be sent to surveyor	Rooms 8 feet high, attic to average 7½ feet. One room at least 100 square feet. All rooms except cellar to have a window of at least 3 feet x 5 feet	Medical Officer of Health and Inspector of Nuisances to be appointed. Council assumes powers to pave and sewer from Highway Commission. Nightly lodgings subject to inspection

not be underestimated. Entrepreneurs certainly responded like economic men to the threat of increased local regulation when they hurriedly ran up hundreds of court houses in the interval between the two acts (see Figure 3.1). On the other hand, the crude political economics which produced this reaction also indicated, in respect of cellar closures, that misery could be the only outcome of an attempt to reduce the supply of cheap accommodation (cellars) at a time of increased demand from the 'sickly and half starved Irish'. The sad tale of the Council's attempts to enforce its building acts while the town was inundated by the effects of Europe's worst human disaster of the nineteenth century has already been told.[16] Only one-third of the inhabited street cellars could be altered to comply with the terms of even the act of 1842. From July 1844 to February 1845, 1,058 inhabited cellars were cleared of their inhabitants and by 1851 over 5,000 had been closed and 'upwards of 20,000 inmates ejected'.[17]

The results of these actions were all too predictable, and the one-sided interference with free market forces was to aggravate severely the housing situation as families were forced into multiple occupance of already overcrowded court and street houses.[18] In this, the predictions of the anti-reformers came depressingly true.[19] Furthermore the market showed little incentive to respond to the new demands placed upon it and Figure 3.1 clearly indicates the speculative response to the changing rules of the housing game. The building boom of mid-1840s, which in 1845 saw the construction of more housing in Liverpool than in any other year of the century, slumped within a few years to the century's lowest level. The poorer end of the market, at annual rentals of £12 or under, suffered particularly and 1846 virtually marked the last year in which housing for the poor was built in Liverpool. 'As most builders knew only too well, the enhanced economic rent — the sure corollary of an increase in construction costs — would be beyond the means of most working men.'[20] The poor henceforth were to squeeze themselves almost entirely into that ever-diminishing stock of increasingly insanitary court housing provided in the speculative booms of the 1830s and 1840s.

Slum Cleaning and Slum Clearing

The philosophy of the Health Committee that was to guide its early operations in the matter of insanitary housing stemmed from a belief that the inhabitants themselves would, with Corporation help and guidance, be capable of maintaining their own environmental standards. The Corporation was now committed to providing basic drainage and cleansing. If landlords and tenants undertook their obligations in the same spirit, the problem would, it was tacitly assumed, solve itself. The approach was one of accepting 'the courts as they stood and of attempting to ameliorate their surroundings ... this depended on securing a higher standard of cleanliness within the area of the courts and the houses themselves'.[21] Even under the terms of its own assumptions, however, the policy had severe limitations, for apart from the system of *nightly* lodging house inspection instituted under the act, no controls were available to regulate internal occupation apart from the power to lime-wash 'filthy and unwholesome dwellings'. Health Committee control was otherwise limited to external matters and their jurisdiction ceased at the threshold.

Despite the sad coincidence of the commencement of sanitary operations with the cholera and typhus epidemics of 1847 and 1849 (when death rates reached the highest levels ever recorded [Figure 3.2]), optimism and activity were initially high. In 1850 for instance there were 10,028 inspections of courts and 55,240 inspections of houses.[22] Yet apart from white-washed walls and the ban on cellar occupation, little of the Corporation's activity impinged greatly on the rights of owners of already existing property and only gradually did its sacrosanctity come into question. Despite the generally lower mortality rates of the 1850s and the £3½ million expended by the Health Committee, the town stubbornly remained the unhealthiest in the land. Attacking the slum dwellings themselves now began to appear a more realistic policy. Duncan in 1846 had mentioned it as a possibility,[23] but it was the special study by Greenhow of the General Board of Health that sparked off the debate.[24] Despite vehement refutations of his statistics,[25] there were nagging suspicions that different tactics were required. Dr. Holland, on inspection, found the courts improved but pointed out that cleanliness alone was not enough and that 'nothing short of extensive reconstruction will reduce the death rate to the level of healthy places'.[26] Finally, the climbing death rates of the 1860s put an end to the Council's arguments which pointed to the supposed amelioration of sanitary conditions. With the onset of the typhus and cholera epidemics of 1865 and 1866 mortality again climbed to the heights last reached in the 1840s.

The failure of the 'good-housekeeping' policy indicated that it was illogical to expect that crumbling fabric and the structural inadequacies of poorly arranged houses, when combined with the social habits of a

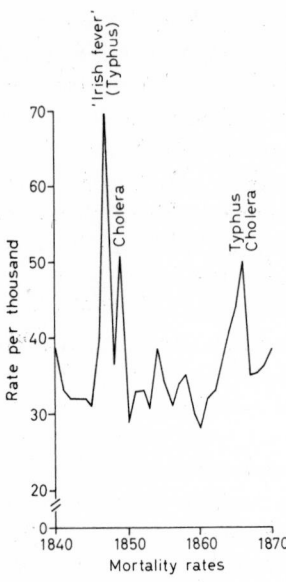

3.2 Mortality rates in the registration district of Liverpool, 1840–1870.

population grown insensitive to the barbarities of urban existence, could be cured by even the most zealous of carbolic remedies. The failure to alter substantially conditions in the courts was made plain to the respectable and influential classes, most of whom had never stepped into a court of the dwelling variety, by the campaigning journalism of Hugh Shimmin, editor of the town's prickly periodical *The Porcupine*. In a series of articles which must rate alongside those of Mayhew as pioneers of sociological journalism, he savagely exposed the extent of squalor at the base and indifference at the apex of Liverpool's steep social pyramid.[27]

'Some people seem to think that this question of the courts can stand; that with the slight improvement made and the inspection adopted and proposed, there is nothing to fear; but let all such people who are disposed to cry "peace, peace" look to the Registrar's returns. There can be no cooking the accounts of this sort ... so long as our local rulers shut their eyes to their duty respecting these places, we will lay the deaths of all who die in courts in excess of the minimum rate at the doors of the Town Council and of those numbers who make a large profession of regard for their unfortunate fellow creatures and when the time for action arrives neglect them.'[28]

By the time Shimmin had completed his series of articles, the publicity and the climbing death rates had stimulated the Council to apply for wider powers under the Liverpool Sanitary Amendment Act of 1864.[29] The act gave powers held by no other Corporation except Glasgow, which had obtained a similar act that year.[30] It empowered the Corporation to buy and clear any court, alley or house unfit for habitation or prejudicial to health. Rights of property were however well protected by generous compensation terms and by a limit on expenditure of £6,000 per annum (one-tenth of the annual expenditure under Liverpool's improvement acts). Responsibility for the clearances rested heavily on the discretionary powers of the Medical Officer of Health; unfortunately Dr Trench was cautious and lacked vision. He was guided by 'no theoretical considerations, but solely by the number of deaths from typhus'.[31] Thin resources were widely spread and spent on minor improvements but even this activity was hampered by the growing strength of the Liverpool Land and House Owners Association.

If the pace of Corporation clearance was slow other factors had combined to restrict the supply of cheap housing. The main line railways and termini, goods yards, dock and warehouse expansion and extension of retail trading were all quietly and continuously nibbling into inner area housing stocks. These were the very districts where working-class housing was most conveniently situated for access to the chief labour markets. Reference to Table 3.4 indicates that though there were overall declines in the proportion of population in overcrowded districts between 1851 and 1871, the size of the population in these districts diminished by only 6.8 per cent in the borough, and in two sub-districts there were even substantial increases in the proportions. New overcrowded districts were being created further away from the town centre (Figure 3.3) and it is clear that a generation after the first housing acts a quarter of Liverpool's total population, over 100,000 people, were confined to a shrinking and physically decaying stock of cheap pre-legislation housing, which the Corporation's cautious if well-meaning policies were incapable of improving. The question of how to supply new dwellings for the lower classes was beginning to occupy the minds of administrators who did not need elaborate statistical tables to know that the housing market in this sphere at least was not self-adjusting. Could it be that private enterprise might respond to a degree of stimulation and inspiration?

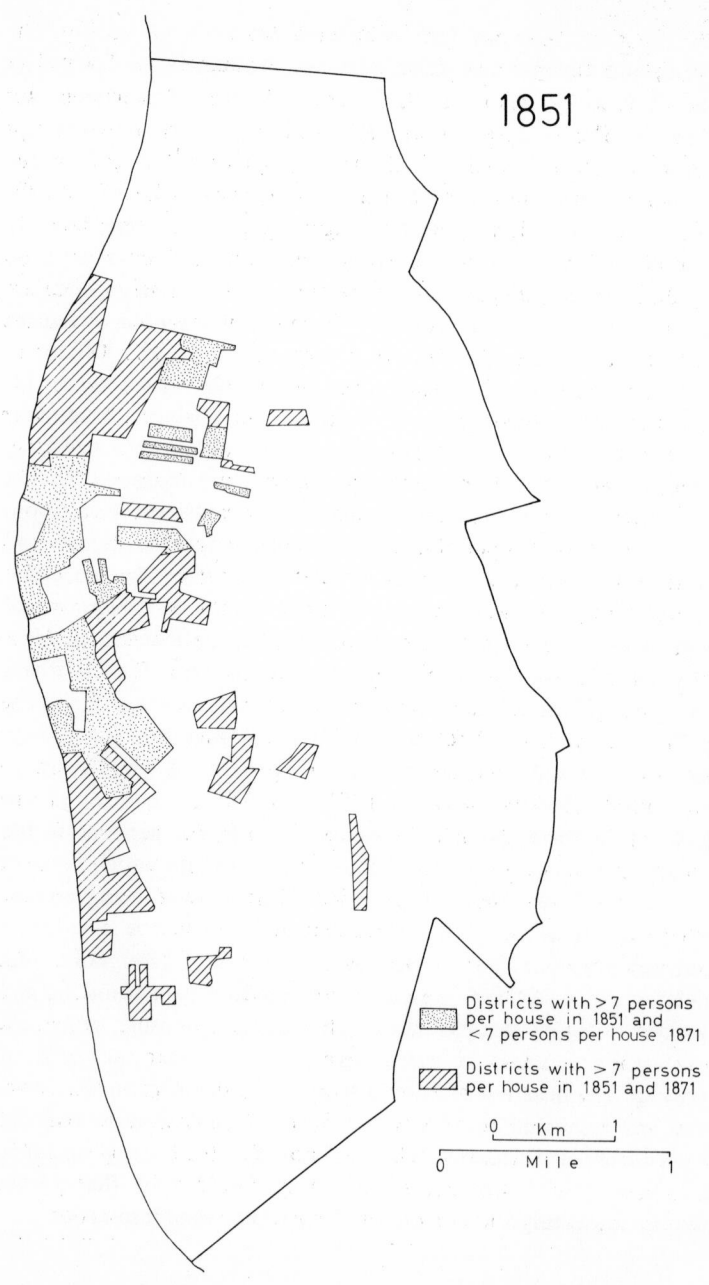

3.3 Overcrowded districts in the Borough of Liverpool in 1851 and 1871.

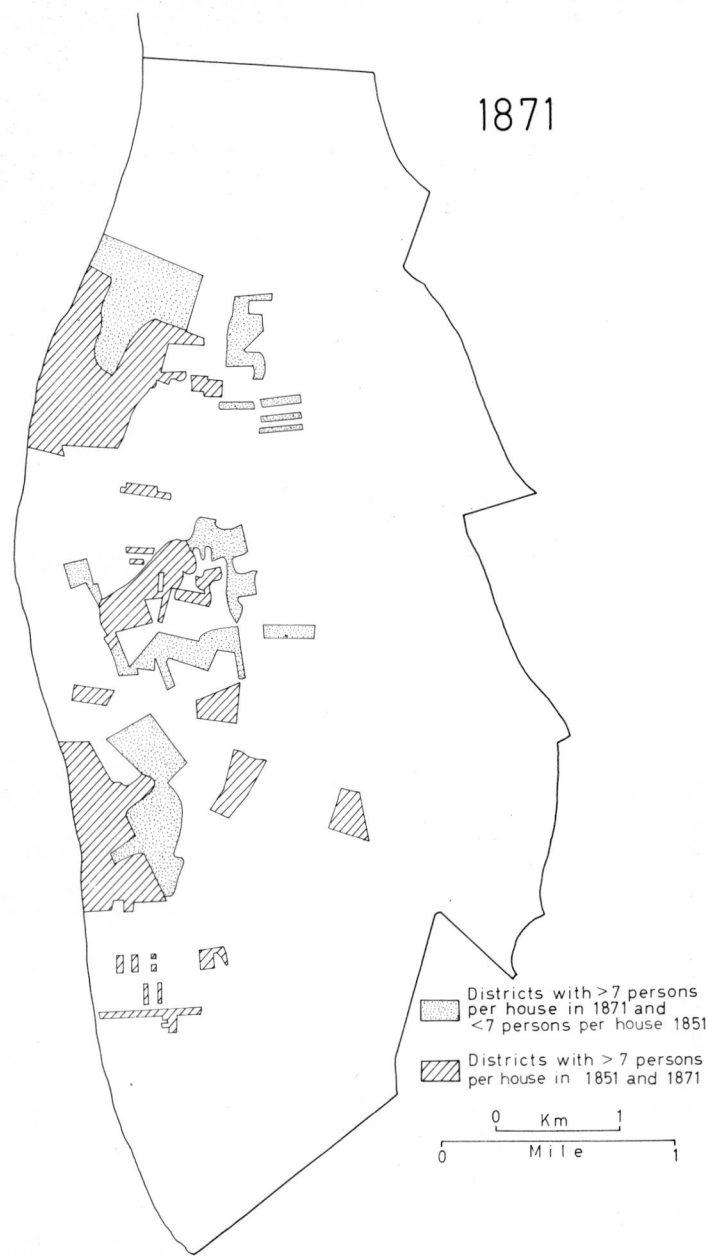

1871

Districts with > 7 persons
per house in 1871 and
< 7 persons per house 1851

Districts with > 7 persons
per house in 1851 and 1871

0   Km   1

0   Mile   1

Table 3.4   Overcrowded Dwellings in Liverpool 1851 and 1871
Average of more than 7 Persons per House

Sub-District	No. of EDs		Population in EDs			
	1851	1871	1851		1871	
			No.	%	No.	%
1. St Martins	17	21	25,536	41.3	30,203	39.2
2. Great Howard	15	4	16,206	58.0	4,302	22.7
3. Dale Street	17	9	20,271	63.8	10,518	44.0
4. St George	8	3	9,178	46.3	3,650	38.7
5. St Thomas	17	14	24,386	71.8	20,546	88.3
6. Mount Pleasant	6	6	8,097	19.3	7,823	17.2
7. Islington	4	12	6,556	16.0	14,185	35.3
Liverpool Registration District	84	69	110,230	42.7	91,227	33.8
8. Toxteth Park	19	9	14,707	24.0	10,008	11.7
9. Everton	1	9	1,314	3.7	10,604	8.6
10. West Derby	1	0	1,200	3.6	0	0
Liverpool Borough	104	87	127,451	33.8	111,839	24.0

Source: Author's computer output from enumeration Summary Data. (1871 basic data kindly supplied by R. Lawton and C. Pooley, Nineteenth Century Merseyside Project.)

The First Model Tenements

The preceding pages have attempted to demonstrate that in trying to remedy the most glaring examples of the town's slum housing, the Council were to some considerable degree exacerbating it. Negative remedies – those of prohibition and demolition – were perhaps inevitably the first to be attempted, but the unstated assumption was that the market would automatically respond to the new demands for cheap housing. However, the relationship between the lack of new cheap housing evidenced in the building surveyor's annual returns and the persistence of overcrowding with its high death rates went largely unnoticed until the 1860s. The arrival of the 1864 Act made some members of the Health Committee aware that the Council would thereby be assisting further the reduction of the housing stock for the poor. They felt, therefore, that the Council was obliged at least to encourage alternative provisions. It was for these reasons that Wilson and Bowring introduced a resolution to the Council calling for the construction of a block of model cottages.[32] A demonstration that such an enterprise could be profitable might persuade private builders to follow suit.

In approaching the question the Council had the experience of private ventures into this field, both in London and on Merseyside. The national associations dedicated to raising the standards of working-class housing had been in existence for twenty years. The Metropolitan Association for Improving the Dwellings of the Industrious Classes, for instance, had already erected eight blocks in London.[33] Closer at hand the Corporation could turn to a number of examples of such dwellings on Merseyside itself.

The earliest of these, and probably the oldest such working-class tenement development in England, lay across the river in Birkenhead. As a 'new town', built essentially around Laird's iron and ship-making enterprises founded in the 1820s, Birkenhead seemed to contemporaries to embody the spirit, hopes and aspirations of the age. Dr Hunter Robertson, admittedly a local man, felt it had

' . . . ready materials to mould and fashion towards a high destiny by providing for all the means of pursuing life with knowledge, principles, and purposes calculated to dignify humanity and advance the progress of one portion of the country towards their proud prerogative of teaching others how to live'.[34]

The town had been laid out on a virtually virgin site to a grid-iron ground plan of broad, straight streets. The prospect of continued rapid growth seemed assured once major dock construction in Wallasey Pool had commenced in 1845. However, the lack of housing accommodation brought problems.

'The dock company finding that they must either provide accommodation for the numerous workmen required for the construction of their warehouses and docks or submit to great inconvenience, expense and delay in consequence of the want of it, they determined to erect a number of dwellings for their labourers and mechanics.'[35]

Contemporary reviews of the resulting company tenements stressed their healthiness, for they seemed to embody many of the proposals put forward by the sanitary reformers. The provision of individual water closets provides indirect evidence to show that the company itself took sanitary matters into consideration. However, the development should probably be placed in the category of housing built for industrial investment. Its isolated position several miles distant from the town centre and the uni-occupational structure which was envisaged evoke obvious comparisons with the nineteenth-century mining village or railway town and in style it is close to the later blocks of Barrow-in-Furness. Perhaps of equal importance was a concern not to affect neighbouring site values. The author of the popular *Land We Live In* felt the district would probably soon be occupied by 'good houses either for shops or private residence' and the promoters were anxious not to detract from them by the construction of dwellings 'mean and poverty stricken in appearance'.[36]

The block was certainly planned as an element in a larger townscape, for it occupied an angle between two of eight converging roads. At other corners a parsonage and school house were planned and the island was occupied by St James Church. The first dwellings (Figure 3.4) were arranged in six parallel blocks (B to G) and it appears that the others were completed subsequently. They were 'elegant' red brick, finished with sandstone, and stood separated by 'avenues', eighteen feet in width. These were considered to be 'narrow alleys' by Henry Roberts, who was not alone in considering that they were less than half the desirable width (Fig.3.4).[37] There were four or five 'houses' in each block, each house having a central stone staircase giving access to two flats on four floors (a plan is given in Roberts).[38] The dwellings themselves consisted of three rooms, a sitting room and two bedrooms opening into each other. The smallness of the bedrooms (9′ 6″ by 7′ and 9′ 6″ by 6′) was criticised by Roberts and others.[39]

> 'The little republic of each house — the denizens of eight dwellings or 24 rooms — are eight independent states so far as regards their domestic arrangements; but they form a sort of feudal union in general matters.'[40]

These 'general matters' were the water tank and what would now be called the central service core, consisting of water, gas and drainage pipes together with a dust chute. The flat roof formed a 'pleasant substitute' for a garden on which to dry clothes. With rents ranging from 3s 6d to 5s, the flats were not intended as a charity. 'The dwellings are really for *working* and not for *poor* men.'[41] Unfortunately there is no indication what return these dwellings made on the large sum of money outlaid, for there are notes of both optimism and pessimism in the literature.[42] It was hoped that 'the experiment may prove to the speculative buyer that he could provide for the humbler classes a very superior kind of accommodation at a profit to himself.'[43]

Plate I. Dock Cottages, Birkenhead, erected 1844. This photograph was taken in the 1930s and shows a number of unemployed residents, probably dockers. The view is from St James' Road (south). Note the block letters, the narrow 'avenues' and the position of the W.C.s. Most striking is the imposing solidity of the dwellings, with their simple detailing reminiscent of contemporary warehouse and dock architecture. (By permission of Birkenhead Corporation).

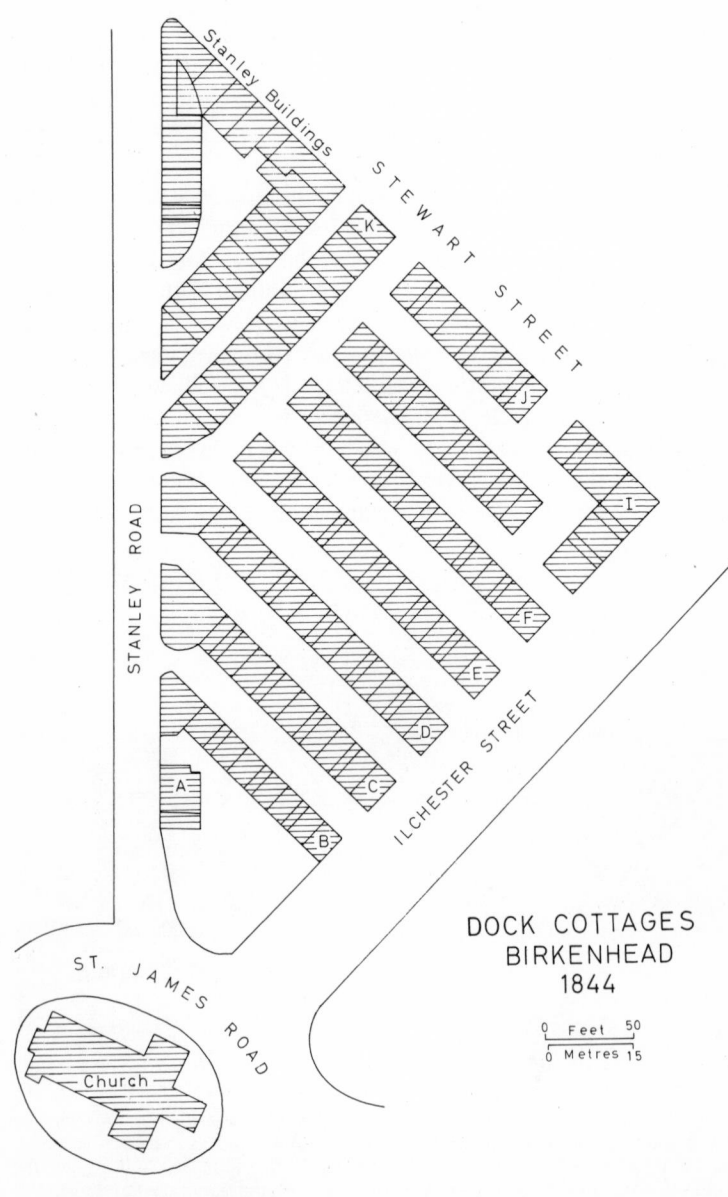

3.4 Birkenhead Dock Cottages, 1844.

A return of 8 or 10 per cent was hoped for by *The Builder*'s correspondent, though the local doctor feared 'the investment will turn out an unprofitable one' owing to the unnecessarily ornate finish,[44] which *The Times* suggested was reminiscent of an inn of court or Chancery building.[45] The structure was certainly imposing even to twentieth-century eyes, though conditions in the cramped three-room space must have become severely overcrowded when occupied by large families. The 'cottages', as they came to be called, were demolished in the 1930s; the tenements built to replace them achieved only half that life and were taken down in 1972.

At least four smaller developments were erected in Birkenhead during this period. Morpeth Buildings was built by the industrialist William Laird,[46] whose incentives for engaging in tenement building were in all probability similar to those of the Dock Company, namely the need to provide housing for industrial workers where none existed previously. Laird, the son of a Greenock rope-maker, may have been especially disposed towards dwellings on the 'Scotch plan'. His four-storey block, built in brick, consisted of eight terraced 'houses', each containing eight dwellings. Each landing served two flats in an arrangement similar to the Dock Cottages. Room dimensions and interior arrangements also appear to have been almost identical and as Laird was a chief partner in the Dock Company it may be that the similarities were not accidental. Air bricks, a feature not noted in descriptions of the Dock Cottages, were a positive proof that sanitary ideas were to some extent in the mind of the architect. One was placed near the floor to admit fresh air and the other near the ceiling for the escape of 'heated or vitiated air'. These sanitary draughts were the subject of complaint from all four tenants interviewed by Robertson, though one stated he had had no trouble since pasting paper over them! The tenants were unanimous in singling out the small area of the flats (320 sq. ft.) as the greatest disadvantage, thus demonstrating a surprising contemporary awareness of the need for more liberal space standards. For example, the sink, water closet, cooker and coals were all crammed into an area eight feet square. The private water closet appeared to be the main attraction, especially as general health levels now seemed higher.

Robertson was provided with a detailed cost breakdown of the buildings which is reproduced in Table 3.5. At 30s per yard, the cost of land in Birkenhead was surprisingly high and it indicates how substantially land speculation had added to building costs. Another expensive feature was the window tax which in Robertson's view

Plate II. No.3 Court, Everton Terrace, from Netherfield Road South, Liverpool. Photograph taken in 1927. High housing densities were not left behind with bye-law housing. The slopes of Everton Brow were covered by this terraced housing (of the 1870s?) despite its seemingly forbidding gradients. The changes in grade allowed the incorporation of three-storey 'Scotch housing' with two-storey terraces behind, incidentally creating a visually fascinating arrangement of architectural spaces.

tended to discourage the construction of healthy dwellings, especially in the form of flats.

Much less is known about the tenements known as the 'Scotch Flats' at 50 and 52, Jackson Street, which were demolished in 1962. They probably dated from the 1840s and as they appear to have been earlier in date than the buildings on either side, it may be that they were intended as part of a larger development which fell victim to the economic uncertainties which afflicted the town in that decade. The two 'houses' each had a ground plan thirty feet square and consisted of three storeys and a basement. Each floor contained two one-bedroom flats. The yards, which measured thirty feet by forty-five, were built at cellar floor level and originally contained privy middens.

Little is known about the 'barracks' on Brougham (later Fox) Street beyond what can be gleaned from the 1:500 O.S. map of 1876. There were seven pairs of 'houses', each pair measuring about thirty feet by twenty-five on a lot thirty feet by thirty-five. Each pair of 'houses' had a small yard and, probably, outdoor privies. Manuscript additions to the map appear to point to the existence of semi-basements and the numbering is consistent with a total of six dwellings in each 'house', which would suggest a height of three storeys.

Finally, though they are not strictly flats, Mr Hughes' development of seventy cottages provides a further indication of land pressures in Birkenhead. Consisting of three storeys above and one below ground, they appeared to be a variation on the four-room 'straight up and down' dwelling common in Liverpool. Each of the five blocks contained fourteen houses consisting of four rooms one on top of the other. Room sizes were larger than in either Morpeth Buildings or the Dock Cottages. The two bedrooms and kitchen were twelve feet square and the sitting room was twelve by nine feet and each dwelling was provided with a water closet and each kitchen with a range and oven, while the avenues were lit by gas. The accounts, given in Table 3.6, indicate a higher return on capital (5.4 per cent) than either of the other tenement blocks. However rentals were also higher, about 4s 8d per week, no doubt reflecting the greater space standards and higher construction costs. At £180 each the dwellings were almost double the price of a typical Liverpool court house.[47]

These Birkenhead housing experiments of the 1840s, which reformers hoped would pave the way to new standards, emphasised at the movement's very start the discouraging financial aspects of sanitary housing for the poor on Merseyside. Experience over the next two generations would merely confirm the evidence provided in these first

Table 3.5

LAND

Length of 8 blocks		292′ 3″
Width of cottage	25 feet	..
Passage behind	5	..
Given up to make a 12 feet street		
into an 18 feet street	3	33

292′ 3″ x 33 1071 yards, 3 roods, at 30s per yard	£1607	0 0
Contract for building 61 cottages, by Messrs Walker	5965	0 0
Extras: fitting shelves, cupboards, tables, each		
cottage, £3	192	0 0
Architect's commission, 3 per cent on £5965	178 19 0
	£7912 19 0	

RETURNS

1 block, containing 8 dwellings, produces the following rental.

On ground floor, 2 cottages at		
4s. 6d. per week, or £11. 11s.		
per annum each	£23 8 0	
On first floor, 2 cottages at 4s.		
per week, or £10 8s. per annum		
each	20 16 0	
On second floor, 2 cottages at		
3s. 6d. per week, or £9. 2s.		
per annum each	18 4 0	
On third floor, 2 cottages at 3s.		
per week, or £7 16s. per annum		
each	15 12 0	
	78 0 0	
8 blocks at £78 each, gross rental of 64 cottages		£624 0 0

DEDUCTIONS

Window-tax, 5 windows to each dwelling,		
or 40 per block, and 3 staircase windows:		
43 windows per block,		
£14 8 9 x 8	115 10 0	
10 per cent additonal	11 10 0	
	127 0 0	
Township rates –		
64 cottages, at 30s. per cottage		
per annum	96 0 0	
Water –		
64 cottages, at 6s. per cottage		
per annum	19 4 0	
Insurance –		
4s. 6d. per cent on £7000	15 15 0	130 19 0
Deduct		257 19 0
Net rental	**£366 1 0**	

Or a little more than 4½ per cent.

Table 3.6

Land for 70 cottages.			
2250 yards, at £1 per yard	£2,250 0 0		
Building account.	10,350 0 0		
		12,600 0 0	
Gross rental of 70 cottages		£850 0 0	

DEDUCTIONS

Township rates,			
70 cottages, at 30s. per an. . .	£105 0 0		
Extra public gas lights for			
avenues	21 15 0		
Water, 6s. per annum on			
70 cottages	24 0 0		
		150 15 0	
Insurance, 4s. 6d. per cent on £8000		18 0 0	
		168 15 0	
Net rental	£681 5 0		

Or equal to 5½ per cent.

accountancy tables. Two variables were crucial in the housing equation; the rent that the tenants could afford, which determined the return on the capital outlay and, secondly, the competitiveness of this return compared with other housing types or other forms of investment. Rent levels were largely determined by those of wages and where low wages and low employment reliability were prevalent as in Merseyside it was usually estimated that casual labourers could afford no more than 3s per week (1s per week per room). Table 3.7 indicates that to be profitable at a 3s rental, a house would need to be constructed for less than £100. The Birkenhead dwellings, which provided what could be considered as the minimum sanitary and space standards consistent with prevailing thinking, clearly did not cater to the cheaper end of the market. Table 3.7 indicates that even at these rent levels, they were quite close to the limit of acceptable contemporary profit margins. Clearly, if healthy dwellings were barely affordable by the fully-employed skilled mechanics, they were unattainable by the mass of the poor.

In Liverpool, the example of Birkenhead was to be followed by Kent Terrace.[48] The O.S. plan and the descriptions that exist make it clear that the site was not a good one. It lay on the east side of Kent Street between Mr Tomkinson's stone-yard, the Mersey Brewery and a boat-building yard. To the front on Kent Street were shops, and

Table 3.7   Percentage Return on Housing in the Nineteenth Century

Per Dwelling

Gross Rent Per Week	Net Return Per Annum*	Capital Cost of Dwelling				
		£60	£80	£100	£120	£140
2/–	£3–18	6.5	4.9	3.9	3.2	2.8
3/–	£5–17	9.7	7.3	5.8	4.9	4.2
4/–	£7–16	15.6	9.7	7.8	6.5	5.6
5/–	£9–15	16.2	12.2	9.7	8.1	7.0

* Allowing 25 per cent as running expenses etc. Laird's deductions (excluding window tax) were 20.8 per cent and Hughes's 19.8 per cent of gross rents (see Table 3.6). Liverpool's City Engineer calculated 30 per cent for expenses.

between them a fifteen-foot passage led to a 'species of double court', the flags of which lay below street level. The housing was arranged in three blocks. The inner block consisted of two rows apparently three storeys high facing outwards into the separate branches of the court; the outer blocks were four storeys high and consisted of two tiers of housing whose upper levels were approached by a balcony. The layout is curious, for this was a very early attempt to provide outside yards and privies in working-class dwellings. The inner houses consisted of a living room about twelve feet square with two bedrooms over. The tiny yards were common to two houses and in them were two sinks under cover and the common privy. The houses on the outside of the court contained a parlour, kitchen and separate yard with convenience, a lobby to the entrance door and, above, two bedrooms.

Opinion about the scheme appears to have been divided. James Aspinall, chairman of the Health Committee, refers to it (albeit anonymously, but with a detailed plan) as an example of how a shrewd builder could evade the spirit of the 1842 Act to obtain two courts for the entrance width of one. Joseph Boult, a local architect, who had given the subject of cottage housing 'much careful attention', considered this type of dwelling 'a remedy'. The only features to which he objected could be blamed on the Council. A sewer had been provided by the builder to connect to a cesspool at the west end but, as the bye-laws did not allow it to connect to the main drains in the street, the cesspool had quickly filled and was causing a nuisance. The buildings were erected by the 'enterprising builder', Hughes and Jones of Elizabeth Street, from designs by a local architect, Mr Ellis. The return on capital was stated to be 9 per cent in 1846.

More is known about Prince Albert Cottages on Upper Frederick Street (Figure 3.5). They appear to have been built as a private venture by George Melly and 'some friends' and had as their inspiration the Prince' Consort's 'model lodging houses' (sic).[49] Unlike the original, however, the Liverpool site was cramped in the extreme. Only fifteen feet separated the two blocks; the rear building was approached through narrow entries and the upper floors from a steep, iron exterior stair. The twenty-two dwellings were let from 4s to 5s 9d. Expectations of philanthropy and more than 5 per cent were initially high, Melly recalled:

'We wished to show what may be done. What have we achieved? These cottages supplied with gas and water, let at the *highest prices* they would command have never been empty, no case of fever has occurred there; they have been inhabited by a particularly industrious and sober community, who have paid their rents regularly . . . ' (my italics)[50]

Yet despite the maximised income from the property it paid a bare 4½ to 5 per cent. 'As a charity then they are a success; as an example to others they are a failure.'[51] The Liverpool merchant was clearly not a man to be satisfied with the return *hoped for* by the Metropolitan Association. Melly drew the conclusion that the artisan must 'have the will to afford a healthy home' by paying the higher rents needed to ensure a reasonable return.[52]

The dwellings had not long been completed and their profit limitations realised when 'an influential meeting' was held, Archdeacon Brooks presiding, which resolved to set up a Liverpool branch of the Association for Improving the Dwellings of the Industrious Classes.[53] This association was the builder of Northumberland Buildings in Toxteth Park which were opened in 1857 (Figure 3.5). The dwellings included one-, two- and three-bedroomed flats. Gas and lighting were provided and 'each dwelling supplied with a scullery, sink, water tap, shelves, plate rack, larder, coal place and WC'.[54] The total cost was £6,360 and though a dividend of 5 per cent was hoped for, only 3½ per

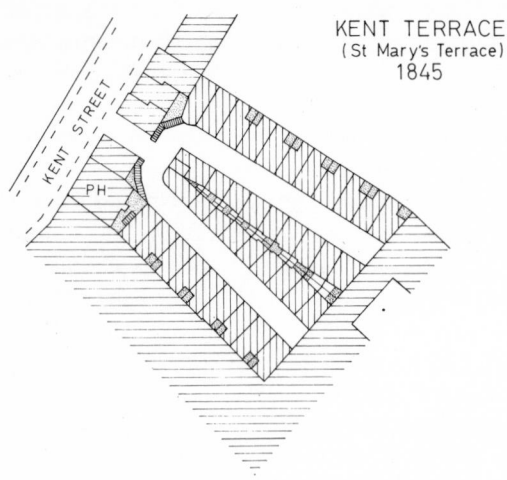

KENT TERRACE
(St Mary's Terrace)
1845

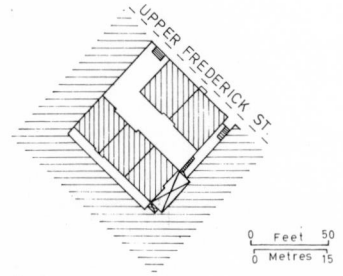

PRINCE ALBERT COTTAGES
1852

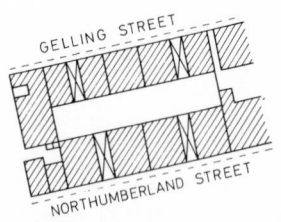

NORTHUMBERLAND BUILDINGS
1857

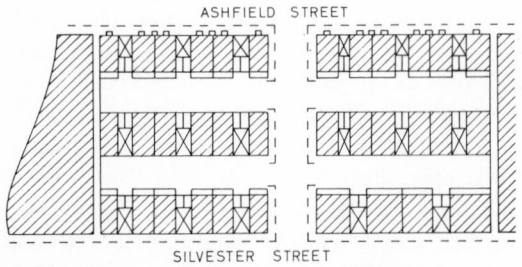

ST. MARTINS COTTAGES
1869

3.5 Tenement dwellings in Liverpool, 1845–1869.

cent was paid in the first year, perhaps because the state of trade had depressed the market.

The Liverpool Corporation's first venture into the housing field is best seen as an extension of the model dwelling concept, a third Liverpool attempt to demonstrate that a builder's economic interests might be served by investing again in working-class housing. It did not mark a significant change of attitude, either as perceived at the time or in retrospect. It was not the commencement of a housing programme linked to the clearances ordered by the MOH. It was not even the result of a bold, imaginative stroke but was the outcome of a series of decisions taken largely to achieve other ends. Following the adoption of the 1864 Act some members of Council saw the need for more provision of cheap housing and they persuaded the Finance Committee to 'give every facility for the erection of model cottages on land belonging to the Corporation'.[55] Five sites were then purchased and Newlands was instructed to draw up a model scheme for the St Martin's site. It was then hoped to auction off the land for the erection of housing similar to that contained in the model scheme.[56] However, considerable apathy was shown among potential buyers[57] and in October 1866 the Council decided, on the recommendation of the Health Committee, to build the dwellings itself.

The period between this decision and the commencement of building was not a happy one, with the Council changing its mind several times and re-submitting designs for amendments to effect greater economies. Eventually it was put to a competition and first prize was awarded to a scheme not subsequently used! The problem continued to be one of cost; the competition had called for plans 'at the lowest cost (having regard both to expense of building and quantity of land occupied), the greater number of healthy and convenient dwellings, substantially built and suitable to the wants of the labouring classes'.[58] The designs were assessed on sanitary principles, namely a free circulation of air, rooms of adequate size and provision of WC's. A large proportion of designs fell foul of Liverpool's local regulations, 'the rock upon which they have split'.[59] The difficulties encountered were not surprising: ' . . . the building act, of which it is impossible to obtain a copy now, it being out of print, was a sealed book, a Liverpool Talmud, to most competitors.'[60] Even when known, the regulations and interpretations of them were difficult to follow and the problem was made worse by the Corporation's willingness to waive several of its own bye-laws regarding building heights and separation widths 'in order to get as many houses on the land as possible'.[61]

Plate III. St Martin's Cottages, Liverpool, erected 1869. Rear view to the east of blocks fronting Sylvester Street. To the left are the three-storey blocks demolished in 1953. The narrowness of the space between the buildings is evident, as is the closed cul-de-sac defined as a 'street' by the Corporation (though it is in many senses a 'court', to avoid their own bye-law restrictions.

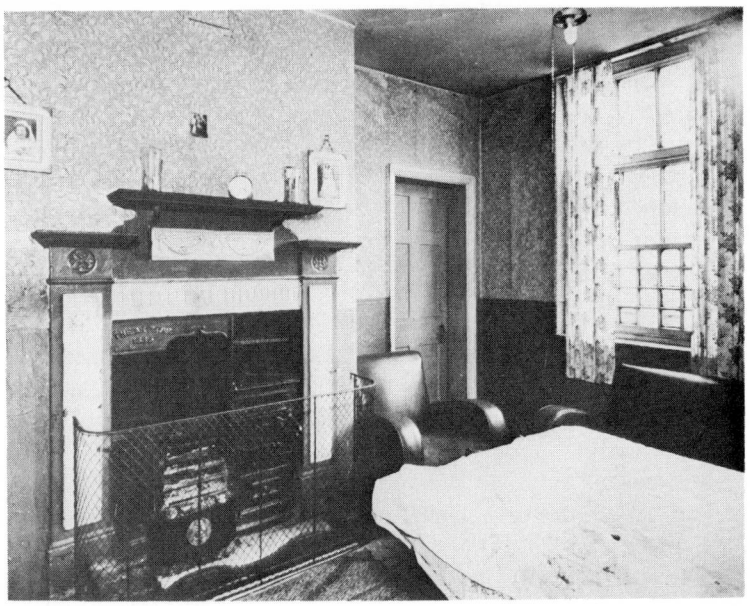

Plate IV. St Martin's Cottages, Liverpool, 1869. Living room, photographed between the wars. Gas lighting and 'The Artisan' ranges were removed in the modernisation of 1953. Ventilation was by means of the usual triple window frames.

When built St Martin's Cottages contained 146 dwellings in four blocks of five storeys and two blocks of three (Figure 3.5). The flats were of one, two and three bedrooms and were entered from landings off the open stone staircase. Two WC's were placed on alternate landings. *The Builder* objected particularly to this arrangement and would have liked to have seen them 'a little less prominently and publicly placed; the seat is opposite the street entrance on the lower floors'. If the lower classes cared little for such delicacies, *The Builder* went on, 'one of the ends of improved dwellings is to raise their occupants, the more the latter are encouraged towards that refinement of habits which forms so large an element in civilisation, the better for them'.[62] Not objected to by *The Builder* or anyone else except Hugh Shimmin was the inclusion of 'basement residences'.[63] The euphemism did little to disguise the fact that to increase its return the Corporation was in effect building cellar dwellings and this on 'made land' created by infilling with chemical refuse. *The Porcupine* pointed out the Council's hypocrisy in condemning such dwellings in private houses while committing 'the sinful practice' themselves. Up in Everton even the 'Welsh jerry builders' were providing new, four-roomed houses with separate yards and WC's at 5s rents (though densities here were not low). In dwellings to be let at lower rates 'cheapness must not be accomplished at the expense of nastiness.'[64]

In attempting to achieve the maximum possible use of its site, the Corporation had bent its own bye-laws, built cellar dwellings, attained a population density of over a thousand persons to the acre and charged the highest market rents. Even so the 5½ per cent return could 'not be considered a very paying speculation' and *The Builder* felt that

' . . . those who undertake to provide for the labouring population in our towns, must be content for the present to mix a little philanthropy with their calculations . . . to make any tangible improvement (. . .) we must not wait too warily for large percentages . . . It is to be hoped that the Corporation of Liverpool having made on the whole a fair first experiment, will not stop in so desirable a work'.[65]

Soon after the opening of St Martin's Cottages, the Liverpool Labourers Dwelling Company had decided to erect their first and the town's fifth model dwellings, called Ashfield Cottages (Figure 3.6). The formula was now a familiar one; financially the venture was to be self-supporting, not charitable; tenants would pay a fair rent and 'thus their self-respect would not be lessened by any consciousness of living in almshouses'.[66] A Mr Shaw Brown had pointed out that labourers could not afford 3s 6p a week but the chairman, Lord Derby, said, to cheers, that labourers apparently managed to do so in London. The dwellings were similar to their close neighbours, St Martin's Cottages, and like them also included basement residences which were later closed.[67]

This quickening in sanitary activity slackened once the death rates assumed their more normal, though by outside standards highly abnormal, levels. Beyond a small circle of enthusiasts Liverpool's interest in sanitary reform was never high and was quick to dissipate; 'the wave of sanitary progress rolled over rapidly and a calm set in'.[68]

Rehousing the Dispossessed

In Liverpool the 'calm' of the 1870s in sanitary matters corresponded with the 'great depression' in charitable effort and indifference to social questions noted by Simey.[69] With every slum clearance presentment the MOH was subject to violent and persistent attacks in Council and 'at length got tired of maintaining the fight and ceased troubling himself to any great extent'. Thereafter the 'patch-work policy set in and if an evil could be tinkered with it was thought to be cured'.[70] From 1871 to 1884 only one presentment, in 1880, was made to Council (Figure 3.7), despite the publication in 1871 of a report by the eminent medical men, Parkes and Sanderson, which restated the basic elements of the sanitary case. A sense of deep shock produced by their contact with Liverpool's slum conditions permeates this report and although not called upon to suggest solutions they recognised that despite the Corporation's efforts of cleansing and demolition, 'the essential features of the labyrinth of courts remain and

Plate V. Ashfield Cottages, Liverpool, erected 1871 by the Liverpool Labourers' Dwelling Company. This photograph was taken in 1955 shortly before demolition. The bricked-up 'basement residences', closed in the nineteenth century, are evident. Access to the upper storeys was by stone stairways at either end of the block. A photograph of the internal arrangements survives showing the W.C. in the kitchen adjacent to the flat doorway. There is some external similarity to Gatliff Buildings, London, built four years earlier by the Metropolitan Association for Improving the Dwellings of the Industrious Classes. (By permission of Liverpool Corporation).

ASHFIELD COTTAGES
1871

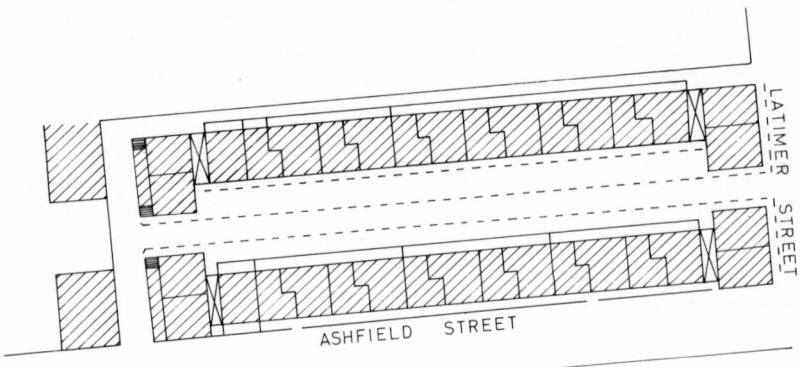

ALEXANDRA TERRACE
1880

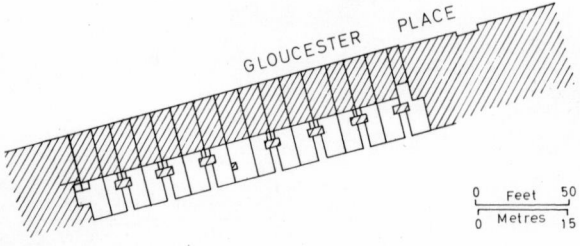

3.6 Tenement dwellings in Liverpool, 1871–1891.

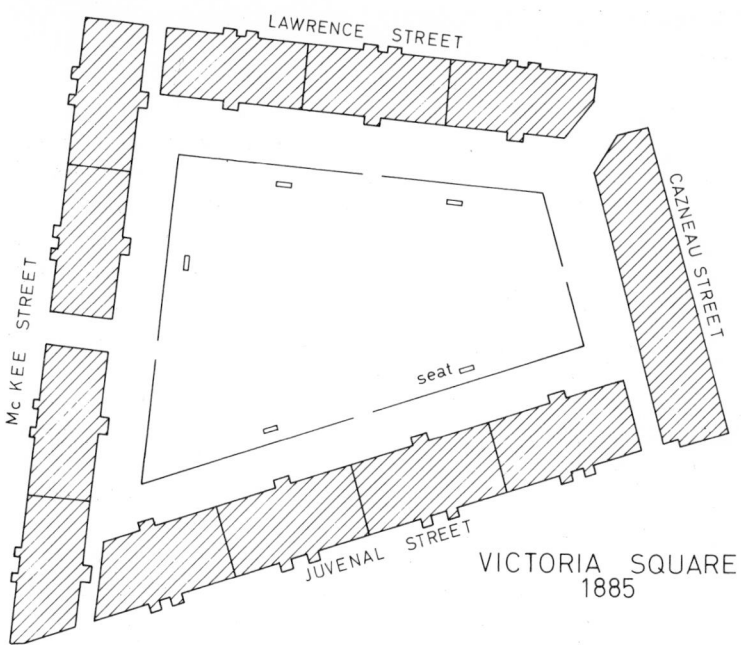

VICTORIA SQUARE
1885

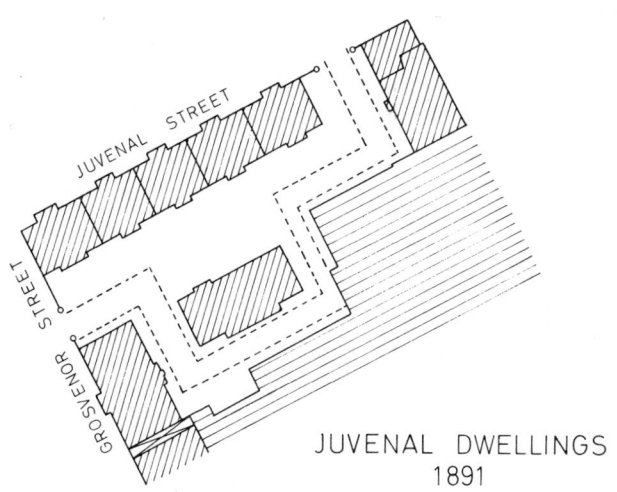

JUVENAL DWELLINGS
1891

can only be removed by demolition *on a much larger scale*' (my italics.[71] Nevertheless, they baulked at the idea of publicly provided housing: 'that would be simply offering a premium to pauperism'.[72]

With the passage of the Artisans' and Labourers' Dwellings Act of 1875 Liverpool for the first time considered using an act of general legislation. As an area-wide instrument the act might have been thought well-suited to the Liverpool situation and indeed two districts were examined as to their suitability for treatment.[73] One of these, the Marybone-Byrom Street area, had been notorious since Duncan's days and, significantly, had already been 'improved' by the Health Committee at a cost of £20,000. Despite these efforts its average death rates still exceeded forty-six per thousand in 1874.

Dr Trench, the MOH, emerges at this time as a major stumbling-block to real reform. As a man with limited vision, perhaps over-cautious from his early political encounters, he lacked a clear conception of the scale of Liverpool's slum problem and the radical approaches needed to eliminate it. He began with the proposition that the back-to-back courts alone needed clearance but even here he was worried that the demolition of badly-constructed courts would force 'poor decent families to seek shelter and herd with the improvident and vicious in those days of misery in the low, sub-let districts of the town'.[74] So he favoured scattered demolitions, for area-wide clearance

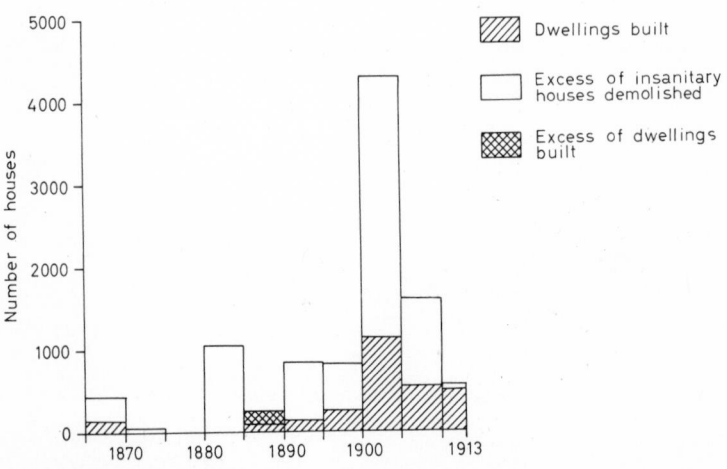

3.7 **Dwellings built and insanitary houses demolished by Liverpool Corporation, 1865–1913.**

programmes would inevitably have included some healthy dwellings. He regretted Parliament's failure to encourage the improvement of existing dwellings rather than demolition. He hoped too that slum clearance could be made to pay for itself by the sale of cleared sites for trade purposes, though he did concede that new, improved dwellings would be needed to receive some of the displaced population.[75] It was as an essential preliminary to the latter proposal that he recommended the clearance of 117 unfit houses and sixty-two other dwellings to allow private tenders for the construction of labourers' dwellings.

The history of the Nash Grove scheme, as it became known, in many ways mirrored that of St Martin's. The Corporation and its officials were loth to allow the construction of publicly-owned dwellings until private enterprise had been given every opportunity to utilise the site for low-rental housing and again these builders were notable by their absence. The stalemate persisted until the arrival of Liverpool's reliable friend of sanitary progress – the epidemic. In 1881 typhus fever returned and the Council was prodded into renewed activity.[76] The condition of the masses re-emerged as a popular debating subject with the now familiar descriptions of squalor and its favourite haunts.[77]

Among speeches addressed to the subject was one by Sir Arthur Forwood, chairman of the Insanitary Property Committee, leader of the local Conservative Party and later MP for the borough. This address is in many ways a landmark in the history of municipal housing for he had come almost reluctantly to the opinion that the housing role of a public authority should be one of saving the 'toiling thousands from the evil consequences which the avarice and greed of individuals might inflict'.[78] He proposed a comprehensive scheme of slum clearance linked with a re-housing programme that would rid the town for ever of its 15,000 court houses and would rehouse their 60,000 occupants. Furthermore, his reasoning provides us with evidence concerning the conclusive arguments for the adoption of the tenement block as the instrument of Liverpool's pre-war housing programme. Forwood pointed out that the local bye-laws, with their not over-generous space standards, would allow only about a quarter of the existing dwellings to be replaced on the same area. Land was too scarce and expensive (the borough, not extended until 1895, was now entirely built up) for housing on 'the self-contained cottage principle'. The only solution was that a 'system of building separate tenements in flats, so common and so popular in London, must be considered as a necessity also in Liverpool'.[79] He did, however, foresee some smaller blocks of cheap, self-contained cottages in small cleared areas.[80] Rents would have to be no higher than 1s per week per room but at £150 per cottage no private person would accept such a return. The Corporation would therefore be forced to undertake the re-housing programme itself, though by providing only two new dwellings for every three demolished it would still stimulate the private sector.[81] The total cost to the Corporation ratepayer would amount to £1.4 million, the equivalent of a penny rate and well within the means of a prosperous city accustomed to spending on such a grand scale for prestigious improvements. Sefton Park alone had cost almost half a million pounds.

The Engineer's report in the following year provides conclusive proof of the economic advantages of the tenement solution.[82] He was asked to report on the

'best examples of buildings erected for the accommodation of the lower classes, at the lowest possible scale of rentals, in blocks and self-contained, and . . . to report as to the advisability of endeavouring to remodel . . . insanitary property . . . so as to make them healthy dwellings at a moderate cost'.[83]

The ceiling rent of 1s per week per room was a 'most difficult' problem and he admitted that it might be 'beyond a successful solution from a purely financial point of view'. On the question of structures he came to the same conclusion as Forwood that in areas where large numbers did not need to be catered for, self-contained houses of two or three storeys would be

'the most suitable and . . . *best appreciated by the labouring classes*. If however it was necessary to provide for a large number of persons on a limited area recourse must be had to dwellings in blocks several storeys in height.' (my italics)[84]

Cost curves derived from his statistics bear out the economic logic of these statements (Figure 3.8). With low land values, two-storey cottages were the most economic in terms of cost per room; as land costs increased this dwelling type became the third-cheapest and five- or six-storeyed blocks of flats became most economical. Once land surpassed £2 per square yard these multi-storeyed blocks (as high as stairs could reasonably take people) became the only dwelling type yielding more than 3½ per cent. If the ability to re-house maximum numbers *in situ* were considered, five- and six-storeyed blocks were again favourable (Figure 3.9).

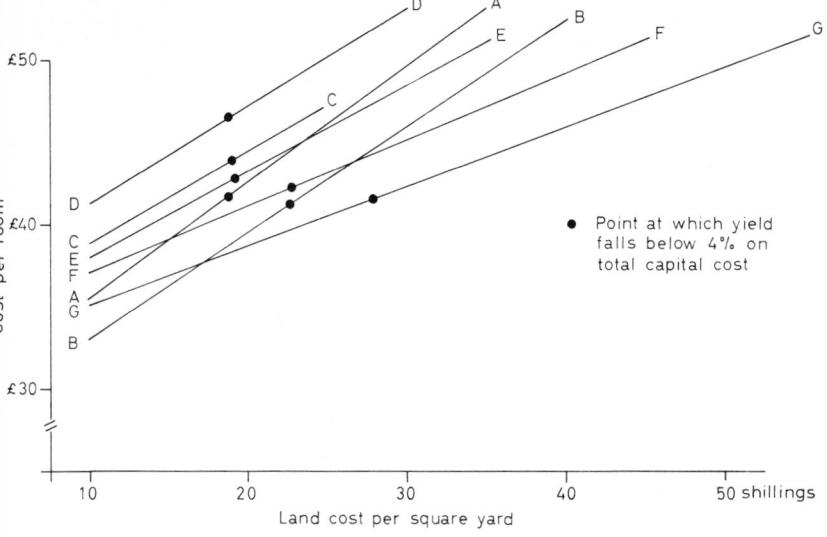

3.8 Cost per room by housing type and land cost, 1884.

The inclusion in the report of elaborate schemes for court-house conversion indicates how far the 'improvement' policy of Trench was, even at this stage, still viewed as an alternative or addition to a new housing programme. Indeed the Engineer felt the scheme had 'much to recommend it',[85] despite the fact that the conversion costs per room amounted to £54, 15 per cent higher than the most expensive new housing schemes at the same land cost.[86]

The papers by Forwood and Dunscombe were clear indications of the likely shape of any coherent future housing policy. For the time being however the proposals were greeted with a barrage of opposition from the Liverpool Land and House Owners Association and little more was heard of the proposals for another fifteen years.[87] Meanwhile, after considerable debate, it was decided to erect Corporation dwellings on the Nash Grove site, the displaced poor having been left for eight years without alternative housing, to which they were entitled under the 1875 Act. The new Insanitary Property and Artisans Dwellings Committee now aimed at providing dwellings of

'the best class, to be an example hereafter to be aimed at by future private enterprise . . . [for residents] whose earnings are sufficient to enable them to pay the moderate rental fixed for the high class accommodation that will be afforded'.[88]

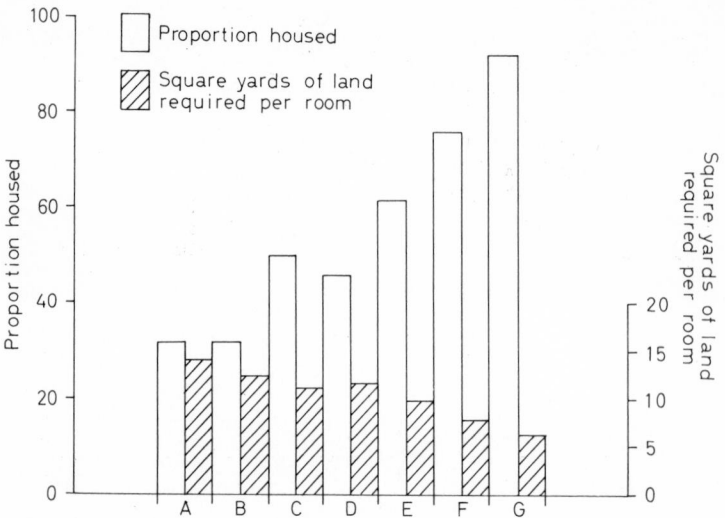

3.9 Proportion of displaced population housed and area required by housing type, 1884.

The 272 dwellings of one to three rooms were to be rented at from 2s 9d to 5s 3d. Victoria Square, which has been fully described elsewhere, was opened by Sir Richard Cross in 1885 and received a diploma of honour at the International Health Exhibition in 1884 (Figure 3.6).[89]

Once more, the modest flurry of sanitary activity passed and the late 1880s were years in which little demolition and no municipal house building took place. The more frequent presentments made after 1889 (involving the demolition of 1,272 houses in the following five years) began to run into political opposition from a new quarter – that of organised labour. The Council's record on the slum housing problem was criticised as anti-working class; admittedly it had resulted in slum clearance but that was little consolation when virtually no alternative housing was being made available. Through Labour and Irish Nationalist representatives, pressure was exerted on the Council to try to ensure a policy of re-housing linked to demolition. As a token gesture in this direction Juvenal Dwellings were completed in 1891, the last municipal housing for six years, but demolition in fact increased and the closing years of the century saw the continued failure to balance the demolition of insanitary dwellings with new housing.

Plate VI. Victoria Square (Nash Grove site), Liverpool, erected in 1885 by Liverpool Corporation. This photograph was taken in 1944 following war damage. The buildings were improved in 1954 and demolished in 1961. The central open space of 5,200 sq. yds. (almost double that required by bye-law) was considered of great sanitary benefit. The scale and expensive detailing of both the exterior and interior (which included communal laundries and liver-crested doorknockers) point to this as a prestige development intended for the better-off artisans. (By permission of Liverpool Corporation).

Prospect and Retrospect

The new century marked a real turning point in Liverpool's public housing policies, symbolised by the substitution of the name 'Housing Committee' for 'Insanitary Property Committee'. With this change came a general recognition that the Corporation was not morally unjustified in building houses itself. It was this attitude, rather than any supposed lack of finance, that had been the greatest single impediment to positive housing progress since 1864. Another vital principle established at the century's end was the recognition that all suitable cleared sites should as far as possible be used for re-housing. These changes were the result of the adoption by the ruling Conservative party of Forwood's populist housing programme designed to attract the workers' vote. In the first fourteen years of the new century the

Corporation was to build 2,392 dwellings, the majority in tenements, compared with the previous total of 503.[90] By 1914 Liverpool had more of its population housed municipally than any other city and was second only to London in terms of the absolute numbers involved.[91] Yet this transformation in the conception of civic responsibility had been long in gestation, even if its actual birth was to a degree dramatically sudden.

This paper has attempted to show that the determination to engage in a large scale publicly-financed housing programme was to a large extent the natural outgrowth of decisions made by the Council to play an active role in shaping the urban environment after the public health crisis of the 1840s. Initially concerned only to regulate and later to clear the worst abuses, the Corporation was forced by the failure of the private housing sector in providing cheap, sanitary housing, to contemplate active participation in the market itself. It has been shown that investment reluctance of private enterprise was a logical outcome of the operation of free market forces which had as their prime determinant the low level of casual wages in a glutted labour market. Despite the Council's clearance programme, and to an extent because of it, the problem of insanitary, overcrowded dwellings remained acute in Liverpool's inner wards and death rates in excess of forty per thousand still occurred until the end of the century. If Liverpool's overall mortality rates diminished it was as much due to the extension of new sanitary housing of the post-bye-law era as to dramatic improvements in general health levels in inner city areas.

Faced with continued high inner-area mortality, the Corporation at first attempted to stimulate the interest of the private market by its first two tenement blocks, but it was not until the end of the century that the political climate had changed sufficiently to permit the contemplation of an uneconomic return on Corporation investment. The transformation was achieved too late to put Liverpool in the forefront of publicly-financed housing in the nineteenth century, a position it might have been expected to occupy following its early legislation and the construction of St Martin's Cottages. Nevertheless it should be added that much lost ground was quickly made up in the first two decades of the twentieth century. In part this lag can be attributed to the strong and well-placed opposition of vested interests but more probably to a general lack of concern over matters which to middle-class councillors would have seemed economically unorthodox, politically embarrassing and of little direct electoral appeal.

The lack of emphasis placed on building form in this paper is a reflection of the paucity of debate on these matters, compared with the controversy over the actual *need* for public housing. Once the principle of council housing was accepted, the building form became a matter of direct economics. As in London high land values automatically meant the adoption of tall structures. Forwood refers to the 'prejudice against dwellings erected in flats and large blocks'[92] but there is no evidence to indicate that such prejudice affected the Corporation's decision to rely on the tenement block for virtually all of its twenty-five pre-war housing schemes.[93]

Name		Date	Location
1.	Dock Cottages	1844–6	Stanley–Illchester Streets, Birkenhead
2.	Morpeth Dwellings	c. 1845	Wood Street. Birkenhead
3.	[Hughes's Cottages]	c. 1845	?
4.	Kent Terrace	c. 1845	Kent Street, Liverpool
5.	Prince Albert Cottages	1852–4	Upper Frederick Street, Liverpool
6.	Northumberland Buildings	1857	Northumberland – George Streets, Liverpool
7.	St Martins Cottages	1869	Ashfield–Sylvester Streets, Liverpool
8.	[Jackson Street]	?(1840s?)	Jackson Street, Birkenhead
9.	[Brougham Street]	?(pre-1870)	Brougham St., Birkenhead
10.	Ashfield Cottages	1871	Ashfield Street, Liverpool
11.	Alexandra Terrace	c. 1880	Gloucester Place, Liverpool
12.	Victoria Square [Nash Grove]	1885	Cazneau Street, Liverpool
13.	Juvenal Dwellings	1890	Juvenal Street, Liverpool
14.	Arley Street Dwellings	1897, 1902–3	Arley Street, Liverpool
15.	Gildarts Gardens	1897, 1904	Gildart Street, Liverpool

Tenement Housing on Merseyside 1844—1900

Owners	Description No. of Dwellings	Blocks	Storeys	Rent	Cost
Birkenhead Dock Co. (Arch. C.E. Lang, London)	324	6	4	3/6 – 5/0	£50,000
William Laird	64	8	4	3/6 – 4/6	£7,942
Robert Hughes	70	5	3+C	4/8	£12,600
?	94?	4	4?	?	?
George Melly 'and friends' (Arch. G. Williams)	22	2	4?	4/0 – 5/9	£4,200
Liverpool Association for the Improvement of Dwellings of the Industrious Classes	35?	2	4?	c.4/8	£6,360
Liverpool Corporation (Arch. Redman & Hesketh)	146	6	2x3+C 4x5+C	3/0 – 6/0	£17,800
?	8	2	3+B	?	?
?	42	7	2+B	?	?
Liverpool Labourers Dwellings Co.	132	2	3+C	c.3/6?	£22,000
Liverpool Labourers Dwellings Co.	32?	1	4	?	?
Liverpool Corporation (Arch. C. Dunscombe)	271	5	5	2/3 – 6/0	£70,000
Liverpool Corporation (Arch. C. Dunscombe)	282	4	3x4 1x3	3/6 – 5/6	£20,000
Liverpool Corporation (Arch. C. Dunscombe)	46	1	2	4/0 – 5/9	£11,000
Liverpool Corporation (Arch. C. Dunscombe)	88 (1897) 141 (1904)	9	3	2/3 – 4/6	£45,000

Notes

1. 'If the map of England were shaded to represent the rates of mortality of the last quarter, the eye travelling from the lighter south to the darker north would be instantly drawn to a spot of portentious darkness on the Mersey'. *Report of the Registrar General*, Second Quarter, 1866.

2. It was called 'an unmerited libel on the old town' by J.P. Halton, *The Results of the Great Operations of Surgery*, Liverpool, 1843, pp.24–7. Duncan's reply to Halton's statistical naivety is contained in W.H. Duncan, *Letter to John P. Halton Esq. . . .*, Liverpool, 1844.

3. W. Moss, *A Familiar Medical Survey of Liverpool*, London, 1784, p.84, and W. Enfield, *An Essay Towards the History of Leverpool* (sic), Warrington, 1773, p.29.

4. The main body of Duncan's evidence is contained in three submissions before government enquiries: Select Committee on Health of Towns, P.P. (H. of C.), 1840, XI, pp.441–53; 'On the Sanitary State of Liverpool', *Local Report No.19 to the Sanitary Enquiry*, P.P. (H. of L.), 1842, XXVII, pp.282–94. (Also published separately by Clowes); 'On the Physical Causes of the High Rate of Mortality in Liverpool', first read as three papers before the Liverpool Literary and Philosophical Society, February and March, 1843, later presented to the Commission on the State of Large Towns and Populous Districts, P.P. (H. of C.), 1844, XVII, pp.12–33. (Also published separately by Clowes, pp.122–60.)

5. I.C. Taylor, 'The Court and Cellar Dwelling: The Eighteenth Century Origin of the Liverpool Slum', *Transactions of the Historic Society of Lancashire and Cheshire*, Vol.CXII, 1970, pp.75 ff.

6. W.H. Duncan's evidence to *A Report on the Proceedings of a Court of Enquiry . . . [Municipal Corporations Enquiry] in November, 1833*, Liverpool, 1833, p.401.

7. *Report of a Committee of the Manchester Statistical Society on the Condition of the Working Classes in an Extensive Manufacturing District in 1834, 1835, 1836*, London, 1838, pp.8–10, also reported in *British Association for the Advancement of Science, Proceedings*, Vol.VI, 1837, p.143. Both the original survey and Whitty's checking survey are described in the above. The MSS agents' figures are preserved in more detail in *Parliamentary Gazetteer of England and Wales, 1842*, Vol.III, Glasgow, 1842, p.132.

   The Corporation survey is found in Liverpool, Health of Town Committee Minute Books, Vol.I, i April 1841; This return together with the district surveyors' accompanying account has been published in an appendix to the evidence given by the Borough Surveyor, J. Franklin, to the Select Committee on Regulation of Buildings and Improvement of Boroughs, P.P. (H. of C.), 1842, X, pp.299–304. The return has also been misinterpreted and inaccurately reprinted in J.H. Treble, 'Liverpool Working Class Housing, 1801–1851', in *The History of Working Class Housing. A Symposium*, ed. S.D. Chapman, David and Charles, Newton Abbot, 1971.

8. W.H. Duncan (1844), Table 7.

9. I.C. Taylor, 'Environment and Society in Georgian and Victorian Liverpool', Liverpool University Ph.D., in progress.

10. Letter from Dr Trench to Board of Health, 18 September 1866 (P.R.O., Board of Health Correspondence).

11. Passed as 'Act for the promotion of health of Liverpool and the better regulation of buildings', 1842, 5 and 6 Vic., XLIV, 18 June 1842 (took effect 1 November 1842).

12. W.H. Duncan (1844), pp.160–61.

13. Appendix No.3, 'Abstract of Petitions presented to the Select Committee on the Building Regulations and Borough Improvement Bills', P.P. (H. of C.), 1842, X, p.304 (my italics).
14. *Ibid.*, Appendix No.2.
15. *Ibid.*, p.188 (q.284).
16. J.H. Treble, *loc. cit.*
17. Liverpool, Health Committee [Thomas Fresh], *Report on the Sanitary Operations of the Nuisance Department from June 1847 to March 1851*, Liverpool, 1851, p.102.
18. J. Aspinall, chairman of the Health Committee, had already foreseen this and admitted the Council's lack of policy in the matter of re-housing in his evidence to the Health of Towns Commission, P.P. (H. of C.), 1845, XVII, q.30.
19. 'Abstract of Petitions . . . ', *loc. cit.*
20. J.H. Treble, *loc. cit.*, p.193.
21. W. Bate, 'Sanitary Administration in Liverpool, 1847–1900', unpublished M.A. thesis, University of Liverpool, 1955, p.39.
22. *Ibid.*, p.105.
23. W.H. Duncan (1844), p.161. Newlands was even more visionary, proposing the erection of detached blocks of four cottages with yards, standards not achieved in Liverpool until 1919, *Report of Sewerage and Other Works*, Liverpool, 1848, p.110.
24. E.H. Greenhow, General Board of Health, 'Papers Relating to the Sanitary State of the People, England', P.P. (H. of C.), 1857–8, XXIII.
25. Duncan pointed out that among major towns Liverpool Registration District consisted only of the central parish and excluded the healthy suburbs. Duncan had himself used comparisons of this type earlier in his career *(Medical Officer of Health Report for 1859*, p.12). See also W.T. McGowen (the Council's legal assistant), *Sanitary Legislation with Illustration from Experience in Liverpool*, Liverpool, 1859, and *The Air We Breathe*, Liverpool, 1860.
26. W. Bate, *op. cit.*, p.41.
27. H. Shimmin, 'The Mysteries of the Courts', *The Porcupine*, 15 Nov. 1862 to 10 Oct. 1863. Later published as *The Courts and Alleys of Liverpool Described from Personal Inspection*, Liverpool, 1864.
28. *Ibid.*, p.73.
29. Liverpool Sanitary Amendment Act, 1864, 27 and 28 Vic., LXXIII, 23 Jan. 1864.
30. J.N. Tarn, 'Housing in Liverpool and Glasgow', *Town Planning Review*, Vol.XXXIX, 1969, pp.319–34.
31. W. Bate, *op. cit.*, p.142.
32. Liverpool, *Council Proceedings*, 7 Dec. 1864, p.36.
33. J.N. Tarn, *Working Class Housing in Nineteenth-Century Britain*, Lund Humphries, London, 1971, chap.3.
34. Quoted in *Land We Live In*, [Anon.], 1854 (and earlier eds.?). I have not been able to trace Robertson's original paper. The dwellings were also described in *The Builder*, Vol.III, 1845, pp.220–1. This has been summarised in N. Pevsner, 'Model Houses for the Labouring Classes', *Architectural Review*, Vol.XCIII, 1943, p.123.
35. *Land We Live In*, p.165.
36. *Ibid.*, p.166.
37. H. Roberts, *The Dwellings of the Labouring Classes*, 1850, p.13. Chadwick attended the opening and while expressing general approval he had doubts on the system of fresh air ventilation *(The Builder*, Vol.IV, 1846, p.537).

38. H. Roberts, *op. cit.*, p.109. The plan has been reprinted in N. Pevsner, *loc. cit.*, p.124.
39. H. Roberts, *op. cit.*, p.14.
40. *Land We Live In*, p.167.
41. *Ibid.*, p.168.
42. J.H. Robertson, 'Remarks on the Dwellings for the Labouring Classes at Birkenhead: Evils of the Window Tax', *Journal of Public Health and Monthly Record of Sanitary Improvement*, Vol.I, 1848, pp.63–6.
43. *The Builder*, Vol.III, 1845, p.221.
44. J.H. Robertson, *op. cit.*, p.64.
45. Quoted in *The Builder*, Vol.IV, 1846, p.537.
46. For Morpeth Buildings, see J.H. Robertson, *op. cit.*, and H. Roberts, *op. cit.* These sources have been kindly supplemented by the Chief Public Health Inspector, Birkenhead.
47. Information and photographs relating to the Jackson Street and Brougham Street dwellings have been kindly supplied by the Chief Public Health Inspector. They are mentioned in Birkenhead M.O.H., *Report for 1870* (unpag.). For 'Hughes' Cottages' see Robertson, *op. cit.*
48. *The Builder*, Vol.III, 1845, p.221; J. Boult, *Transactions of the Liverpool Polytechnic Society*, 1844–6, pp.78–86; evidence of J. Aspinall (qq.46–9) to Commission on the state of Large Towns and Populous Districts, *Second Report*, P.P., 1845, XVIII, pp.85–6. Aspinall gives details of the ground floor plan of the west end of the property. The architect Ellis referred to by Boult had also designed houses 'being built' at Gerard and Byrom Street, 'three houses' in height (5 or 6 storeys?). The builders of Kent Terrace, Hughes and Jones, were also engaged in providing artisan housing in blocks of four, back-to-back with separate yards on Paddington Street, a rare example in Liverpool of non-court back-to-back housing.
49. G. Melly, *Self Help*, London, 1864, p.10; H. Roberts, 'The Dwellings of the Labouring Classes', *Transactions of the National Association for the Promotion of Social Science*, 1858, p.609.
50. *Ibid.*
51. *Ibid.*
52. *Ibid.*
53. *The Builder*, Vol.XII, 1854, p.283. Also in *Labourer's Friend*, 1854, p.95.
54. *The Builder*, Vol.XV, 1857, p.68. The dwellings were later disposed of, for they were included in the estate of Robertson Gladstone in 1876. An internal plan was included in the prospectus of the sale (information provided by M. Stammers, City of Liverpool Museums).
55. *The Builder*, Vol.XXII, 1864, p.907.
56. *The Builder*, Vol.XXIV, 1864, pp.276, 373.
57. *The Builder*, Vol.XXV, 1867, p.174.
58. *The Builder*, Vol.XXVII, 1869, p.98.
59. *The Builder*, Vol.XXV, 1867, p.174.
60. *Ibid.*
61. Liverpool, *Council Proceedings*, 10 Oct. 1866, quoted in W. Bate, *op. cit.*, p.155.
62. *The Builder*, Vol.XXVII, 1869, p.98.
63. 'Basement Residences', *The Porcupine*, 16 May 1868, p.66.
64. 'Workmen's Dwellings', *The Porcupine*, 9 May 1868, p.56.
65. Within a few years the offending basements were closed, thus reducing the number of dwellings to 124. They were modernised in 1953, electricity was introduced and structural alterations were made. The two inner blocks of three storeys were demolished. (The life of these last surviving nineteenth-

century tenements in Liverpool has been extended yet again by recent proposals.) See F. Walter, 'Conversions, Number Six, Liverpool: Improvement to Sub-standard Houses', *Architectural Journal*, 18 March 1954, pp.337—8.

66. *The Builder*, Vol.XXIX, 1871, p.453.
67. *Ibid*. The dwellings are also described in J. Rayner, *Sanitary and Social Improvement*, Liverpool, 1875. They were demolished in the 1950s.
68. *The Porcupine*, 6 Jan. 1875.
69. M.B. Simey, *Charitable Effort in Liverpool in the Nineteenth Century*, Liverpool, 1951.
70. *The Porcupine*, 6 Feb. 1875.
71. E.A. Parkes and J.S. Burdon Sanderson, *Report on the Sanitary Condition of Liverpool*, Liverpool, 1871, p.69.
72. *Ibid*., p.76.
73. Liverpool, Health Committee, 'Report of the Medical Officer of Health as to the Area, Population and Death Rates of Two Districts of the Borough', in *Council Proceedings*, 1875, pp.647—61.
74. Quoted in A.B. Forwood, *The Dwellings of the Working Classes and How to Improve Them*, Liverpool, 1873, p.17.
75. *Ibid*.
76. Investigated in the MOH's report for the Health Committee, *Causes of Fever and Other Zymotic Diseases in the City*, Liverpool, 1884.
77. Articles republished by the *Liverpool Daily Post* as *Squalid Liverpool: Report by a Commission*, Liverpool, 1883. Also, C.S. Pain and W. Carter, *Concerning Insanitary Houses, Light, Pure Air and Water*, Liverpool, 1884.
78. A.B. Forwood, *op. cit.*, p.4.
79. *Ibid*., p.20.
80. *Ibid*., p.29.
81. *Ibid*., p.28.
82. Liverpool, City Engineer, *Labourers Dwellings, Report*, Liverpool, 1884.
83. *Ibid*., p.3.
84. *Ibid*., p.6.
85. *Ibid*., p.8.
86. *Ibid*., p.12.
87. W. Pierce, O. Williams,, J. Murphy, *Letters on the Insanitary Dwellings and Housing of the Poor*, Liverpool, 1884. (Owen Williams was a prominent Welsh 'jerry-builder').
88. Liverpool, City Engineer, 1884, *op. cit.*, p.14. Though there were very few imitations of model dwellings on the lines hoped for by the Corporation, Liverpool's three or four storey 'Scotch or workmens' dwellings', often built above shops, might be considered as the multi-storey response of the private market. They were erected on Whittle, Back Colquitt, Parr, Tetlow, Lattimer, Hopwood, Smith, Salisbury, Back Salisbury and Field Streets, on York, Wilmot and Byrom Terraces, and on Wellington and Everton Roads (this list is not complete).
89. *The Builder*, 19 June 1886, p.881. The post-war conversions are described in W. Felix, *loc. cit.*, pp.339—40.
90. B.D. White, *A History of the Corporation of Liverpool, 1835—1914*, Liverpool, 1951, p.136.
91. *Ibid*., p.140.
92. A.B. Forwood, *op. cit.*, p.26.
93. Only parts of the Bevington Street and Sparling Street schemes contained two storey houses, though the Arley and Kew Street schemes contained two storey flats.

Chapter 4 A Landscape of Small Houses: the failure of the workers' flat in Lancashire and Yorkshire in the nineteenth century *S. Martin Gaskell*

'Notwithstanding these present points in its favour, we doubt whether at present this system of building in blocks will be very successful anywhere but in the metropolis where the enormous value of land renders any other impossible, especially for that large number of artisans whose residence near to their work is almost indispensable. But in provincial towns, the independent artisan . . . would not readily reconcile himself to dwellings of this description.'
J. Hole, *The Homes of the Working Classes* (1866), p.62.

At a time when the advantages of building dwellings in tenement form were being strongly advocated in London,[1] the North's leading housing reformer, James Hole, was virtually discounting such a remedy for the West Riding.[2] He did so for reasons that were to be invoked in opposition to the building of flats for the remainder of the century in Lancashire and Yorkshire. There the pressure on land was never so great that sheer cost made the ideal of an individual house impossible for a large proportion of working-class families. Nor did the industrial towns of the cotton and woollen areas ever develop to such an extent over the century that travelling presented such real difficulties as to make rehousing in central districts an essential requirement. The arguments that housing reformers brought forward in favour of building dwellings in London could never be applied with equal justification in the provinces.

Furthermore, in Lancashire and Yorkshire there was not, as there was further north, any tradition of tenement living.[3] This was so despite the fact that in some of the narrow West Riding valleys the steepness of the slope necessitated building upwards. But such towering terraces as still survive at Todmorden and Hebden Bridge, Halifax and Sowerby Bridge were not flat dwellings in the accepted sense of the term.[4] It was simply for reasons of physical necessity that the houses were placed one on top of the other, and each was entered completely separately from different levels on the hillside. There were no common entrances or stairways; the individual front door remained inviolate. Nor did the practice of private flat building, which seems to have begun in Birkenhead in 1845, spread further into Lancashire than the port of

Liverpool itself.[5] The early and continued interest which both philanthropic societies and the Corporation in that city displayed in the provision of model dwelling blocks was in no like matched in any of the other large industrial centres of the North.[6]

Tenement dwellings, both in their basic concept and their design, were importations onto the northern scene. They seem frequently to have been but adaptations of national trends and changing fashions in housing. They never really took root. The northern working man was too attached to the ideal of his individual home.[7] Artisans traditionally lived in separate houses and the number of persons per house was low.[8] This state of affairs was even more true in the West Riding than in Lancashire. In Sheffield, Dr G.C. Holland noted in 1843 that the artisans generally had a house for themselves and those in the suburbs frequently also had a garden.[9] In good times it was unusual to find two families under the same roof though, of course, such accommodation was not available for all the working class. That in Manchester in 1851 nearly 12 per cent of the population lived in cellars clearly testified to this,[10] but individual occupation, if not individual ownership, remained an attainable ideal for many working-class families in the North and the persistence of this ideal ultimately exercised a modifying influence on the design of such flats as were built in Lancashire and Yorkshire. By the end of the century, the concept of the block dwelling was giving way to that of the cottage flat. Fear of tenement blocks and northern individuality, as well as the differing economics of land use in the provincial town, all combined to devalue the architectural tenets of London housing reformers. As a result the basic division in housing reform schemes — between tenement and terrace, between central and suburban — was questioned and out of the debate emerged a type of flat that in some ways broke down these sharp distinctions.

The original dislike and distrust of tenement blocks was not lessened in the North by the early essays there in block building. The dwellings erected by the Dock Company at Birkenhead had been considered rather grim, being too closely built and inadequately ventilated.[11] Each row was four storeys high and was serviced by an internal public staircase communicating with the flats on each floor. The dangers inherent in such a plan in terms of hygiene and privacy were readily seized on by housing reformers and, by the 1860s, in order to overcome these weaknesses most dwelling blocks in London were being constructed on a more open plan.[12] Such considerations, however, did not apparently trouble those companies and industrialists who built, either out of managerial necessity or for investment purposes, blocks of dwellings to accommodate their labour force and for many northern towns such blocks were the first intimation of what tenement living might mean. At Barrow-in-Furness, in response to the growing housing shortage, the Haemetite Steel Company engaged the Dundee firm of Smith and Caird in 1871 to erect flats on the Scottish model.[13] These were followed by blocks built by the Duke of Devonshire on Barrow Island in 1872 and by the Furness Railway Company in 1879.[14] All were oppressive stone blocks with long iron balconies and limited accommodation. They were designed with the intention of building as cheaply as possible and, in the latter case for instance, the cost per room was £49 10s, compared with the estimated cost of £75 per room in the new Peabody buildings.[15] These limitations were part of the developers' intention of making the maximum use of the land. As a result, on the various sites in Barrow, there were 69.85 structurally separate dwellings per acre. By 1881, 3,590 people in Old Barrow, nearly all flat dwellers, occupied 392 house units, covering less than seven acres.[16] Their not surprising condemnation as 'barracks' was typical of contemporary reaction to several similar developments.[17]

In 1870, the Lancashire and Yorkshire Railway Company erected a four-storey block of dwellings in Oldfield Road, Salford, on land close to their tracks into Victoria Station, Manchester.[18] There was accommodation, at rents varying from 3s to 5s per week, for sixty-two families and each set of rooms was furnished with sinks for washing and a grate with an oven; water closets and dust chutes were provided for each floor. The scheme also included two shops in addition to wash houses and drying grounds. But neither the provision of these facilities nor the careful arrangement of the dwellings themselves could compensate for the austere and unwelcoming appearance of the buildings.[19] The series of forbidding blocks, with their dark and cramped internal staircases, were constructed of common red brick without the slightest relief of ornamentation and their appearance was in no sense improved by their position as close to the high wall of the Company's coal depot as the bye-laws would permit. The grim and unwholesome character of this scheme was matched by another effort in the following year in Manchester when a disused mill in Jersey Street, Ancoats, was converted into 149 dwellings.[20] The first two storeys contained single-roomed dwellings, while the remaining floors provided two- and three-roomed apartments with shared water closets and wash houses on each level. Here again considerations of light and ventilation were overlooked and against such buildings the criticisms of block dwellings were to be justly levelled.[21]

It is not surprising that such tenements earned the title of barracks and that in the public mind they were linked, in their grimness and austerity, to the public lodging houses, now slowly appearing under the 1851 Lodging Houses Acts.[22] The shared facilities and restrictive rules gave such buildings considerable points of similarity and for the working classes both became associated with a decline in economic standards, with a loss of social position. Throughout the century, flat dwelling remained a second-rate alternative for the working men of Lancashire and Yorkshire.

This fundamental dislike of the flat survived the limited efforts of individuals and societies to bring to the provinces the latest conceptions of the design of dwellings that were being formulated in the metropolis. As early as 1844, the Society for Improving the Condition of the Labouring Classes had been formed under the presidency of Lord Ashley and among its objectives was the intention to build what was called 'a planned dwelling or cottages' which would combine 'comfort with economy'.[23] After various London ventures, virtually the last work of the Society was undertaken in Hull in 1862 as a result of a local gift of £5,000 to the Society for the purpose of establishing at Hull 'an example of suitable dwellings for the labouring poor of that town'.[24] The dwellings provided accommodation for thirty-two families, of which five had one bedroom, nineteen two bedrooms and eight had three bedrooms. The buildings formed three sides of a square with a courtyard in the centre and consisted of two storeys with a centre of three storeys on each side. Each dwelling on the ground floor had an entrance from the street and one from the courtyard, while the dwellings on the first floor were approached by stone stairs from the courtyard. Thus each dwelling had separate access and the façade of the building appeared as an ordinary terrace of houses rather than as a block of dwellings.[25] In these ways the Hull Dwellings differed from the blocks that the Society had previously erected in London. The Model Dwellings, built in Streatham Street, Bloomsbury, in 1849, were in a U-shaped block of five storeys with gallery access, while the Thanksgiving Buildings in Grays Inn Road of the same year had internal staircases and were, in fact, designed to show that the staircase access system, if carefully designed, could be quite satisfactory.[26] It is interesting, therefore, that in their one provincial experiment the Society adopted a very different form — one that was considerably more extravagant in terms of land, but a form that was considerably less distinctive in terms of style. In this first experiment in the erection of model dwellings in Yorkshire, the features of the cottage flat system had already made their appearance. But, as an example of what might be undertaken without undue outlay and with the reasonable hope of a modest profit, the Hull Dwellings found few imitators.

Over the next decade, only two schemes envisaged as model dwellings were apparently undertaken in the counties of Yorkshire and Lancashire, excluding Liverpool. In 1873 the Salford Improved Industrial Dwellings Company provided flats for forty-six families in Greengates.[27] The dwellings took the form of four three-storeyed buildings and so here again there was little in external appearance to distinguish these model dwellings from the surrounding terraced property, though this did not enable them to escape the stigma attached to other contemporary multi-dwelling blocks in Manchester.[28] The most notable features of this undertaking were the liberal provision made for the supply of open space around the dwellings and the care taken in fitting out the apartments with washing and cooking facilities.

This concern with internal arrangements was not matched in the model block erected in Shannon Street, Leeds, in 1867.[29] The aim of the Leeds Industrial Dwellings Company was to provide dwellings that would go some way towards meeting the huge demand in the town for cheap accommodation which could be let for a satisfactory profit. The local architects, Adams and Kelly, thus produced a design whose cost was as low as could be compatible with the modest standards of the Company.[30] The small block of eighteen two- or three-roomed dwellings cost £1,440. The rooms were small and the bedrooms inadequately ventilated. But more serious was the fact that though each flat was provided with a slop stone, the washing facilities and lavatories were shared. The latter were grouped on each landing with only three privies to serve the six apartments on each floor. This was the main criticism that *The Builder* made against the dwellings, which in general layout were like their London counterparts, having gallery access in order to avoid the house tax.[31] This block is important, therefore, as probably the only model undertaking in the area, before the municipal efforts at the end of the century, which tried, admittedly on a limited scale, simply to copy current metropolitan fashions. Though it was a small block, the long façade with its front galleries and open staircases, with its Gothic trimmings and gables, obviously looked like a block of model dwellings, as the term was understood in architectural and housing reform circles in the 1860s. Perhaps this was the reason for its later manifest unpopularity.[32] Certainly the last effort by a private company in the North to build model dwellings for the working class shunned the conditions of such a design and deliberately set out to produce one which met the requirements of a provincial town as distinct from those of the capital.

This was the work of the Manchester and Salford Workmen's Dwellings Company (Limited).[33] In its origin, the company was experimental and its first (and only) block, designed by Lawrence Booth of Manchester, in 1883, was intended to be demonstrative. The general policy of the Company was to provide independent household life, at a cost of on average only 2s 6d per week, for the very poor people who then herded together in the slums and low lodging houses.

> 'Good sanitary arrangements, privacy and the possibility of decency in the domestic life of the tenants are the objects sought to be attained.'[34]

As a basic principle of design, 'the large flat system' was to be avoided and a plan that could be called 'the semi-detached cottage' adopted. Moreover, the promoters considered that it was undesirable to build anything like a 'colony' of such dwellings in any particular place, but rather sought to distribute them in smaller groups wherever land could be secured. Thus a main consideration was to reduce to a minimum, in this case, the distinctiveness that could accrue to tenement dwellings through their size and design.

As with the contemporary East End Dwellings Company Ltd in London, the aim was to provide for the poorest class of labourers at the very cheapest cost compatible with realising a fair rate of interest upon the capital employed.[35] The design reflected these considerations. The layout was to consist of three-storey blocks which contained two dwellings on each floor, while the blocks themselves were separated by open staircases. Behind the dwellings there was a communal drying yard and playing area which the architect considered preferable to small independent backyards, for a large open rear space combined with a wide front street would provide for 'such a complete circulation of air around each block as will secure immunity from the spread of fire and even infective diseases'. This was considered particularly important when dealing with a class whose habits and ways were notoriously difficult. Each dwelling contained two rooms, with the bedroom again divided by a wooden screen in order to allow a certain degree of privacy at a minimum cost. The tenant was supplied with an earthenware slop sink, a ventilated pantry cupboard and an oven range, in addition to an individual water closet and coal bunker on the landing. Privacy in such arrangements was felt to be essential if cleanliness was to be enjoined among the lower classes[36] and it was fear of the destructive habits of such tenants that invoked the view that the fittings should be of the simplest form.[37] To this end the floors were constructed of concrete and the walls were not plastered but built in glazed brick up to the height of five feet and the remainder in common brick which was whitewashed. In these ways the architect laid down forms and standards of development which he felt the Company might apply with equal success in a variety of situations.

A site was finally found in 1883 on which to put the ideas into practice. Even in Manchester it had been difficult to procure suitable land at an annual ground rent of less then 1s a square yard. A plot, however, was secured in Holt Town, Ancoats, at the cost of about 7d a square yard and twenty-four tenements were built along the lines proposed. The cost was £78 for each. The only deviation from the original plan was the substitution, at the surprising request of the Corporation, of pail closets for the intended water closets.[38] Otherwise the structural and sanitary arrangements of the dwellings appear to have fully realised the expectations of the promoters and were considered well adapted to their intended purpose.

However, the Company suffered a setback when it came to the question of finding suitable tenants who could pay the rent and would assist in the proper upkeep of the property. Though the tenements were situated in the heart of a poor district and were surrounded by industrial works, there was not the 'anticipated rush to secure the chance of decent household life at a cheap price'.[39] When completed, the tenements were offered publicly without undue restrictions and 'in order not to offend the sensibility of any would-be-tenant, all mention of such things as charity and philanthropy was carefully avoided'. Nevertheless, the dwellings, though so few in number. were never properly and fully tenanted at any one time. Moreover. the tenements were soon invaded by the 'nomadic householder' – a character very much fostered and encouraged by speculative builders in and around Manchester in order to enable them to dispose of newly erected property under apparently favourable conditions of occupancy.[40] The Company attempted to evade the depredations of this group by demanding the payment of rent in advance, but such a condition was wholly unpalatable to the working classes of Manchester. It is impossible to say whether or not strict adherence to this original proviso would have caused the property to remain unoccupied, but it is certain that it would have prevented letting to several worthless tenants. As it was, the Company failed to realise its anticipated 4½ per cent and it withdrew from any future endeavour, so the inhabitants of Manchester and district were denied the further benefits of the extension of the Company's plans which, in addition to blocks of dwellings, had included the provision of co-operative shops and coffee taverns. The directors, however, felt that nothing worthwhile could be done for the homeless poor until they themselves assumed a more responsive and responsible attitude.

'The Company, having carried out its own part of its philanthropic purpose amid a great deal of head shaking, it is tolerably certain that, unless those intended to be benefitted evince a warmer appreciation of its efforts, no other attempt of a similar character is likely to be made . . .'[41]

Such model agencies might, therefore, attempt to show, at a local level, the manner in which the careful design of dwellings could benefit both the moral and physical health of the working class. They failed, however, to stimulate any further building of tenements in Lancashire and Yorkshire, either by philanthropic organisations or by speculative builders. Their example did not encourage a sense of responsibility in an area where the need for model dwellings, though not as great as in the metropolis, was increasing.[42] The housing agencies of the North had been unable to make themselves attractive as forms of commercial investment and to stimulate philanthropic involvement in a task that was so urgently required. Yet this disinterest in model dwellings was not a reflection of markedly better housing conditions in the North as compared with London.

In 1866 James Hole had drawn attention to the atrociously low quality of speculative house building in Leeds and to the need for proper building regulations.[43] In 1874 the Leeds Social Improvement Society submitted a memorial to the town council of Leeds on the insanitary and overcrowded condition of the town, and drew attention to the fact that there had been no improvement since their own previous report of 1860.[44] In strong language, they urged on their fellow citizens the duty of assistance in the struggle for better housing standards. In Sheffield, in the following year, ratepayers, acting under the Cross Act, instigated a Corporation inquiry into a central, though not the worst, area of the city where it was disclosed that the density was 182 per acre and that most of the houses were damp and many were back-to-back.[45] In Manchester too at this period the Statistical Society was noting the rapid pace at which the city was expanding, with jerry-built houses that formed a continuing threat to the health and well-being of the working-class population.[46] All such provincial towns were faced with the difficulties posed by the indifference of local authorities to housing problems, the inadequacies of the housing bye-laws and the disinclination to expend money on reform.[47]

Nevertheless, reports such as these during the 1870s and 1880s, though they failed to effect direct action by the municipalities involved, did serve to change greatly the attitude of the public towards housing reform. In marked contrast to London, however, this growing awareness of the need for a new effort did not lead to the stimulation of new improved dwelling schemes. Significantly, both the Leeds Industrial Dwellings Company and the Manchester and Salford Workmen's Dwellings Company, after their initial experiments with model dwellings, transferred their attention to schemes on the lines of the work originally undertaken by Octavia Hill. In 1875 the Leeds Social Improvement Society had suggested remedial action along these lines and in the following year the Directors of the Dwellings Company, after nearly a decade's inactivity, decided to undertake the purchase and reconditioning of insanitary house property in the town.[48] By the end of the century they owned over 1,000 houses. Likewise in Manchester, the Dwellings Company, after initial disappointment in the attempt to raise the standards of accommodation of the working population, redirected its energies to buying up neglected, though structurally sound, properties and bringing them up to a respectable standard.[49]

It was the success of the efforts of Miss Hill and her followers that encouraged Manchester Corporation to undertake similar work in its primary assault on the housing problems of the city.[50] It was considered that a sum of money which would have been expended on the barrack system and so serve to improve only a very limited district could by such means be spread over a large area and thus make a distinct impression on the general health of a large proportion of the community. Under the Manchester Improvement Act of 1867 a dwelling could be peremptorily closed and the owner required to repair it.[51] The houses condemned were generally of the back-to-back type and the Corporation made a small contribution towards the cost if such houses were thinned out in order to provide yard space and ventilation. Between 1886 and 1899 about half the houses thus closed were re-opened and by the end of the century Manchester's stock of back-to-back houses had been reduced to 5,000. It was a task that Manchester always looked back on with pride as being more practically effective an answer to the housing problem than many grander and costlier schemes of model dwellings.[52]

Reconditioning remained the major element in Manchester's housing policy right up to the First World War and the nature of this work is indicative of the approach to the problem in the northern towns. The emphasis remained on the terraced unit. The tenants in unhealthy areas might have been rehoused in flats as in London, and as to some extent in Liverpool, but in Manchester in 1878 the Medical Officer of Health was not yet convinced that flat dwellings were healthy and he preferred to suspend judgement until the Liverpool experiment had been given a longer trial.[53] And for the time being the Council remained unwilling to recognise the improvement of housing conditions as an immediate civic responsibility.[54] The Medical Officer was favourably impressed with the idea that voluntary societies of workmen should combine to build owner-occupied dwellings and pointed to successful experiments in Chorlton-upon-Medlock and Birmingham.[55] A similar response to the housing problem had been current in Leeds since the work of James Hole in 1866.[56] The Leeds Permanent Building Society claimed that, in a freehold area where a working-class house cost an average of £160, working men could become house owners and that the working people as a class could solve their own housing problems.[57] Such an attitude failed to realise that action of this nature would only be possible among the relatively well-paid artisans and would be quite beyond the means of the poorest workers in the worst dwellings, who were most in need of better living conditions.[58]

The reality of the situation only gradually dawned on the public and the authorities. In 1889 the Sheffield Association for the Better Housing of the Poor, while advocating similar self-help remedies, recognised the need for assistance for the poor working man and for controls to curb the activity of the jerry-builder.[59] During the previous decade the Co-operative News had been urging like modification in the work of the various co-operative building societies that flourished in the North.[60] Nevertheless, the emphasis in all the proposed solutions remained on the provision by individuals of low-rise traditional housing. To build high was never as necessary in these provincial towns as in London.[61] For just as the lower cost of land in the provinces meant that the cost of the average terraced house could be within the range of a larger proportion of the working class, so it also theoretically widened the opportunities for action under both the Torrens and the Cross Acts. In London, by the 1880s, rising costs faced housing reformers with two alternatives: either to encourage the growing movement of the population from central London to the suburbs where land values and building costs were lower, or to provide, with local government assistance, housing in central London for those who could not be enticed to move out by the hope of cheap transport and lower rents. The solutions to the housing problem were thus becoming polarised — suburban housing as opposed to central tenements, private enterprise as distinct from municipal action.[62]

Certainly prior to the 1890 Housing of the Working Classes Act, this dichotomy did not apply in the provinces. Though land values were rising in the commercial centres of the northern towns, they still bore no comparison to costs in the capital. Vacant land close to the city centres of Manchester, Leeds and Sheffield could, up to the last decade of the century, economically support the building of two-storeyed terraced housing. Moreover, the suburban alternative was never so distinctive an alternative as in London for, even in these cities, expansion was limited and the journey to work was never excessive. With the radius of the continuous built-up area rarely extending beyond a mile, the walk to work remained a possibility even with migration outwards, and the working class was not deterred from this migration by fear of unreasonable transport costs.[63] There were then very clearly not the same pressures at work in Lancashire and Yorkshire as there were in London where they led to a considerable development of working-class tenement dwellings during the years after 1875.[64] Outside the metropolis, the overwhelming economic incentive in favour of tenement building was removed and the debate as to the relative merits of flats as against the separate house was thus freed, to concentrate on the positive aspects of the problem. In addition, such circumstances favoured the continuation of the experiments with smaller blocks of flats of the type already begun in Manchester. As a result, by the time the local authorities in the North came to be involved with the consideration of tenement building as a means of rehousing in areas of slum clearance under the 1890 Act, their options were less narrowly defined than those of the London County Council and the possibilities in the variation of the design of dwellings had been more widely explored.

The modification in tenement design and, in particular, the break away from the monolithic block that was to appear at various times and places in Lancashire and Yorkshire was largely the outcome of the continuing hostility towards such dwellings among both the working population and local housing reformers. The basis of such criticism had been established by James Hole in Leeds. He emphasised the dangers to health that could arise with high buildings, especially when crowded together onto inadequate sites without proper provision for light and ventilation. He warned his fellow housing reformers of the need to take extra precautions to secure the health of the population when it was densely concentrated.[65]

High density was clearly established as a factor which in itself prevented the exercise of the good life.[66] Sanitarians feared the direct correlation between high density and the prevalence of disease, with its ensuing high death rate. As it was not elicited whether this relationship held true in the high densities of the new tenement blocks, many housing reformers and sanitarians assumed that it was so; despite much conflicting evidence they included in their arguments all areas of high density regardless of the housing pattern employed. The newer tenement schemes were considered along with older areas of over-crowding as equally productive of bad housing. There were some, however, who considered block dwellings, of whatever quality, as a greater threat to health than densely packed traditional dwellings.[67] It was this fear that sustained the opposition to flats of Manchester's first Medical Officer of Health, Dr Leigh.[68] He voiced the concern of many that large tenements posed a particular health hazard since the greater degree of communication between the occupants, especially when facilities were shared, encouraged the more rapid dissemination of epidemics. At the 1866 meeting of the Social Science Association, during the Health and Social Economy Section debate on 'The Dwellings of the Labouring Classes', Mr Rumsey, a delegate from Cheltenham, drew attention to the growing fears raised by this connection.

'It is not only the black clouds of smoke or even the sulphurous fumes and other chemical impurities of our atmosphere that destroy life, but it is to a still greater extent the exhalation and emanation from human bodies that cause the evil . . . The evil reaches its climax in what are called model lodging houses. The present death rate is not to be taken as the slightest evidence of the ultimate result of this new method of packing the masses, for the inhabitants of these blocks include at first the ablest portion of the population. After twenty to thirty years the death rate will be increasing, for Mr Peabody, whose dwellings are of the best, places 625 people on an acre, which is nearly seven times the density of population in Liverpool, with ninety-five per acre.'[69]

High density thus came to be associated with a particular kind of housing which was usually on a scale that was large and inhuman.

Reforming concern over the danger to health involved in the conventional tenement design combined with other criticism of model dwellings to produce a positive movement of many facets in favour of an alternative answer to the problem of housing the working-class population in large cities. Flat dwellings were unpopular among those for whom they were intended. Overtones of charity and the connotations of barrack building combined with the working classes' natural antipathy to organisation and regulation.[70] This was even more true in the North where the habit of shared dwellings was less common than in London.[71] However, this form of building had always been justified on the grounds of economic necessity in areas of high land values.[72] The opposition to block building was thus greatly strengthened when it could be demonstrated that, even by building high in central areas, the housing companies had not been able to produce, at an economic rate, dwellings within the reach of the labouring population.[73] Despite lower land costs in the cities of Lancashire and Yorkshire, the dwelling companies there had been no more successful financially than those in the metropolis, since they had to cater for a working population dependent on even lower wage scales.[74]

The decades of the 1860s and 1870s thus produced considerable dissatisfaction among housing reformers and sanitarians with regard to the planning and design of tenement blocks.[75] The misgivings were summed up in *The Architect* of 1875 with a sharp rejoinder to Henry Darbishire's earlier exposition of the virtues of block building. The journal considered that it was the responsibility of the architectural profession to evolve a housing pattern which would meet the needs and means of the class for whom it was intended.[76] It was, of course, part of the problem that during the 1860s architects had, as a profession, neglected the issue of working-class housing. Such individual architects as were concerned concentrated on tenements rather than cottages. Their attention was, however, primarily devoted to the architectural appearance of the buildings. The design of large tenement blocks remained monotonous and the planning of the sites often paid little attention to the needs of aspect or ventilation, but simply sought to crowd as many tenants as possible onto a small unit of land. Economic pressures prevented housing companies from giving weight to environmental considerations and the uniform designs largely employed did nothing to improve the architectural quality of the tenement buildings, whose drab and forbidding appearance contributed to their unpopularity.[77]

Despite the numerous architectural competitions for the design of model dwellings between 1860 and 1880, most of the companies continued to rely on well-tried methods.[78] In any case, for all their varieties in layout and accommodation, the architectural solutions remained basically high impersonal blocks of grim brickwork. The only fundamental alternative in flat design was the concept of the two-storey cottage flat. It was an approach that was traditionally common on Tyneside, and had been adopted for model dwellings by the Edinburgh Co-operative Building Company Limited in 1861.[79] The Company, following the advice of earlier reformers in the city, turned its back on the usual 'Scottish tenement' with its dark internal staircase and adopted the idea of the cottage flat. The houses as built were all two-storeyed with a flat on each floor, with separate access to the upper flat being gained by individual external stairs.[80] The possibilities inherent in this approach were really first worked out in architectural terms in 1871 by Bannister Fletcher in his book *Model Houses for the Industrial Classes*.[81] He considered that the reason for failure, both in financial and aesthetic terms, of existing model dwellings was their want of adaptation to the feelings, wishes and habits of the inhabitants.

'Most of them are huge hives, containing such large numbers that privacy is next to impossible, and a superintendent is necessary, whose continued interference makes the inhabitants feel rather too much like inmates of a public establishment, and prefer any miserable tenement where their actions are comparatively uncontrolled.'[82]

In particular, he condemned existing tenement plans on the grounds of their extremely narrow staircases, the great loss of space in passages, the awkward shape of rooms and the darkness of the living rooms.[83]

The alternative that Fletcher proposed was a system of flats whose external appearance closely resembled a normal 'middle-class' terrace with nothing to show that the building was occupied by more than one family. *The Building News* particularly commended this feature and the arrangement of the elevation in the cottage style.[84] It also praised, for its simplicity, the internal plan with its central corridor leading from the front door to a staircase set halfway down its length and giving access to four separate sets of rooms arranged on each floor. The plan allowed for the careful disposition of well-shaped, spacious, airy and light rooms with the suitable location of water-closets and coal-houses adjoining an internal yard. The considerable depth of the property in relation to its width allowed for economy on the land occupied. For the humbler class of artisan, Fletcher provided a series of designs for two-roomed dwellings based on similar principles.[85] The concept evolved out of a genuine consideration of the sensibilities of the working class and was an attempt to arrive at an acceptable *via media* between the large tenement block and the self-contained cottage. As such it aroused considerable interest among architects and in 1875 *The Architect*, continuing its attack on Darbishire's plans for dwelling blocks, promoted the idea.[86]

As a concession to the preference of the English workman for his self-contained house, the building of cottage flats was first considered by Birmingham Corporation in 1884.[87] In Lancashire and Yorkshire the architectural interest in smaller units of dwellings coincided with the traditional hostility to high-rise building in that area and with the influence of earlier practical efforts to realise alternatives to the design of dwellings as practised in the metropolis. Yet it was not until the very end of the century that flats of this nature were erected by any local authority in the North.

Meanwhile, the motivation of tenement building and considerations relative to the design of flats had undergone a considerable revision in the provinces, as in London. After the 1890 Housing of the Working Classes Act, the legislative framework existed for new steps to be taken in housing reform and it was clear that local authorities would henceforth play a much more considerable role than in previous decades. The municipalities of the North, faced with the failure of philanthropic capitalism to provide an adequate number of low-cost dwellings for working men in the city centres, had now to accept not only the need for more energetic slum clearance but had also to face the problem of building fresh accommodation for those evicted by such schemes. Under the 1890 Act, however, local authorities had to build according to the standards formulated by the Local Government Board. Basically it was required that rehousing be on the cleared sites and be of such character as would cater for the class of person displaced. These considerations combined with growing economic pressures on land to produce a situation in which provincial experiments in flat building were seemingly subject to the same demands and conditions as influenced the design of tenements in the capital.

The first northern town to experiment with block building in this changed atmosphere was Manchester, where a new urgency was given to the housing problem by the extraordinary increase in the city's population which occurred during the last decade of the nineteenth century. According to the Medical Officer of Health, it was this growth in population that was basically responsible for the critical increase in overcrowding.[88] But by this time there were also other considerations which influenced the attitude of the Council. The large boundary extensions of 1890 had doubled the area of the city and had incorporated within it several districts where great numbers of Manchester workers had gone to live.[89] This meant that it was no longer possible for Manchester to delegate to its neighbours the responsibility for housing the city's workpeople. The Corporation had itself to deal with the consequences of overcrowding and decay in the inner districts of the city.

The first Manchester Reconstruction Scheme was presented to the Council in 1891.[90] It covered certain of the worst areas in Ancoats and it proposed to widen and clear the approaches, to provide proper ventilation and open spaces. The houses and buildings in that area were to be demolished and the sites left as open spaces or for the erection of suitable dwellings for the working class. Such a scheme was subject to the sanction of the Local Government Board, which ultimately required that the Sanitary Committee undertake the demolition in progressive stages and so, it was hoped, incur the minimum of displacement. The Board also required the provision, on the sites cleared, of adequate rehousing.[91] These demands meant that not only had the Corporation to undertake rehousing according to the standards and conceptions of the Local Government Board, but it also had to work within limitations that now matched those which the London County Council had to face. The land in Ancoats, cleared and afterwards built on at Oldham Road, cost £5 6s 9d per square yard.[92] Thus the basic land costs had risen to a figure comparable with those in the capital, where for six recent clearance schemes the London County Council had been compelled to pay between £4 12s 7d and £8 13s 7d per square yard for the land.[93] Moreover, while the Sanitary Committee was required by its own Corporation to produce a scheme that was financially viable and that would not impose too heavy a burden on the sinking fund, it was also required by the Local Government Board to rehouse those people displaced and this meant the rehousing of the very poorest.[94] With such conditions, a provincial town now had to face a situation that had long been current in housing reform in the capital. In seeking a solution, therefore, it is not surprising that the Manchester Sanitary Committee turned for advice to Henry Spalding, one of the architects employed by the London County Council.

Spalding, who designed the first block of dwellings for the Oldham Road site, had no sympathy with current romantic notions that dwellings should be so designed as to elevate the standards of the working classes. His concern was to build at a reasonable rate and to produce an adequate return, even if this was at the expense of architectural distinction.[95]

'What we have to aim at, as architects, is the practice of the most rigid economy in planning and fittings. And as this, of course, applies to the designing of the elevations also, we cannot as a rule spend much money on ornamentation of any kind; but by judicious use of materials at our disposal a good effect can always be obtained.'[96]

As a result, the Oldham Road Block No.2 was externally depressing in appearance, with its dark red brickwork relieved only on its façade by the pretentious use of repeated and inexpensive terra cotta trimmings

Plate VII. Victoria Buildings, Oldham Road, Manchester, erected in 1894. The architects were Spalding and Cross. (By permission of the City Librarian, Manchester).

and frilly gables. With regard to meeting the requirements of dwellings for artisans, they were described by Mrs Sidney Webb, who visited them in 1896, shortly after they were opened, as being of a 'fair average character, large and bright and airy, every two tenements having a water closet'.[97] The dwellings were arranged in a five-storey block enclosing a large quadrangle and were entered from the balconies which extended all around the court with stone steps approaching them at each corner of the building.[98] Much of the ground floor was utilised for shops and laundries and drying rooms were provided at the top of the building at each of the four corners. The dwellings themselves were arranged in pairs and were normally of two rooms, though some contained only one. It was with the internal fittings that Henry Spalding exercised the most strict economy. Every two dwellings shared a sink and water closet, while the rooms themselves had cement skirtings and iron pipes since he considered, from his London experience, that wooden skirtings were removed for firewood and lead piping for sale. There was, he felt, neither the need nor the incentive to provide the poor with housing of a higher standard than that to which they were commonly accustomed.

'We seem to have taken it for granted that, if we design the tenements on the most approved methods of hygiene, the working classes will adapt themselves to their new surroundings. I do not wish to under-rate the importance of hygiene, but hygiene is not valued by the working man and so for its advantages he does not care to pay. For example, if we provide a system of fresh-air inlets and outlets to his rooms, we shall find that in a very short time they will all be blocked up. I fear it is not much good to argue with the working man about sanitation or ventilation. He does not appreciate them . . . Some years ago it was the custom to provide baths in many of the dwellings; now it is seldom done, and considering that public baths are accessible in most neighbourhoods, I think it is an open question whether these should be provided in these buildings. Also it is no great hardship for people of this class to share a scullery with another family; they have for the most part been used to it all their lives, living as they do in houses with sanitary accommodation for one family and with rooms let to three or four. The first thing, then, is to find out the mode of living and habits of the working people, for unless we give them what they are accustomed to we shall find the class of people for whom we intend to provide will not live in our buildings.'[99]

Plate VIII. Pollard Street Dwellings, Manchester, erected in 1894. Architects, Spalding and Cross. (By permission of the City Librarian, Manchester).

Despite such a low estimation of the requirements of the tenants and despite the rigid economy exercised in the erection of this block of tenements, the Corporation rapidly discovered that the building costs had remained disproportionately high and, as a result, the economic rents were beyond the means of those of the working class for whom these spartan dwellings were clearly intended.[100] Excluding the cost of the land, the Oldham Road No.2 Block cost £116 per room.[101] At the only other major block of this type undertaken by the Manchester Corporation – the Pollard Street Dwellings (1896) – even greater economy of design was exercised and no decoration of any kind was allowed to relieve the external or internal dreariness of this 135-roomed block. Nevertheless, building costs per room rose to £98.[102] These figures compare with the cost of £81 to £138 per room in the block dwellings erected by the London County Council in the period from 1893 to 1901.[103] Though slightly lower land costs on average meant that rents never rose as high as they did in central London, a two-roomed dwelling in either of the blocks was let at between 3s 6d and 5s a week, and this was an amount that simply could not be paid by tenants evicted from property of which the average rent had been 2s 6d a week.[104] This, combined with the persistent hostility to such blocks in Manchester, meant that neither of these undertakings was ever fully tenanted during the next two decades.[105]

Within the Health Committee during this period, though there was never any doubt that whatever dwellings the Corporation built should be economically viable, there was a growing feeling that municipal dwellings should manage to cater for the poorest in the community.[106] In their attempts at building high it seemed the committee had not found the answer to the problem. So in meeting the remainder of the Local Government Board's rebuilding requirements for the Oldham Road and Chester Street Improvement Areas, the City Architect was requested to prepare alternative schemes, and these were on the lines that became known as 'tenement houses'.[107] These usually consisted of two- or three-storey buildings arranged in rows like ordinary houses and they contained up to six apartments in each 'house'. Access was internal as in the earliest northern tenements and the external appearance, though less fanciful in design, was akin to what had been proposed by Bannister Fletcher. Tenement houses differed from block dwellings in the height and construction of their main walls and also in the arrangement of scullery and water-closet which were generally integrated within the dwelling unit. In appearance as in their provisions, they were intermediate between the cottage and the block dwelling.[108] For instance, though greater privacy was secured to each dwelling by the limited number of people using each entrance, the rear yard still remained in common use. This form of building was first put into practice in Manchester in 1899 in the Pott Street area of Ancoats, where seventy-eight dwellings were erected in two three-storeyed rows and it remained the principal type of building undertaken by the Corporation through until 1918.[109] In all, some 278 houses were provided in such tenements. Even at the Alexandra Place Dwellings, begun in 1903, though the frontage of the building was given an architectural unity befitting its position on the main Rochdale Road into the city, the dwellings themselves were divided into four units with separate access and private facilities.[110] After the 1896 experiments, block building of the conventional kind never appeared again in Manchester.

It could not, however, be claimed that these tenement houses were the financial success anticipated. The demands of the bye-laws meant that despite the reduction in height, building costs were not proportionately lower. The cost per room remained between £80 and £90.[111]

Rents for a two-roomed dwelling in the Pott Street, Chester Street and
Sanitary Street dwellings were fixed at between 4s and 4s 6d per
week.[112] The dwellings, however, contained a considerable number of
three-roomed flats renting at between 5s and 6s per week and this
placed an even greater part of the dwellings beyond the means of the
poorest tenants. Nevertheless, these dwellings were always more
popular than those in blocks and never failed to find tenants.[113] This
factor, along with the lower maintenance costs, naturally made them a
more attractive alternative for the hard-pressed Sanitary Committee
struggling to meet the demands of the Local Government Board
without loss to the Corporation's sinking fund.

However, these tenement houses, with their crowded positions, their
grim exteriors and their austere fittings, did nothing to meet the views
of those housing reformers who considered that Corporation dwellings
should set a higher standard for other builders of workmen's dwellings.
Increasingly it was felt that such standards could only be achieved by
means of suburban low-density housing. In Manchester, strong support
was given to such opinions in the speeches and writings of T.C. Horsfall
and T.R.Marr.[114] The belief that all the ills of the working classes
would be assuaged by the development of low-density housing estates
was reflected, by the end of the century, in the City Council's decision
to purchase the 238 acre Blackley Estate on the City boundary for this
purpose.[115] However, the higher cost of the houses than anticipated
and the continuing delays in development meant that by 1904 only 200
dwellings had been completed and no further work was contemplated
on the Estate until shortly before the outbreak of war.[116] By 1904 it
was clear that, whatever its virtues, the garden suburb, municipal or
otherwise, was not to be the panacea for all the problems which had
baffled housing reformers throughout the Victorian period.[117] By then
the failings of the Blackley Estate were as strongly urged in the Council
and in the city press as were the more common complaints against
tenement dwellings – the isolation and lack of facilities of the former
were now set against the lack of light and air, the low standard of
decency and the problem of numerous stairs to climb in the latter.[118]
The later tenement houses of the Corporation, though more popular
than the original block dwellings, had done nothing to win over the
bulk of popular opinion in favour of the building of centrally placed
flats for the working class.

As a result, therefore, the Sanitary Committee, after 1904, began to
investigate a new solution to the problem. Discussion arose over
whether or not houses of the traditional character, when sanitarily

satisfactory, were not completely adequate for working-class habitation.[119] Clearly the Conservative-controlled Council thought so. The need, it was felt, was not for grand schemes but for slow advances causing the minimum of disturbance.[120] The Council turned its attention, therefore, to insanitary property beyond the confines of the immediate city centre, at Cheetham Hill and Bradford.[121] Though development costs were lower, so not necessitating multi-storey building, land remained costly and the Council determined on the preparation of a compromise scheme for cottage flats. There had been forerunners of this type in the North, but they had recently been extensively promoted by the propagandist activities of Councillor Thompson of Richmond, where such buildings had been highly successful.[122] All told, some 590 flats of this type had been erected in twelve towns by 1905 and of these some had separate access to each first-storey flat, while others had limited balcony access.[123] In every case, building costs were much lower than for block dwellings or for tenement houses, averaging £67 per room. Once again the cost of the site would determine the economic feasibility of the scheme. It was this factor that had led the Medical Officer of Southampton to comment on such a scheme there that: 'The rents . . . must of necessity exceed that which the unhoused class from this area can afford to pay.'[124] On the other hand, Manchester's neighbour, Stretford Urban District Council, had built forty such cottage flats on land that cost only £7 per room and had thus been able to rent them at no more than 3s 3d to 3s 9d per week for a two-roomed dwelling.[125]

Such a scheme had much to commend it to a Housing Committee. It avoided the need for extensive formal planning and of moving large numbers of people to new areas. At the same time it provided a smaller dwelling unit which made a concession to people's continuing fears of multi-storey dwellings, while achieving a higher density on the land than did the ordinary terraced housing. Dewsnup considered that the two-storeyed cottage flat presented the most favourable type for securing economy of building with more privacy of family life than barrack dwellings could possibly give.[126] A plan for ninety-nine such flats was therefore drawn up by the Manchester Housing Committee in 1908 for the Cheetham Hill site.[127] Unfortunately, it was rejected because of the high clearance costs involved.[128] With the approval of the Local Government Board, the scheme was abandoned and Manchester was to undertake no more municipal house building prior to the First World War. However, this last effort to find a way between conflicting alternatives had drawn attention to the fundamental problem which remained in housing reform.[129] This was the problem of catering for the needs of those earning less than £1 per week. Such people could not afford a suburban life style, yet Manchester's efforts at tenement building had also been revealed as financially impractical. The problem remained intractable as long as the Council conceived of municipal enterprise in this field in terms of only immediate loss and gain. Until the necessity of subsidisation was accepted, the concept and design of dwellings remained subordinate to the economic interest.

Similar problems and restrictions naturally bedevilled other municipalities in the area, though both Sheffield and Leeds came into the field later and clearly learned from Manchester's earlier efforts. The Sheffield Corporation's slum clearance scheme – the Crofts – was sanctioned in 1894 but, as a result of the difficulties involved in acquiring the properties, rebuilding did not begin until 1900.[130] In the meantime, many schemes of development were considered and the Health Committee would probably have favoured the erection of cottage property[131] as this had been the form of the Corporation's first housing endeavour in Hands Lane in 1899 and had proved popular and remunerative.[132] However, the density of development required by the Local Government Board on the Crofts site meant that some form of

Plate IX. The Crofts, Sheffield, erected in 1900, from Townhead Street. The architect was C.F. Wike. (By permission of the City Librarian, Sheffield).

Plate X. The Crofts, the rear courtyard. (By permission of the City Librarian, Sheffield).

multi-storey development was inevitable.[133] Before deciding on its exact nature, deputations from the Council visited several cities and, acting principally on their investigations in Manchester, decided on a compromise design.[134] They criticised the block buildings from the sanitary point of view, considering that the grouping of flats in five and six storeys was a danger to health, while at the same time it was felt that the tenement houses were ill-positioned for the adequate provision of light and air. The Crofts scheme, therefore, eventually consisted of dwellings which were very similar to those erected in Pott Street, Manchester, but which were built in a long, curved terrace around the perimeter of the site, so allowing the retention of a large open communal area in the centre. 124 tenements, containing one to three rooms each, were provided in this scheme with rents varying from 3s to 6s per week.[135]

Despite the fact that these tenements let fairly well, the average of empties was low and the loss of rent was very small, the undertaking was not financially satisfactory.[136] The cost of compensation payments to the owners had been exorbitant and the final cost of the land in the Crofts had averaged £5 8s per square yard. The Housing Scheme was charged only 12s 6d per square yard, but the balance remained a serious annual charge on the ratepayers.[137] Furthermore, the Health Committee was never satisfied with the barrack-like appearance of the buildings.[138] There had, for some time, been strong support both in the city and in the Council for the garden city movement, and already in 1900 the Corporation had acquired land for a suburban estate at High Wincobank.[139] Consequently, by 1905 the Health Committee had determined that it would erect in the Crofts only a sufficient number of houses to accommodate the actual number required by the Local Government Board and would sell the surplus land on building leases.[140] Though it was considered that the Crofts tenements were a vast improvement on what had been there before and that they were, in fact, the best means of rehousing the displaced tenants who could not practically move to the suburbs, the committee now decided to concentrate their future activity in the garden suburb.[141] As in Manchester, however, the slow rate of development on the suburban scheme led to the renewal of demands for the building of low-cost centrally placed tenements.[142] By 1910 this had become a major issue in local politics and had resolved itself on a party-political basis. With the return of the Liberals in the 1911 municipal elections, plans for the further development of the Wincobank estate were revived and no other schemes of clearance and subsequent tenement building were to be considered in Sheffield prior to the First World War.[143]

The endeavours of the Corporation in Sheffield, as in Manchester, had shown that tenement construction on central sites was neither popular nor financially viable if the rents were to be within the reach of the majority of the working class. A short-lived experiment of the Health Committee in Sheffield did, however, illustrate the possibilities inherent in a different concept of the flat. This involved viewing the flat not as part of a clearance scheme, but as a desirable form of accommodation for the upper working class and lower middle class.[144] Between 1902 and 1905 the Corporation, acting under the powers of their Local Acts and Orders, erected on surplus lands five blocks of shops with flats above.[145] In design these buildings followed a pattern that had already become known in the city during the 1890s when several private tradesmen had erected new premises with flats above.[146] The dwellings were in small groups with between five and seven units, depending on size, on each floor which were reached by external iron staircases. They were considered to be much superior to the dwellings put up for artisans and were let at quarterly rentals to 'people in fairly good positions'.[147] A four-roomed flat costing on average £200 could be reasonably let at a rent equal to a 4 per cent return on the building.

The architects responsible for these schemes were Messrs Flockton and Gibbs and it was to them that the Health Committee turned when it considered similar developments on its surplus land. The properties, erected in Snig Hill, Westbar, Gibraltar Street and two in Infirmary Road, contained respectively seventeen, two, eight, six, and eight dwellings.[148] The majority of these were three- or four-roomed flats, though Corporation Buildings in Snig Hill contained four five-roomed and four six-roomed units. The water closets were grouped away from the dwellings which backed on to open yards. Weekly rents averaged from 5s 9d to 8s 0d. Appealing to prosperous artisans and shopkeepers whose work made it advantageous to live as close to the city centre as possible, these dwellings were never vacant and their arrangement was widely appreciated, if length of tenancy is any sure guide.[149]

This municipal enterprise, though financially successful, was not extended. Nor was it repeated elsewhere. For, by the first decade of this century, flats, in their various guises, had become synonymous with certain attitudes and considerations in the housing reform movement. The ascendency of the garden city movement after this time determined that the erection of tenements would be entertained by local authorities only as a secondary alternative. The term 'flat' was, more than ever, to be indistinguishable from the idea of the low-priced dwelling. In the council chambers of provincial cities, the debate hardened into the question of whether municipal dwellings should cater in central tenements for the level of the lowest, or attempt through garden suburbs to elevate the standards of the working classes. With the growing support of the Local Government Board for a low-density solution, combined with the traditional mistrust of high-rise building, prevarication became the rule of most housing committees.

In the decade prior to 1914, flat building came to a virtual halt in Lancashire and Yorkshire, though in most cases schemes for town planning and garden suburbs were but welcome relief from a subject that had never held great appeal in the region. At the turn of the century northern advocates of tenement building were still fighting the battles against hostility and prejudice which the London housing reformers had begun half a century earlier. Fears for health and privacy remained predominant among the majority of the working class and local authorities continued to want to see the answer to bad housing either in the prevailing system of traditional terraced housing or in the natural extension of the urban area. In Leeds, for instance, the Council resisted the Local Government Board's demands for rebuilding with regard to the Quarry Hill and York Street Clearance Areas begun in 1894, maintaining that there were more than sufficient empty houses in the city to cater for the dishoused.[150] Only in 1900 did they agree to comply with the Board's minimum requirement by providing thirty-nine dwellings in a three-storey balconied block.[151] Likewise in Hull, it was the outside pressure of the Local Government Board that forced the Council to spend £10,000 on providing three four-storeyed blocks containing forty dwellings for the accommodation of 200 persons displaced from the central clearance area.[152] Even at the opening ceremony the Mayor expressed his disapproval of the scheme and it was considered that new houses would readily have been found on the expanding perimeter of the city.[153]

As it always had been in Lancashire and Yorkshire, the tenement was an alien idea that had to be imposed on an unwilling population. Few private builders undertook schemes for flats, either for middle or working-class occupation, and those that did contemplate such developments were far from encouraged by the local authorities.[154] As a means of housing reform, the flat was doomed in an age that would not countenance subsidisation once it became apparent that it, no more than any other single system, did not hold the financial solution to the problem. Since building costs were comparable, this failure was perhaps even more significant than in London for it showed that land costs did not account for all the problem. No company or municipality in the region was able to produce a tenement which could be let at a rent that was within the means of the lowest classes and at the same time ensure an adequate financial return. In the last resort, however, it was the hostility of the working classes in Lancashire and Yorkshire to the idea and to the appearance of the multi-storey dwelling that determined its unpopularity and its failure to become established.[155] The insistence on one's own front door was consistent throughout this period. Despite all the efforts to modify in various ways the appearance of the monolithic block dwelling as it had developed in London, the tenement dwelling never secured the approbation of either the majority of the working-class or of the authorities, and it never overcame that hurdle of hostility which had faced its first appearance in the region.

Notes

1. *The Builder*, Vol.XX, 1862, pp.56, 71, 107. H. Roberts, 'The Progress and Present Aspect of the Movement for Improving the Dwellings of the Labouring Classes', *Transactions of the National Association for the Promotion of Social Science*, 1860, p.766. R. Kerr, 'Problems of Providing Dwellings for the Poor', *Transactions of the Royal Institute of British Architects*, 1866–7, p.37.
2. J. Hole, *The Homes of the Working Classes*, London, 1866, pp.62–5.
3. J.N. Tarn, *Working Class Housing in Nineteenth Century Britain*, London, 1971, p.38.
4. V. Parker, *The English House in the Nineteenth Century*, London, 1970, p.31. J.L. Berbiers, 'Back-to-Back Housing, Halifax', *Official Architecture and Planning*, December 1968, pp.1595–9.
5. *The Builder*, Vol.III, 1845, p.220; Vol.IV, 1846, p.537. *The Labourers' Friend*, 1847, p.182.
6. J.N. Tarn, 'Housing in Liverpool and Glasgow: The Growth of Civic Responsibility', *Town Planning Review*, Vol.XXXIX, 1968–9, pp.322–6.
7. *Transactions of the National Association for the Promotion of Social Science*, 1866, p.621. *Building News*, Vol.XIII, 1866, pp.2–3. *The Architect*, Vol.XVIII, 1877, p.49; Vol.LXI, 1899, Supplement, p.21.
8. Select Committee on Town Holdings, *Third Report*, 1888, A.A. 312–20. Royal Commission on the Depression of Trade, *Second Report*, 1886, A.1289. Sheffield Medical Officer of Health, *Annual Reports*, 1873, p.34; 1874, p.30; 1888, p.60; 1893, p.13. *Manchester City News*, 10 Feb. 1906.
9. G.C. Holland, *The Vital Statistics of Sheffield*, Sheffield, 1843, pp.46, 70–2.
10. E.D. Simon and J.D. Inman, *The Rebuilding of Manchester*, London, 1935, p.7.
11. H. Roberts, *The Dwellings of the Labouring Classes*, London, 1850, p.13. *The Builder*, Vol.III, 1845, p.220; Vol.IV, 1846, p.537.
12. N. Pevsner, 'Model Houses for the Labouring Classes', *Architectural Review*, Vol.XCIII, 1943, pp.123–8.
13. J.D. Marshall, *Furness in the Industrial Revolution*, Barrow-in-Furness, 1958, p.348. *Barrow Herald*, 22 July 1871.
14. J.D. Marshall, *op. cit.*, pp.348, 413. *Barrow Herald*, 28 June 1873. *The Builder*, Vol.XXI, 1873, p.910.
15. J.D. Marshall, *op. cit.*, p.413. A. Newsholme, 'The Vital Statistics of Peabody Buildings and other Artisans' and Labourers' Block Dwellings', *Journal of the Royal Statistical Society*, Vol.LIV, 1891, pp.91–2. J.N. Tarn, 'Housing in Urban Areas' (Univ. of Cambridge Ph.D. thesis 1961), p.75.
16. J.D. Marshall, *op. cit.*, p.348.
17. *Barrow Herald*, 22 July 1871. *The Builder*, Vol.XXX, 1872, p.240.
18. W. Pearlman, 'The Dwellings of Manchester' (R.I.B.A. thesis 1956), p.31. *Manchester City News*, 6 May 1871. I am grateful to Mr P.T. Wilby of Rothwell and Evans, Solicitors, Salford, for information on the site of these dwellings.
19. W.H. Wood, *The History of Salford*, Salford, 1890, p.8. These dwellings were demolished under a Clearance Order in 1971.
20. W. Pearlman, *op. cit.*, p.31.
21. *Transactions of the National Association for the Promotion of Social Science*, 1866, p.732. *Building News*, Vol.XIII, 1866, p.426; Vol.XXIII, 1872, p.255. *The Architect*, Vol.XIV, 1875, p.342.
22. The Common Lodging Houses Act, 14 & 15 Vict., c. 28. The Labouring Classes' Lodging Houses Act, 14 & 15 Vict., c. 34.

23. *The Labourers' Friend*, June 1844, pp.1–2.
24. *The Builder*, Vol.XX, 1862, p.571.
25. *Ibid.*, p.569.
26. J.N. Tarn, *Working Class Housing in Nineteenth-Century Britain*, London, 1971, p.7.
27. *Salford Chronicle*, 8 April 1873. E.R. Dewsnup, *The Housing Problem in England*, Manchester, 1907, p.141.
28. Manchester Medical Officer of Health, *Annual Report*, 1876, p.37. Manchester and Salford Wesleyan Methodist Mission, *Second Annual Report*, 1889, p.34. W.H. Wood, *op. cit.*, p.8.
29. *The Builder*, Vol.XXV, 1867, p.173, E.R. Dewsnup, *op. cit.*, p.141.
30. J. Hole, *op. cit.*, pp.210–11.
31. *The Builder*, Vol.XXV, 1867, p.173.
32. F.M. Lupton, *Housing Improvement: A Summary of Ten Years Work in Leeds*, Leeds, 1906, p.3.
33. *The Builder*, Vol.XL, 1881, p.291. W. Pearlman, *op. cit.*, p.32.
34. *The Builder*, Vol.XLV, 1883, p.747.
35. J.N. Tarn, *Working Class Housing in Nineteenth-Century Britain*, London, 1971, pp.26–8.
36. *Transactions of the National Association for the Promotion of Social Science*, 1862, p.754; 1864, p.588; 1868, p.624. *Building News*, Vol.XVI, 1869, p.258; Vol.XXIII, 1872, p.255; Vol.XXX, 1876, p.316. *The Architect*, Vol.XXV, 1881, p.128. *The Builder*, Vol.XLVI, 1884, pp.192, 249.
37. *Transactions of the National Association for the Promotion of Social Science*, 1869, p.605; 1874, p.617; 1881, p.583; 1884, p.475.
38. A. Redford, *History of Local Government in Manchester*, 3 vols., London, 1939, Vol.II, p.424.
39. *The Builder*, Vol.XLV, 1883, p.748.
40. W. Pearlman, *op. cit.*, pp.32–3.
41. *The Builder*, Vol.XLV, 1883, p.748.
42. The availability of good cheap housing in the northern towns seems to have decreased from 1860 with the introduction of building bye-laws which served to force up rents and restrict the amount of building undertaken. Even so, the problem remained more severe in London. See: *The Builder*, Vol.XXXIV, 1876, p.149. *Building News*, Vol.XXXVI, 1879, p.337.
43. J. Hole, *op. cit.*, pp.125–8. *The Builder*, Vol.XXIV, 1866, p.57.
44. *The Builder*, Vol.XXXII, 1874, p.844. *Building News*, Vol.XXVI, 1874, p.690.
45. Sheffield Medical Officer of Health, *Annual Report*, 1875, p.27. *Sheffield Independent*, 8 Feb. 1876; 14 March 1877. E.R. Dewsnup, *op. cit.*, pp.146–8.
46. *Building News*, Vol.XXII, 1872, p.52.
47. *Transactions of the National Association for the Promotion of Social Science*, 1871, pp.523–4, 531; 1881, pp.577–8, 611, 687.
48. *Building News*, Vol.XXVII, 1874, p.690. *The Architect*, Vol.LXIII, 1900, p.155. *Journal of the Society of Arts*, Vol.XLVIII, 1900, pp.254–8. B.S. Rowntree, *Poverty, A Study of Town Life*, London, 1902, p.180. T.R. Marr, *Housing Conditions in Manchester and Salford*, Manchester, 1904, p.75. E.R. Dewsnup, *op. cit.*, p.188.
49. *Manchester City News*, 25 May 1912. *Building News*, Vol.XCVIII, 1910, p.324.
50. Manchester Medical Officer of Health, *Annual Report*, 1870, pp.33–4.
51. The Manchester Corporation Waterworks and Improvement Act, 1867, 30 and 31 Vict., c. xxxvi. *Manchester Guardian*, 31 Oct. 1934.

52. E.D. Simon and J. Inman, *op. cit.*, p.18. A. Redford, *op. cit.*, Vol.II, p.418.
53. Manchester City Council Proceedings, 10 July 1878.
54. Manchester City Council Proceedings, 3 March 1875; 31 May 1876.
55. Manchester City Council Proceedings, 1 May 1872; 31 May 1876.
56. J. Hole, *op. cit.*, pp.87–8.
57. Select Committee on Town Holdings, *Third Report*, 1888, A. 381.
58. J. Hole, *op. cit.*, p.73. *Building News*, Vol.XIII, 1866, p.2. Select Committee on Town Holdings, *Third Report*, 1888, A.A. 381, 3530–6, 3605–11. Cf. S.M. Gaskell, 'Yorkshire Estate Development and the Freehold Land Societies in the Nineteenth Century', *Yorkshire Archaeological Journal*, 1972, p.161.
59. *Sheffield Independent*, 9 Oct. 1889, 13 May 1890. Sheffield Medical Officer of Health, *Annual Report*, 1890, p.12.
60. *Cooperative News*, Vol.II, 1872, p.266; Vol.VII, 1876, p.136. *The Cooperator, Anti-Vacinator and Herald of Health*, Vol.XI, 1871, p.214. Rochdale Equitable Pioneers' Cooperative Society, *Almanack*, 1867.
61. *Building News*, Vol.XIII, 1866, p.2. *The Architect*, Vol.XLV, 1891, p.136. W. Thompson, *The Housing Handbook*, London, 1903, pp.175–7. A.S. Wohl, 'The Housing of the Working Classes in London, 1815–1914", in *The History of Working Class Housing*, ed. S.D. Chapman, Newton Abbot, 1971, p.28.
62. *Transactions of the National Association for the Promotion of Social Science*, 1877, pp.498–515; 1879, p.459; 1881, p.580; 1884, pp.479, 482. *Building News*, Vol.LXVII, 1894, p.457.
63. G.C. Dickinson, 'The Development of Suburban Road Passenger Transport in Leeds, 1840–95', *Journal of Transport History*, Vol.IV, 1960, pp.214–23. H.B. Rodgers, 'The Suburban Growth of Victorian Manchester', *Transactions of the Manchester Geographical Society*, 1961–2, pp.1–12. M.J. Mortimore, 'Urban Growth in Bradford and Environs, 1800–1960' (Univ. of Leeds M.A. thesis 1963), pp.139–53.
64. E.R. Dewsnup, *op. cit.*, pp.140–1, 165–9. J.N. Tarn, *Working-class Housing in Nineteenth Century Britain*, London, 1971, pp.25–8. London County Council, *Housing of the Working Classes in London*, 1913, pp.146–52.
65. J. Hole, *op. cit.*, p.62.
66. *Transactions of the National Association for the Promotion of Social Science*, 1864, p.586; 1865, pp.452–4; 1871, p.424; 1874, pp.596, 621.
67. Ibid., 1884, p.482. *Building News*, Vol.XVI, 1869, p.258; Vol.XXVI, 1874, p.449; Vol.XXX, 1876, p.316. *Daily News*, 19 Feb. 1887. *The British Architect*, Vol.XXXV, 1891, p.147. *The Architect*, Vol.XLV, 1891, p.136. *The Builder*, Vol.XXXVIII, 1881, p.810.
68. Manchester City Council Proceedings, 31 May 1871; 10 July 1878; 6 June 1883.
69. *Transactions of the National Association for the Promotion of Social Science*, 1866, p.738.
70. Ibid., 1874, p.618; 1877, p.510; 1884, p.482. *Building News*, Vol.VII, 1861, p.408; Vol.IX, 1862, p.25; Vol.X, 1863, p.866.
71. *The Times*, 29 Apr. 1864. 'Manchester and London: A Comparison of the Homes of the Artisans', *Manchester City News*, 10 Feb. 1906.
72. *Building News*, Vol.VII, 1861, p.408; Vol.VIII, 1862, p.157.
73. *Building News*, Vol.VIII, 1862, pp.157–8; Vol.XIII, 1866, p.810. *The Architect*, Vol.V, 1871, p.295; Vol.XIV, 1875, p.342.
74. By the 1880s in London the average rent for a single room was 4s 9d and the cost of two rooms was 7s 6d to 10s. The average weekly wage of Peabody tenants (heads of families only) was £1 3s 10d in 1881 and £1 4s in 1891. The bulk of the Trust's flats were let out to families whose heads were earning between 20s and 30s per week. See: Select Committee on Artisans'

and Labourers' Dwellings Improvement, 1881, *Minutes of Evidence*, p.126. Royal Commission on the Housing of the Working Classes, 1884–5, *Minutes of Evidence*, p.126; *Report*, p.21. *Pall Mall Gazette*, 5 Feb. 1884. *Journal of the Statistical Society of London*, Vol.LIV, 1891, p.90. A. Bowley, *Wages and Income since 1860*, London, 1951, pp.10ff.

75. H.A. Darbishire, 'Dwellings for the Poor', *Building News*, Vol.X, 1863, pp.866–7, 889. *Building News*, Vol.XIII, 1866, p.2; Vol.XXVII, 1874, p.449; Vol.XXX, 1876, p.316. *The Architect*, Vol.VIII, 1872, p.142; Vol.IX, 1873, p.83; Vol.XII, 1874, p.43; Vol.XV, 1876, p.151; Supplement, p.8.

76. *The Architect*, Vol.XIV, 1875, p.342.

77. *Building News*, Vol.XXIII, 1872, p.255. *The Architect*, Vol.XIV, 1875, p.342. *The Builder*, Vol.XLII, 1882, p.457. *Transactions of the National Association for the Promotion of Social Science*, 1869, p.605; 1877, p.510; 1881, p.614. *Daily News*, 19 Feb. 1887. J.N. Tarn, 'The Peabody Donation Fund: The Role of a Housing Society in the Nineteenth Century', *Victorian Studies*, Vol.X, 1966, p.30.

78. J.N. Tarn, *Working-class Housing in Nineteenth Century Britain*, London, 1971, p.21.

79. *Transactions of the National Association for the Promotion of Social Science*, 1863, p.627. *The Builder*, Vol.XXI, 1863, p.281. H. Gilzean Reid, *Housing the People, An Example in Cooperation*, Paisley, 1895, *passim*.

80. *The Cooperator*, Vol.IV, 1863, p.8; Vol.VIII, 1868, pp.615, 635, 650.

81. B.F. Fletcher, *Model Houses for the Industrial Classes*, London, 1871.

82. *Building News*, Vol.XXI, 1871, p.319.

83. B.F. Fletcher, *op. cit.*, p.2.

84. *Building News*, Vol.XXI, 1871, pp.319–20.

85. B.F. Fletcher, *op. cit.*, pp.8–15.

86. *The Architect*, Vol.XIV, 1875, p.342.

87. *Transactions of the National Association for the Promotion of Social Science*, 1884, p.474. *The Architect*, Vol.XXXI, 1884, p.360. These proposed cottage flats were not in fact built. For details see: W. Thompson, *op. cit.*, pp.72–3, 108–9.

88. The increase in the population of Manchester between 1891 and 1901 was from 505,000 to 544,000. See: Manchester City Council Proceedings, 20 Oct. 1897. E.R. Dewsnup, *op. cit.*, pp.309–11. E.D. Simon and J. Inman, *op. cit.*, p.30.

89. A. Redford, *op. cit.*, Vol.II, p.422.

90. Manchester City Council Proceedings, 22 Jan. 1891, 5 Apr. 1891; *Epitome of Proceedings*, 4 Feb. 1891.

91. Manchester City Council, *Epitome of Proceedings*, 2 Sept. 1891, 7 Oct. 1891, 4 May 1892, 4 Sept. 1892, 5 Oct. 1892, 9 Nov. 1892.

92. City of Manchester, Sanitary Committee, *Housing of the Working Classes: History of the Schemes and Descriptions of the Corporation's Dwellings*, Manchester, 1904, p.3.

93. W. Thompson, *op. cit.*, p.155.

94. Manchester City Council, *Epitome of Proceedings*, 2 Sept. 1891, 7 Oct. 1891, 4 May 1892, 4 Sept. 1892, 5 Oct. 1892, 9 Nov. 1892.

95. The average return on block dwellings built under Parts I & II of the 1890 Act was estimated in 1903 as 3.5 per cent in London, 2.66 per cent in Liverpool, 1.33 per cent in Manchester, 4.5 per cent in Glasgow and 3.5 per cent in Edinburgh. In order to cover capital outlay on building it was generally reckoned that a return of 4 per cent was necessary. See: W. Thompson, *op. cit.*, pp.170–1. *The Builder*, Vol.LXXVI, · 1899, pp.79–80.

96. H. Spalding, 'Block Dwellings: The Associated and Self Contained Systems', *Journal of the Royal Institute of British Architects,* Vol. VII, 3rd. ser., 1900, p.255.
97. Webb MSS., London School of Economics.
98. City of Manchester, Sanitary Committee, *op. cit.,* pp.27—8.
99. H. Spalding, *op. cit.,* p.254.
100. City of Leeds, The Housing of the Working Classes Act 1890, *Report of the Visit of the Sub-sanitary (Unhealthy Areas) Committee to Salford, Manchester, Liverpool and London,* 1899, pp.15—19. E.D. Simon and J. Inman, *op. cit.,* p.22.
101. W. Thompson, *op. cit.,* p.69.
102. City of Manchester, *op. cit.,* p.29.
103. W. Thompson, *op. cit.,* p.69.
104. City of Manchester, Sanitary Committee, *op. cit.,* pp.28—9.
105. *Manchester City News,* 29 Feb. 1908, 31 Oct. 1903. T.R. Marr, *op. cit.,* p.84.
106. *Manchester City News,* 15 Mar. 1902, 25 Oct. 1902, 25 Apr. 1903, 22 Oct. 1904, 5 Aug. 1905, 20 Oct. 1906, 29 Feb. 1908, 24 Oct. 1908, 22 Oct. 1910.
107. Manchester City Council Proceedings, 2 Sept. 1896. *The Builder,* Vol.LXXI, 1896, p.215. E.D. Simon and J. Inman, *op cit.,* p.22.
108. *Building News,* Vol.LXXII, 1897, p.266. W. Thompson, *op. cit.,* p.70.
109. Manchester City Council Proceedings, 4 Aug. 1909.
110. Ibid., 16 July 1902, 5 Aug. 1903. *Manchester Evening Chronicle,* 3 Feb. 1906. E.D. Simon and J. Inman, *op. cit.,* p.22.
111. W. Thompson, *op. cit.,* p.71.
112. City of Manchester, Sanitary Committee, *op. cit.,* pp.31—6.
113. *Manchester Guardian,* 24 July 1914.
114. T.C. Horsfall, *The Improvement of the Dwellings and the Surroundings of the People: The Example of Germany,* Manchester, 1904, pp.24—6, 39—42. T.R. Marr, *Housing Conditions in Manchester and Salford,* Manchester, 1904, pp.885—95. *Building News,* Vol LXXXVII, 1904, p.285; Vol.IC, 1910, p.396. *The Architect,* Vol.LXXXII, 1909, Supplement, pp.16—19. *Manchester City News,* 20 March 1902, 7 Apr. 1906, 26 Oct. 1907.
115. Manchester City Council Proceedings, 12 Dec. 1899, 3 Jan. 1900.
116. City of Manchester, Sanitary Committee, *op. cit.,* pp.8—19. Manchester City Council Proceedings, 23 Feb. 1910, 27 Feb. 1911, 18 Dec. 1912, 28 Jan. 1914, 27 May 1914, 26 Aug. 1914.
117. *Building News,* Vol.LXXXVI, 1904, pp.87, 396. *The British Architect,* Vol.LXII, 1904, pp.179—80.
118. *Manchester City News,* 15 Mar. 1902, 22 Oct. 1904, 21 Oct. 1905, 29 Feb. 1908.
119. *Ibid.,* 22 Oct. 1904, 21 Oct. 1905.
120. *Ibid.,* 29 Feb. 1908.
121. Manchester City Council Proceedings, 2 March 1904, 4 May 1904, 6 May 1908, 1 Sept. 1909 (Appendix). *Manchester City News,* 4 Sept. 1909.
122. W. Thompson, *op. cit.,* pp.72—3. *The Architect,* Vol.LXI, 1899, Supplement, pp.25—6.
123. W. Thompson, *The Housing Handbook,* London, 1903, pp.54—60, 72—3; *The Housing Handbook Up to Date,* London, 1907. pp.94—5.
124. Southampton Medical Officer of Health, *Annual Report,* 1899, p.30.
125. W. Thompson, *The Housing Handbook,* London, 1903, p.73; *The Housing Handbook Up to Date,* London, 1907, p.183.
126. E.R. Dewsnup, *op. cit.,* p.231.

127. Manchester City Council Proceedings, 6 May 1908. *Manchester City News*, 7 March 1908, 9 May 1908.
128. Manchester City Council Proceedings, 4 Aug. 1909, 1 Sept. 1909, 26 Oct. 1910, 1 Feb. 1911.
129. *Manchester City News*, 22 Oct. 1910, 29 Oct. 1910, 25 Mar. 1911, 22 Apr. 1911, 4 Apr. 1914, 5 Apr. 1919.
130. Sheffield Medical Officer of Health, *Annual Report*, 1892, p.62; 1893, p.47. *Sheffield Independent*, 24 March 1892, 1 March 1894.
131. *Sheffield Independent*, 28 Feb. 1894.
132. Sheffield Corporation Health Committee, *Handbook of Workmen's Dwellings*, Sheffield, 1905, p.14. V.M. Hughes, *History of the Growth and the Location of the Corporation's Housing Schemes*, Sheffield, 1959, p.4.
133. *Sheffield Telegraph*, 9 July 1898. *Sheffield Independent*, 3 Feb. 1900.
134. *Sheffield Telegraph*, 16 July 1898. *Sheffield Independent*, 24 Feb. 1900.
135. Sheffield Corporation Health Committee, *Handbook of Workmen's Dwellings*, Sheffield, 1905, pp.21–5. *Building News*, Vol.LXXX, 1901, p.83. W. Thompson, *Housing Handbook*, London, 1903, p.71.
136. Sheffield Medical Officer of Health, *Annual Report*, 1900, pp.79, 95–7. *Sheffield Independent*, 6 Oct. 1902.
137. Sheffield Corporation Health Committee, *Handbook of Workmen's Dwellings*, Sheffield, 1905, p.7.
138. *Ibid.*, p.8.
139. *Sheffield Independent*, 3 Feb. 1900.
140. Sheffield Health Committee, *Handbook of Workmen's Dwellings*, Sheffield, 1905, pp.8–9.
141. *Sheffield Independent*, 9 Oct. 1905. *Report of the Proceedings of a Conference on the Development of Suburban Areas*, Sheffield, 7 Oct. 1905, p.14.
142. Sheffield City Council Minutes, Estates Committee, 9 Feb. 1911. *Sheffield Independent*, 28 Oct. 1911, 31 Oct. 1911.
143. Sheffield City Council Minutes, 4 July 1917. S. Pollard, *History of Labour in Sheffield*, Liverpool, 1959, pp.187–8.
144. Though this was a common form in London, it seems to have been a novel venture in the provinces. See: *Building News*, Vol.LXXXVI, 1904, p.754.
145. Sheffield Corporation Health Committee, *Handbook of Workmen's Dwellings*, Sheffield, 1905, pp.12–13. V.M. Hughes, *op. cit.*, p.4.
146. Undated newspaper cuttings, Local History Collection, Sheffield City Library. *Sheffield Daily Telegraph*, 3 Oct. 1923. W. White, *Sheffield Directory*, 1896; 1900.
147. *Sheffield Telegraph*, 16 July 1898.
148. Sheffield Corporation Health Committee, *Handbook of Workmen's Dwellings*, Sheffield, 1905, pp.30–5.
149. Ibid., p.13. *Building News*, Vol.LXXXVI, 1904, p.754.
150. *Yorkshire Post*, 23 May 1896. *Leeds Mercury*, 5 Mar. 1897. *The Builder*, Vol.LXXVI, 1899, p.282. *Building News*, Vol.LXIX, 1895, p.504; Vol.LXX, 1891, p.807; Vol.LXXII, 1897; p.292; Vol.LXXIII, 1897, p.429; Vol.LXXVI, 1899, p.763.
151. F.M. Lupton, *Housing Improvement: A Summary of Ten Years Work in Leeds*, Leeds, 1906, pp.7–10. Leeds Corporation Housing Committee, *City of Leeds: A Short History of Civic Housing*, Leeds, 1954, p.3. *Leeds Mercury*, 18 March 1901. *Yorkshire Post*, 18 March 1901.
152. *The Builder*, Vol.LXXV, 1898, p.83; Vol.LXXVII, 1899, p.330.
153. *Yorkshire Post*, 16 Oct. 1900.
154. See, for example, the case in Halifax of the builder, George Buckley, who in

1889 submitted to the Council for approval three successive schemes for flats. Each time the Building Committee refused to approve the erection of flats in the town. Halifax Corporation Building Committee, Plans No.4788 (new series), 3 Sept. 1889, No.4852, 12 Nov. 1889. I am grateful to A. Dingsdale, University of Leeds, for drawing my attention to this venture.

155 *Manchester City News,* 10 Feb. 1906. Sheffield Federated Trades Council, *Annual Report,* 1905–6. Sheffield Labour Representative Committee, *Annual Report,* 1905–6, p.5. *Building News,* Vol.XCIX, 1910, p.396. *The Architect,* Vol.XCII, 1914, pp.337–40. E.R. Dewsnup, *op. cit.,* p.231.

Chapter 5 From Working Class Tenement to Modern Flat: local authorities and multi-storey housing between the wars
Alison Ravetz

Although the word 'flat' was established in English usage by the early 1800s it was still little used after the First World War, when 'tenement' was much the commoner term. Tenements, or flatted dwellings in large blocks, still had an unsavoury, nineteenth-century image. The Tudor Walters Report in 1918 noticed them only to remark that 'no advocate appeared' for them and at best it allowed that 'modified types of such buildings might be a necessity in the centre of areas already partly developed with this class of dwelling or to meet special conditions'.[1] It made no further mention of them, and at a time when the two-storey suburban house was the ideal dwelling this was consistent with the Report's function of codifying and disseminating the most advanced ideas on housing design.

The Dudley Report of 1944 served the same purpose for the post-1945 period, but by this time the position had changed. The tenement was now quite distinctly the modern flat and although the report was 'aware of the keen controversy of the house versus the flat' it did not question the latter's existence.[2] It devoted a long section to discussing how the disadvantages of many flats built between the wars could be avoided in future and recommended that new ones should be as large and well-appointed as houses. It is clear that in the interval between the two reports a minor revolution had taken place in the provision of flats and in public estimation of them.

Throughout the 1920s and 1930s, in public as in private housing, the popular ideal both in theory and practice was the low-density garden suburb. The proportion that flats contributed to all subsidised dwellings between the wars, though it was some 40 per cent in London and some 20 per cent in Liverpool, was nationally only about 5 per cent.[3] These were in blocks at most six storeys high and they do not include the 'cottage flats' which were a common feature of suburban council estates. These latter were built four in a block, resembling houses in external appearance, and they were for practical purposes simply a cheaper version of the suburban house. By 1930 privately-built blocks of upper-class flats were appearing in London, at seaside resorts and in the more important provincial centres. With some partial exceptions, such as Dolphin Square, these did not aspire to providing for complete communities and in general they attracted little public notice, although it is possible that they helped to increase the respectability of council flats of the same period.

The record of flat building by local authorities has the same diversity (and the same difficulty of establishing overall patterns) as most other aspects of local government.[4] The majority of English cities did not use their powers of slum clearance in the 1920s and confined their use of the housing subsidies to suburban estates without undertaking high-density redevelopment. Only in London and Liverpool, where housing and land shortages were acute, was there no break in a tradition of flat building that went back to the middle of the nineteenth century. In these cities it is possible to find continuity of style and of site (as on the Tabard Estate in Southwark, where construction was halted in 1917 and resumed in 1919) and blocks were usually built up to five–six storeys high. Even here, however, flat building took second place to suburban house building during the 1920s. Between 1920 and 1932 in London flats never contributed more than a quarter of the annual completions of new municipal dwellings and in Liverpool in the same period they contributed less than a twelfth – for both cities this was a reversal of the record prior to 1914. Birmingham and Newcastle were unusual among the larger county boroughs in building over a hundred flats under the 1923 and 1925 housing acts. At best, other large housing authorities, like Bradford and Bristol, built only a few dozen three- or four-storey flats in this decade and the majority built none at all. This was perhaps most surprising in Manchester, where the Corporation had built many hundreds of tenements around 1900, but the opposition to flats of E.D. Simon (later Lord Simon of Wythenshawe) may go far to explain it. The Leeds experience was more typical of other cities, for here knowledge of flats was confined to a small housing trust block built in 1866 and one municipal and one private enterprise block of c.1905. After 1919, in the absence of any suburban land shortage, the Council found it easy to build new estates at the fringes of the city and to leave the central slum districts undisturbed.

It was the national slum clearance campaign, inaugurated by Greenwood's Housing Act of 1930, that finally coerced the major cities, as well as some smaller ones, into building flats. This act facilitated procedures for clearance and introduced a new Exchequer subsidy which was attached to the number of people displaced rather than the number of new dwellings provided. This subsidy was increased when rehousing was done in flats over three storeys high on expensive sites. But as long as the general housing subsidy of the Wheatley (1924)

Act remained in force this legislation was not sufficient to lure most authorities away from their established policies of suburban building, to deal with the central slums. It was not until the Health Minister in a coalition government (Sir Hilton Young) abolished the general subsidy in 1933 that Greenwood's Act, with its mandatory five-year programme of slum clearance and rehousing, became widely operative. This act was followed by the 1935 Housing Act, which made overcrowding a statutory offence and replaced the Greenwood subsidies by others that were attached only to certain categories of dwelling. Though these included flats and the subsidies increased for more expensive land, they were less generous than the Greenwood subsidies. These latter were to terminate in 1938 and the prospect of this loss caused a number of authorities to step up their programmes to take advantage of the larger subsidies while they were in force. This meant that outside London and Liverpool, which had not waited on this legislation to clear slums or build flats, the years between 1933 and 1939 constituted the most significant period of flat building between the wars. By 1939 some authorities — notably Leeds, Manchester and Liverpool — still had huge programmes of flat building in hand, which would have been implemented but for the onset of war.

While London and Liverpool were continuing to build flats in thousands, the majority of large cities, including a number who had no previous experience of tenements, built some flats between 1933 and 1939. These might be no more than three storeys high and were sometimes intended only as one- or two-person dwellings, but in most cases they were family dwellings four or five storeys high. Many cities built a few hundred flats in large estates. Newcastle built over 500, Leeds nearly 1,000, Liverpool over 5,000, and Manchester an astonishing total of over 9,000. But even now some of the leading county boroughs still avoided flats for practical or policy reasons and these included Coventry, Leicester and Wolverhampton. The giant estates of the 1930s were a phenomenon of London and the great northern cities. Although the policies of Liverpool, Manchester and Leeds were not formally linked, these cities were connected by an informal chain of personnel who were interested in flats and they rapidly became more important than London as innovators in large, flatted estates.[5]

Although by 1939 flat living had actually been experienced by only a small proportion of the population, slum clearance was a national issue and the resulting interest in flats was almost universal. At the beginning of the slum clearance drive they were still regarded as tenements for the poor, the unpleasant but inevitable building form where maximum density and maximum cheapness were required. By 1939 the cruder prejudices against them were softened and they were now recognisably modern flats, an accepted form of dwelling for normal and respectable families. To understand this development it is necessary to examine the main arguments advanced for flats in the 1930s and the standards of design and fittings that they managed to achieve.

Practical and Ideological Arguments for Flats

Among the arguments advanced for flats between the wars we find the following regularly appearing, either singly or in association:
    the economics of city development
    social exigency
    technical innovation
    social idealism
    continental example
    fine architecture
    the preservation of rural land.
The first two were arguments or rationales used in the nineteenth century and were now similar responses to a similar set of economic and social constraints. The remainder, however, are typically twentieth-century arguments and some of them are peculiar to the 1930s. For the most part they are ideological rather than practical, in that their prime purpose was to motivate councils to build flats and they did not necessarily have to correspond exactly to reality in order to influence policy and action. Together they reflect a conscious reorientation towards flats which was felt not so much as a return to an earlier tradition, or as a new episode in that tradition, but as a new and uncertain venture. This was so even in London and Liverpool, where flat building had never ceased, and in Manchester, whose pre-1914 tenement blocks were still relatively new, as well as in the towns and cities that now embarked on flat building for the first time.

The Economics of Town Development and Social Exigency

The basis of the economic argument was the high price of central land which then (as now) had to be acquired at site valuation even when it carried 'unfit' housing that merited no compensation and was going to be used for working-class housing to replace that demolished. Despite the possibility of using existing services, this made the redevelopment of such sites vastly more expensive than the development of new suburban tracts and the subsidy provisions for central sites reflected this. It was inconceivable to use them for small numbers of houses at low densities and it was assumed then that the only way of accommodating the required densities of dwelling was by building blocks of flats.

The social exigency argument was the traditional argument that some sections of the working-class, including the lowest paid and the shift workers, needed to live within walking distance of their jobs. Thus the docks were the rationale for the thousands of flats built in Liverpool before and after 1914. In some contexts this argument was slightly artificial. In Leeds, for instance, it was advanced for the building of Quarry Hill Flats, on the assumption that market workers needed to live next to their work. In the event no attempt was made to adjust rents to the means of such people, and only a small number of market workers (including some well-to-do stallholders) appear ever to have lived in the flats.

The proximity-to-work argument had originated in a period with no cheap public transport. Such transport was available in the 1930s, but its capacity would have needed to be increased to carry the large slum populations that were eventually rehoused in the major cities, and its cheapness was a matter for dispute. One of the main reasons for distress arising from rehousing in the suburbs was the higher cost of living, in which the fares of the breadwinner played a large part. The people in Hulme and other proposed clearance areas of Manchester were firmly united against suburban rehousing for this very reason; they pleaded against being sent out to Wythenshawe and asked instead for flats in their own neighbourhoods.

Technical Innovation

Aside from the problem of site costs, there was a widespread and vague belief that unit building costs for flats ought to be lower than for houses. The facts were otherwise. Although other countries, including Scotland, could build flats more cheaply than houses, in England they were consistently more expensive than urban, non-parlour houses. The cost of such houses, with three bedrooms, dropped to around £400 in the early 1930s and was further reduced to about £300 before the price of building materials began to escalate in the years leading up to the outbreak of war in 1939. Over the same span of time the cost of flats appears to have been normally rather more than one-third higher than that of houses, until the middle 1930s, when it increased to as much as two-thirds. Flat costs were at their lowest around 1934, when they were normally around £435, but by the later 1930s they were rising to near £600. If the actual floor-area of dwellings was taken into account, the average cost of flats was nearly double that of houses, which were invariably larger than flats with the same number of bedrooms.[6]

Unfortunately it was on the more imaginative and innovating estates that building costs were highest. London's Ossulston Estate, pared down from the estimated £813 unit cost of the original design, achieved an actual unit cost of £617 around 1930. Leeds's Quarry Hill Flats in 1938, achieved a unit cost of £630, which was some 20 per cent above the national average, although this included many important extras, as we shall see. By 1935 it was widely known that building costs for flats escalated when they were higher than five storeys and this, together with the extra cost of installing passenger lifts, acted as a restraint on building flats above the traditional height.[7]

The building costs were reflected in high rents, which made a nonsense of the claims of flats to cater for the poor. Liverpool partly solved the problem by subsidising rents of flats, as well as managing to build them rather more cheaply than the rest of the country. But this was exceptional and rents of over 10s, exclusive of rates, were commonly charged in the provinces and rents of up to £1 8s in London. The sum of 10s represented some 20–25 per cent of an unskilled worker's wage and it compared unfavourably with a normal house rent of 8s or less.

Although English flats were admittedly more spacious and better appointed than continental ones there appears to be no simple explanation why they cost so much more to build than houses. The provision of electricity and other services besides lifts was a contributing factor and details like the need to satisfy fire regulations and building bye-laws helped to make them more expensive than they strictly needed to be. To some extent also cost was a function of design; it was recognised, for instance, that balcony or gallery access flats were cheaper than those with staircase access but, although this presumably influenced the choice of some authorities, they made no concerted effort to use standardised designs in the interest of lowering costs.

With the revival of large-scale slum clearance in the early 1930s some

official and semi-official agencies began to be actively concerned with
the cost problem. Up to this time blocks had been built traditonally,
with either load-bearing brick walls or steel frames. In 1934 the Council
for Research on Housing Construction, Slum Clearance and Rehousing
considered how to reduce the cost of working-class housing and
analysed the relative merits of houses and flats. They advocated flats
rather than houses and believed that frame construction and standard-
isation were the keys to the problem of cost. A departmental
committee of the Ministry of Health produced reports on the
construction of flats for the working classes in 1935 and 1937. They
analysed a number of different building systems, including steel and
reinforced concrete frame structures with many different kinds of
cladding. They found that traditional brick construction was the best in
many respects, but felt that the innovating systems had promise and
ought to be tried, with the help of a relaxation of fire regulations.[8]

The reports had no mandatory force, and the British building
industry, as Marian Bowley has shown, remained unresponsive to new
techniques during this period.[9] The foundation of the British Constructional Steelwork Association and the Reinforced Concrete Association
in 1929 and 1932 and the new codes of practice that each helped to
introduce did not change this inherent conservatism, which ensured
that English building, and particularly the building of flats, was far
behind European practice. The use of reinforced concrete frames and
patent systems promised the local authority architects significant
savings on the cost of construction and many local authorities had
already had some experience of non-traditional building from the
prefabricated houses of the early 1920s. But on the rare occasions when
they considered reinforced concrete construction, as at Kennings Estate
in Kensington, they found that contractors tendered for traditional
brick construction much more cheaply. The City Architect of Liverpool, L.H. (later Sir Lancelot) Keay, was strongly tempted by the
possibilities of reinforced concrete, but even he regretfully conceded
that conservatism in building methods was the best policy for local
officials.[10]

The new interest in building construction was useful in focusing
attention upon some of the technical problems of flats, particularly
that of noise, and systematic research into these was now begun. In
other respects it met with so many of the practical and social obstacles
to innovation (as opposed to the purely technical aspects) that
arguments were bound to be couched in ideal rather than practical
terms. This was most striking in the propaganda for prefabrication

which, as a matter of faith, some believed would give improved production and performance in mass housing as it had already done in the mass production of cars and other goods. Both the Council for Research on Housing Construction and the departmental committee considered schemes that were wholly or partly prefabricated. Among other methods they considered the Mopin System, which was also the subject of a study and report by the Building Research Station in 1934.[11] The most completely prefabricated method then available, it had already been used successfully for flats and houses in France and it promised substantial savings. The Building Research Station were sympathetic to its claims but remarked on the 'unusual organisation' required by so unconventional a system. Impressed with the site organisation at Drancy, however, they recommended its trial on a large cottage estate. The only authority to take up the system was Leeds, where the Housing Committee and the City Architect chose to ignore the warning and adopted it for Quarry Hill Flats – unwisely, as it turned out. In the event all the promised savings of the system were dissipated by problems of co-ordinating the factory production with the erection and the consequent dragging out of the contract over six years. Not only the contractor but also the architect and the structural

Plate XI. Quarry Hill Flats, Leeds. Mopin system buildings under construction, 1936. (By permission of the City Architect, Leeds).

engineers failed to appreciate the subtleties of the method or the fact that, although it did not require skilled bricklayers, plasterers and other trades, it did call for special skills of a non-traditional kind.

Leeds had originally intended to use the same system on its vast schemes of central redevelopment, but as the Mopin System had proved so disappointing it turned to another less ambitious system, Dyke's 'clothed concrete' system of prefabricated panels mounted on a reinforced concrete frame. This had already been used successfully on the Birmingham St Martin's (Emily Street) flats in 1939.[12] Aside from this limited success and the occasional block of reinforced concrete frame flats in London and elsewhere, there was no magical technical breakthrough for the architect of local authority flats before 1939. The arguments for innovation, therefore, were not so important for their practical applications as for helping to reinforce the belief of some that high flats were technically feasible, potentially cheap and, above all, essentially modern dwellings.

Social Idealism

Once the great quinquennium of flat building was under way it generated a great deal of enthusiasm, both social and architectural, that frothed over into newspapers, books and journals. Here the old flats-versus-houses controversy was conducted with a new briskness. It was not, and did not need to be, related to any careful estimate of housing needs or users' reactions. It sufficed that the slum clearance campaign now brought flats within reach of the general idealism of the housing movement. Housing was the gateway to health, education, higher domestic standards – the essentials that were crucial in transforming the culture of poverty into what later became the affluent society. Up to now these goals had been attached to suburban houses and the people who inhabited them. Before flats could be allowed to share them they and their population had to lose the old image of slum culture and tenement, and there was much debate about the ability of people from unhealthy homes to use modern amenities to full advantage.

This is not to say that all the flats now built were well-designed and well-fitted homes. On the contrary there were many that were dreary twentieth-century translations of Peabody tenements.[13] It did mean that those who championed flats did it with militancy and bravado. They often backed up their campaigns with show flats and exhibitions of models and plans which were given maximum publicity in the press, with more than a touch of the millenarianism that inevitably accompanies reports of the newest architecture, while it is still clean, white and original.

Flats had powerful advocates in the churches, politics and industry. Churches of all denominations supported public demand for them in Manchester and Leeds, as doubtless in other places, because they saw this form of development as the only way to avoid the dispersal of neighbourhoods and the break-up of parishes.[14] There was a strong lobby for flats among women's organisations and, once they were satisfied that flats could make healthy homes, many architects and housing reformers shared their concern to lighten the traditional domestic burden of women. In Leeds and elsewhere the Women's Co-operative Guild campaigned for them because they believed they would be convenient homes to keep clean and warm. In Manchester the Women's Advisory Committee of the Borough Labour Party were at first disposed to be critical of the earliest inter-war flats at Kennet House, but after a tour of the building they were so far converted that they took the architect to task only for not providing lifts. The gas industry was another potent propagandist for modern flats. The Ascot Water Heater Company published a large, glossy volume, *Flats*, in 1938, in which the main item described was Kensal House, designed by Maxwell Fry and fitted exclusively with gas fittings by the Gas Light and Coke Company. Various gas boards throughout the country arranged exhibitions and competitions and opened gas-equipped show flats, for the ulterior motive of expanding in this new and promising market.

The purest expression of social idealism in flats was the Leeds estate at Quarry Hill. Before and after 1914 successive councils in Leeds had been complacent and dilatory about its slum problem, so that by 1933 only a few score of houses had been cleared and the back-to-backs (some 75,000 in all) were a national byeword. In 1933 a Labour Council was returned and it hung on by a handful of seats for a brief two years. In that period, with the Reverend Charles Jenkinson as Chairman, the newly-formed Housing Committee appointed their first City Architect (R.A.H. Livett) and embarked on gigantic slum clearance programmes. As well as huge suburban estates, Livett was briefed to build an estate of flats on the notorious and now half-derelict slum of Quarry Hill, less than a mile from Leeds Town Hall. Nothing was to be spared to make it the most advanced, magnificent and luxurious estate the world had yet seen, a fitting compensation to slum dwellers for

Plate XII. Kennet House, Cheetham, Manchester. Photograph taken in 1970.

years of neglect and an architectural embellishment to the centre of Leeds. The city was in an uproar throughout Jenkinson's administration – in pursuit of his vision he had to go against the pleas of his own and other churches – and the flats were drawn into the political controversy time and again. When the first part of the estate was opened in 1938, however, a Conservative Council was pleased to take credit and until well into the 1960s both Corporation and citizens of Leeds were fiercely proud of what they believed to be the largest estate in Europe. Yet even at the beginning there was a contradiction in the concept of flats here. Jenkinson repeatedly referred to Quarry Hill as a decanting centre for people in transition from the slums to suburban houses, which he believed every right-minded person would prefer. His architect, on the other hand, designed them and repeatedly described them as a permanent home for a full and settled population.

Particularly important in the conception of Quarry Hill, and central to most arguments from social idealism, was the example of the Continent. The general public was made aware of this from exhibitions of photographs up and down the country and it was the huge socialist estates of Vienna, built between 1920 and 1933, that were singled out for special notice. These in particular served as magnets for all who worked within the housing and labour movements to improve the condition of life for the working classes, as well as all the young and socially aware architects who 'did not consider their education finished until they had studied these workmen's dwellings of Vienna on the spot'.[15]

The Appeal to Continental Example

A number of cities and official bodies sent delegates to view continental housing schemes. Birmingham's delegation to Germany, Austria and Czechoslovakia in 1930 was one of the earliest and its report, published in 1930, was widely studied and quoted. In 1935 the London County Council (as well as the Department of Health for Scotland) sent delegations to Germany, Austria, Czechoslovakia, Holland and France. The LCC delegates (who included the Chairman of the Housing Committee, then Lewis Silkin, MP) also toured Scandinavia. The Leeds Labour Council, in 1933, leaned heavily on a report of the West Yorkshire Society of Architects, who visited the same countries. The United States, although it was building skyscraper apartments at this time, had not begun its Federal Housing programmes and did not attract similar pilgrimages. On the contrary it was sending to England and Europe for news of good modern housing for low-income families. The USSR, though it was building flats under German tutelage by the early 1930s, was also beyond the range of most English visitors.[16]

The architecture of the German estates was the most advanced and in building techniques the French estates were probably the most interesting; but it was the Viennese estates that most captured the imagination of English visitors. Possibly this was because of their scale, many of them having over 1,000 dwellings and some stretching along frontages of half a mile. In the absence of any national housing subsidies they had been built by the socialist municipality and financed by the summary measure of taxing existing dwellings. In spite of their political connotations, the estates were almost universally admired in England. The scale and public grandeur of the buildings, with formal gardens, pools, sculptures, as well as essential welfare provisions like crèches and canteens, opened a whole world of possibilities to English housing reformers. It seemed that working-class life could be lived here with undreamt of levels of convenience and dignity and it came as a revelation that normal populations, including families with children, could be so accommodated. Outside London and Liverpool English tenements had tended to be identified with the aged and the single, but Vienna demonstrated that whole English populations might similarly live 'quite satisfactorily, comfortably and happily in a flat or tenement dwelling under perfectly healthy conditions, *provided the necessary amenities are included within the scope of the scheme*'.[17]

At the same time it was obvious that the individual flats in Vienna, as in most European cities, were much inferior to the standards that English people had come to regard as essential since the introduction of housing subsidies. The majority of European flats looked at were lacking a private bath or bathroom; some lacked a hot water system; in general they were smaller and less well finished than English flats. Consequently delegates recommended that English dwelling standards be maintained and combined with the European scale and provision of public amenities. Birmingham was advised by its delegation to build a model colony of about 1,000 flats. In Leeds the City Architect was briefed to design estates of not less than 500 flats, with kindergartens and with not more than 25 per cent of the site occupied by buildings.

Like the arguments of the social idealists, continental example was in essence an ideological issue that was largely independent of social reality. So, for instance, the extra costs of combining good English dwelling standards with European amenities were largely glossed over.[18] In practice they meant that such amenities were reduced, deferred to the end of the contract, or eventually left unfinished. The obvious differences between the English estates, when completed, and their continental models were seldom commented on. Quarry Hill Flats was widely believed to be a self-contained estate, when in fact it has lacked a school, a crèche, a health centre, a community hall and post office for some or all of its life. In Birmingham, after several years delay, the Council adopted precisely that course of action which its delegation had advised against; the St Martins Flats, though designed to have several open and covered playgrounds and a bowling green, consisted of only 266 dwellings.[19] Symbolic of the gap between continental model and English performance was the window box, which English visitors had seen with cascades of flowers under summer skies in Vienna, Berlin and other cities. Specifying window boxes for estates must have seemed a relatively inexpensive way of bringing the same riotous profusion to English – even Scottish – schemes, where we find it running like a leitmotif. Unfortunately the rigours of the British climate frustrated these well-meaning intentions and the window boxes failed to produce flowers or any other crop.[20]

Plate XIII. London County Council, Ossulston Estate, Euston. Photograph taken in 1973.

It is possible that much of the development of English flats in the 1930s would have taken place even without the continental model. The Ossulston Estate, planned before 1928, had open spaces with trees, seats and children's playgrounds. The large Liverpool estates of the 1930s, with gardens, playgrounds, shops and other facilities, paid little direct tribute to continental models and were in direct line of development from estates built there in the 1920s. It is not necessary to look outside English tradition for shops and laundries, which are found in Victorian tenements, and as early as 1900 the great LCC estates at Boundary Street and Millbank were creating complete urban environments with an awareness of the architectural contribution that flats could make to a city.

The large estates of the 1930s were not therefore a completely new departure. But this is a judgement made in retrospect. Most of the people who decided on and designed them did so in conscious imitation of European models, even if they might have made similar choices without them. This can be seen in London, where after the Ossulston experiment an 'improved' flat and estate type was introduced in 1934; and even after this, Lewis Silkin's delegation looked at continental estates to see how far they could be imitated in the next phase of rehousing, under the 1935 Act.

Fine Architecture

From the time of the earliest English tenements of the 1840s it was appreciated that blocks of flats could be distinguished architecturally. But so great were the economic and social constraints of tenements for the poor that architects played little active role in designing them and, as J.N. Tarn has shown, it was not until the time of the big LCC estates around 1900 that architects became closely involved in this branch of housing.[21]

After 1919 the housing subsidies enabled architects to become responsible for designing flats, like all other council housing, although for many years numerous authorities did not appoint architects but used engineers to design their estates. The earliest inter-war blocks of flats were safe and dull derivatives of the pre-1914 blocks, lacking the vitality and variety of the styles used at Boundary Street and Millbank. Traditional construction kept heights to five—six storeys (the maximum permitted by load-bearing walls) and later, when new techniques could have lifted this restriction, local authorities, as we have seen, did not adopt them. In so far as these early blocks had style, it was neo-Georgian. The Ossulston Estate was possibly the earliest to strive for some originality and it achieved this with the layout of buildings and the impressive arcading, balconies and other details of some of its blocks.

With the swing towards flats in the 1930s came a renewal of interest in their architectural potential. This was partly for the same reason as in the 1840s; it was felt that estates of flats could make a contribution of a monumental kind to cities. In addition there was now the lobby of the Modern Movement in architecture, whose adherents assumed, with Le Corbusier, that good modern housing would be in tall blocks. The CIAM (Congrès internationaux d'architecture moderne) made mass housing the theme of their conferences and exhibitions throughout the later 1920s and the 1930s and for the most part it was taken for granted that apartment blocks were the most appropriate building form for modern ferro-concrete techniques, as well as offering the most civilised way of life to the working classes and the most visually satisfying urban environments. Aside from demonstration contexts like the Weissenhof (Stuttgart) housing exhibition of 1927, to which van der Rohe, Gropius, Le Corbusier, Behrens and many others contributed, the contribution of the Modern Movement to mass housing depended on national and local housing policies. In England, in spite of the immense effect that the Weimar phase had upon young English architects and housing reformers, it contributed little in practical terms to local authority housing.

Architecture of the Modern Movement entered English housing in a very small and sporadic way, through the medium of private clients building their own houses, or the few enterprising housing associations that built blocks of flats. Its uncompromisingly modern, white-concrete and flat-roofed designs encountered the opposition of planning authorities and often hostile demonstrations from the public as well. No local authority adopted the style. On the contrary, to the despair of Maxwell Fry, member of CIAM and founder member of MARS (Modern Architectural Research Group), the tendency was for every authority that built flats to build 'in a blind faith that the only decency is Georgian.'[22]

Nevertheless a new style for blocks of flats, modernistic rather than modern, appeared in London, Manchester, Leeds, Liverpool and some other cities, along with the estate improvements and reform of dwellings in the middle 1930s. In so far as it had any specific European inspiration this seems to have come mainly from Vienna, whose great estates had nothing original either in structures or aesthetics, but whose scale and monumental grandeur impressed most English visitors with a general suggestion of modernity. All the larger English estates of the 1930s strove after these same qualities, and those that in addition tried to achieve a modern style picked up some of the accidental attributes, rather than essentials that were based on a more adventurous and honest use of modern materials.

Thus the wide windows and angle windows (the close-set metal glazing bars emphasising the width) represented glass curtain walling. Curved facades advertised liberation from conventional structures. These were to be found on estates in Berlin and Vienna and the type example was the famous Schocken store of Mendelsohn at Chemnitz (Karl Marx Stadt). In such buildings as this the continuous glazed bands alternated with solid bands to give the effect of horizontal stripes. This was taken up with enthusiasm in the modernistic blocks in England, where the cantilevered access balconies already provided a strong horizontal emphasis. Kennet House and Quarry Hill Flats, which lacked such balconies, were given a striped polychrome effect by alternate bands of contrasting finishes. A virtue was made of the fact that long ranges of buildings (which were more typical of Vienna than other

European cities) paid no respect to the natural contours of the land, but floated free above them. Like some private blocks at this time, municipal flats were sometimes layered in different heights, in conscious imitation of ocean liners. The more deliberately modernistic blocks had flat roofs, though English space heating from open fires caused difficulties in providing chimneys with sufficient draught. Despite some fanciful propaganda for flat roofs, little use was ever made of them either for play or any other practical purpose.[2 3] Above all, the English blocks made plentiful use of applied decoration, which was supplied by features such as door canopies, balconies, projecting turrets housing staircases, semicircular and elliptical arches (which were carefully constructed within rectangular steel frames), flower troughs and the inevitable window boxes which were arranged in ranks around arches and other points of interest. It was a geometric, self-confident style, which only occasionally seemed to mellow, as at Manchester's Heywood House (1939) where modernism was combined harmoniously with brick and pitched roofs.

R.A.H. Livett, in his Quarry Hill estate, was the only principal architect to try to fuse a modernistic style with a modern building system. He had already thought it out and actually used the style at Kennet House in Manchester, where concrete was simulated by cement rendering over brick and the structure also was traditional. Kennet House was designed a year or more before he resolved to use the Mopin system in Leeds and, although he may have considered this method of construction more appropriate for the style, there was no doubt that this was already fixed and chosen. This shows the extent to which the modernistic style was independent of structural considerations.

The modernistic buildings have a special interest, but the more typical products of the 1930s were the neo-Georgian blocks so common in London and Liverpool, characterised by front facades with high, small-paned windows and rear elevations dominated by the access balconies and staircase turrets. Sometimes they picked up the curved ranges, rounded arches and other features of the modernistic style, but in general they were not so ambitious as the brasher and self-consciously modern estates. Without risking so much, their achievement was more secure but less striking. The neo-Georgian style might not, in itself, have been sufficient to give the necessary architectural impetus to the new-type flats of the 1930s. Modernism, spurious as it was in many ways, reminded observers of international trends, symbolised progress and helped to establish flats as an indispensable ingredient of modern urban environments.

Plate XIV. Melrose Road flats, Liverpool, in about 1938. (By permission of the Divisional Director of Architecture, Liverpool).

Flats as a Means of Preserving the Countryside

Although not many protagonists for flats used this argument explicitly, there was in the 1930s what F.J. Osborn described as 'one moment of real peril for planning', when there was a temporary alliance between rural preservationists and supporters of high-density flats.[24] Even such level-headed spokesmen as L.H. Keay and Elizabeth Denby saw good modern flats as a means of checking suburban sprawl 'at twelve cold and draughty, detached or semi-detached cottages to the acre, in estates banished to the periphery of the town far from friends and work'.[25]

As before, the theoretical possibilities of flats obscured practical difficulties. The opportunities of increasing open space by increasing the height of blocks were demonstrated by Gropius in 1930 and gradually made an impact in England during the following years; but the practical difficulties of making full use of such space and, in particular, the amount of land consumed by access roads, were not appreciated. This misapprehension can be seen carried to an extreme in *The Modern Flat* (1937) of F.R.S. Yorke and Frederick Gibberd. After graphically contrasting the unspoilt countryside which was being sacrificed to the sprawling suburb, the authors referred admiringly to a design by Gropius and Maxwell Fry for flats in Windsor. Here, without the tedious necessity of communications or neighbourhood services, 'the countrydweller would be in the country immediately he left his door'.[26]

The Role of Practical and Ideological Arguments

The various arguments for flats have been discussed here at some length, but it should not therefore be supposed that public opinion generally was in favour of living in flats. The universal ideal continued to be the suburban house and the prevailing propaganda that of the Garden City, or rather its debased derivative, the garden suburb. The protagonists of flats were either, like Sir Hilton Young, militantly defensive about them ('You can get as good if not a better home for the worker in flat blocks as in a cottage')[27] or put their faith in one particular argument for them, to the exclusion of all other considerations. The majority of City Architects, like Leonard Heywood of Manchester, regarded flats as an unfortunate necessity and L.H. Keay of Liverpool was unusual in making a virtue of them. Even Charles Jenkinson invariably maintained that 'for the average English working-class family, from the economic and sociological points of view, the cottage is by far the best dwelling' and it was his declared policy to provide a suburban house and garden for every family who wanted one.[28] In most places we find that the movement to flats, impelled as it seemed by necessity, was excused by selected arguments. Only in Leeds, despite the housing chairman's reservations, were all the arguments (except that of saving rural land) advanced in concert and explicitly and triumphantly used to justify the Quarry Hill estate.

This helps to explain why the break with the earlier tenement tradition, rather than the continuity, was what was emphasised, and why so little effort was made to enquire into the performance and results of the new flatted estates once they were built. A few such investigations were made, some of them, like a study of pre-war tenements and post-war flats made in Manchester, so well reasoned that they could serve as a practical manual today.[29] But though they were born of economic and social exigencies, flats were not so much a social experiment as the application of a set of theories. The social effects, the monitoring of results, or the possibility of authorities comparing their experience, therefore, were of relatively little importance. This is why it is necessary to appreciate the ideological content of arguments for flats.

This lack of objective appraisal is of more than historical interest, for propaganda and counter-propaganda for flats resulted in the attachment of two contrary myths. The 'bad' myth derived from the association with slums, the poor, charity and tenements; the 'good' myth from social progress and modernity. Where, as in London, both bad old tenements and good modern flats were fairly commonplace, the dual myths did not often obtrude; but where, as in Leeds, the new flats were a flamboyant break with tradition and built only after sharp political struggle, the duality had a noticeable influence on life on the estate, and public estimation of it, over a long period.

Design: The Standards Achieved

Beside the rationales and ideologies of flats their contribution to housing standards at this time must be considered. The main benefit of the housing subsidies was that they enabled local-authority flats to become invariably self-contained dwellings. This was not always the case for housing trust flats, some of which were still being built with shared facilities in the later 1920s. There was however little interest in the layout and fittings of flats in this decade. They normally had gas lighting, a coal cooking range in the living room and gas rings for supplementary cooking in the scullery, which also frequently contained the bath.

In the middle 1930s the leading authorities simultaneously, and apparently independently, began to design flats with higher standards of space, comfort and privacy. Manchester led the way with Kennet House, which was planned in 1933 and opened in 1935. Access was by internal stairs, which had doors at ground level and led to two flats on each landing. Every flat had a recessed private balcony, an electric griller in the scullery (as well as electric light throughout) and a bathroom where, to save space, the basin was fitted over the end of the bath. From 1934 London, Liverpool and Leeds also had 'new flats' with stair access, private balconies and better fittings, which included fitted wardrobes, scullery worktops, vermin-proof skirting and picture rails, and the obligatory window boxes. At Quarry Hill Flats the scullery became virtually a fitted kitchen and it contained a back-to-back range which presented an oven to the scullery and an open coke fire (lit by gas poker) to the living room. Even here, however, the living-room fire was still fitted with trivets for cooking, while the scullery was provided with gas rings and griller. The sculleries remained small working kitchens all this time, as was consistent with current dogma that working-class families should be discouraged from cooking and eating in the same room. Overall dwelling sizes, however, were increased in this period, from an earlier level of 680 sq. ft. for a three-bedroom flat to a new standard of 700–725 sq. ft. Very importantly, estates now included a range of flat sizes, from one to four or five bedrooms, to accommodate a balanced population.

At the same time services were improved. The LCC, which had earlier experimented with improved refuse containers at Ossulston, now provided dust chutes to every eight–twelve flats, rather than every thirty. Quarry Hill Flats again led the field with the inclusion of the French Garchey system, which had been adopted at Drancy but never before been used in England. Refuse was placed in containers fitted under each sink and flushed by domestic waste water to underground chambers, from which it was drawn to a central incineration plant on the estate. District heating was tried in the first instalment of the Ossulston estate, but not in the later parts. It was also considered at Leeds in the early stages of planning for Quarry Hill Flats, but it survived only as a fitting to the incinerator that was supposed to transmit heat to the estate laundry above.

It was still normal at this time for lighting in working-class homes to be supplied by gas and in modern flats the gas industry discerned a great potential market. Their show flats included Kensal House, which had no electricity and where even the irons had to be powered by gas. In 1933 the London Gas Light and Coke Company succeeded in getting a private Act passed to prevent housing authorities in their own area of supply from imposing any restrictions on forms of fuel on their tenants and other companies followed suit in the next year.

Gas light was still very much cheaper than electric light, and with the introduction in 1929 of an automatic switch that did not need a pilot light it seemed to offer an equal convenience. Many housing reformers agreed with the gas industry that electric fittings placed a cruel burden on working-class tenants. The cost of electricity varied widely from area to area, but at best it could be obtained at ½–¾d a unit, to which the cost of bulbs had to be added.[30] In spite of this some public authorities and housing trusts anticipated the extension of electricity for lighting, cooking and even space-heating in working-class homes. Liverpool and London experimented with all-electric dwellings and Liverpool seems to have been providing electric lighting in flats as early as the 1920s (just as before 1914 it had led the country in providing gas light in municipal dwellings). At Ossulston the LCC rented washing machines and water heaters to tenants at a charge of 1s 9d to 2s per week and the weekly cost of current for these, with lighting, was reckoned to be 2s to 3s. It was assumed that providing a power circuit was ruled out by cost and plugs for appliances were run off the lighting circuit.[31]

Supplementary to the private dwellings were basement store rooms, estate mortuaries for laying out the dead,[32] radio relay systems and communal laundries and drying rooms. What was thought to be a very generous ratio of open space to building was laid down in Leeds and Birmingham, and the open spaces here and elsewhere were laid out with gardens and playgrounds as well as access roads. Quarry Hill was probably the only estate to include small patches of garden which tenants were supposed to cultivate, and here, as on a handful of estates throughout the country, it was intended to lay out tennis courts and bowling greens for the use of tenants. Swimming pools, which were a fairly common provision with upper class flats, got no further than being considered in the early stages of planning at Quarry Hill. Within the grounds of this and some other large estates were shops, estate management offices, crèches and community halls. The implementation of crèches depended on other departments of local authorities than housing, but under the 1936 Act housing departments did have power to provide community halls, which Livett included in his plans for Kennet House and Quarry Hill Flats. Garages, another common feature of private estates, were considered quite unnecessary for council tenants at this time.

Many of these items can be found in the nineteenth-century tenement estates, but they were then prompted by strictly utilitarian motives. They were now the result of conscious choice, related to the various ideological arguments for flats, particularly that of continental example. Height was another matter that was sensitive to these arguments, but in this respect the inter-war flats only just broke free of inherited standards by 1939. The overwhelming majority of local authority flats at this time were no higher than five—six storeys (and many were no higher than three—four storeys) whereas luxury blocks in London and resort towns were being built up to nine—twelve storeys by the later 1930s. These of course had passenger lifts while at best local authority flats had coal hoists. Even had structural considerations permitted, it was generally agreed that lifts were too costly to provide for working-class tenants.

In Europe inter-war flats were grouped into three height-zones. The great majority did not exceed four—five storeys, the height of the demonstration blocks at Weissenhof in 1927 and of the well-known German estates (*Siedlungen*) at Frankfurt and Berlin. But in Holland, France and Germany English visitors saw a few blocks of ten—eleven storeys (the height chosen by Le Corbusier and Gropius in unbuilt projects for Paris and Berlin) and two outstandingly original French estates, Cité de la Muette at Drancy and Villeurbanne near Lyons, had towers of sixteen and eighteen storeys respectively. These seemed to be reaching towards the much greater heights envisaged by Le Corbusier in his ideal city, but their greatest interest at this time was perhaps in their very rarity.

Viennese estates fell mainly into the lowest height zone, but some of their buildings were transitional. Sometimes the normal heights were raised to six, seven or eight storeys, giving the stepped effect that was imitated in England. The main purpose appears to have been for visual effect and since no lifts were provided there must have been some hardship to residents. In England it was taken for granted that above five storeys lifts ought to be provided and had this been possible it was generally agreed that ten storeys would be the preferred height.[33] Ten-storey blocks were approved (but not built) by Liverpool City Council in 1930; they were considered but rejected by the LCC in 1933; they were considered again by the Council for Research on Housing Construction in 1934 and, in the same year, for an annular shaped block at Liverpool.

In practice the only two estates that broke away from the five—six storey norm were Ossulston and Quarry Hill Flats. As originally proposed, Ossulston had blocks of up to nine storeys, but when implemented six storeys was the maximum. Quarry Hill was the only inter-war council estate to have lifts, which were supposedly paid for out of the savings of the Mopin system.[34] Because of the internal stair access a two-person lift was needed on each staircase and, in all, eighty-eight were provided. At Drancy the Mopin system had been used to build tower blocks of sixteen storeys, but here the architect chose the transitional heights of Vienna, stepping them from three to eight storeys for effect. At Quarry Hill, as on some Manchester estates, the single-person flats were provided in low blocks in the centre, while the repetition of dwelling plans on each floor dictated that large family flats should be stacked up above one another on one staircase. This created social and management problems that were no doubt responsible for much of the continued public reluctance to accept flats as suitable places for families to live.

The innovations of this period, therefore, did not include high-rise flats in the present sense. The improvements that were made can be thought of as deriving on one side from a native tradition of domestic privacy and comfort and on the other from an alien tradition of public amenity. The increase of domestic comfort made living in flats much more acceptable to a wider range of people, but the public amenities encountered a host of social obstacles to their successful implementation and use. The overall achievement, though it did not succeed in abolishing public suspicion of flats, was enough by 1939 to separate them from the tenement name and image; and if the new levels of space, fittings and amenity cost far more than a poor slum family could be expected to afford, this contradiction was soon obscured by full employment and other wartime conditions.

The Legacy of the 'Improved' Inter-War Flats

While nationally the reversion to large-scale flat building waited for the resumption of slum clearance policies in the middle 1950s, London and Liverpool, their traditional housing shortage now aggravated by bomb damage, continued building this type of dwelling immediately after the end of the war. They built thousands of flats, finishing estates begun before 1939 and using up pre-war designs, both for the 'improved' and the older type of dwelling.

Local practice continued to vary widely, according to local needs, traditions and politics. Before the end of the war most of the established centres of flats had looked foward to building a proportion of flats again after the war. The Greater London Plan (1943) envisaged flats of various heights up to ten storeys, which would be used in varying densities where they would form from 45 to 100 per cent of all the dwellings. Liverpool also envisaged building some flats of eight or ten storeys. Leeds made a positive virtue of flats and intended to have an inner ring of Quarry Hill type estates up to ten storeys high. Manchester, however, swung against flats and officially rejected anything higher than three storeys.[35]

National policy, as shown in the Dudley Report of 1944 and the *Housing Manual* of 1949, was to advise against the use of flats as family dwellings, but at the same time their authors were forced to admit that in high-density areas the housing of children in flats could not be avoided. They recommended a mixture of houses and tall blocks and the 1946 Housing Act allowed special subsidies for houses that were included in high-density schemes. Manchester claimed the credit for pioneering this at Greenwood House (1936–8), where single and elderly people were housed in lower blocks in the interior of the estate. It was universally agreed that lifts were necessary for flats of more than three storeys above ground and a subsidy was made available for them. The earliest types were, like the Quarry Hill ones, two-person lifts, but later, with different building forms, it was possible to introduce the three-person lift. With lifts, London was building up to eight storeys in the mid-1940s and the 1949 *Housing Manual* discussed flats of eleven and twelve storeys.

Both nationally and locally it was agreed that the full range of estate amenities should be provided but in practice these were often defeated by haste and economy. The arguments that were now put forward for them were more muted and presented more from utility than social idealism. The huge, self-contained estate, as a self-conscious exercise in model housing and town planning, no longer appeared, except as a late, provincial relic of the earlier movement. At the same time higher dwelling standards achieved by the best of the inter-war flats were coming into more general circulation. It was here that the Quarry Hill estate made its chief contribution. As well as the passenger lifts, its back-to-back grate was adopted in Manchester. The Garchey system was considered, although not used, in Liverpool, in connection with a district heating scheme. Later, in more modern form without on-site incineration, it was adopted at Park Hill (Sheffield) and the Barbican, among other post-war estates. The Manchester and Quarry Hill flat lay-out, with staircase access and private balcony, was widely adopted, while some authorities took the best of the London inter-war estates as their model.

Apart from some practical problems, of which noise was probably the greatest, it was possible from inter-war experience to reach a high level of privacy and comfort. Doubts about the social problems of flats could not be settled so easily. The earlier enthusiasm and burst of innovation that had made the transition to modern flats possible in the 1930s were now wanting and any community items that were proposed were conceived more as compensations for having to live in flats than as good ends in themselves.[36] The new high-rise flats of the 1950s, although they overlapped in time with the last use of inter-war designs, needed not only technological innovation, but the fresh inspiration of another set of practical and ideological arguments, thought out anew.

Notes

1. Local Government Boards for England and Wales and Scotland, *Report of the Committee to consider building construction in connection with the provision of dwellings for the working classes, &c.* Cd.9191, 1918, para.84.
2. Central Housing Advisory Committee, *Design of Dwellings*, HMSO, 1944, para.33.
3. R.H. Reiss, 'Housing floor space standards', *Town and Country Planning*, vol.XXIV, 1956, p.613.
4. I am indebted to the following County Boroughs for sending information of their housing records: Bradford, Bristol, Coventry, Derby, Leeds, Leicester. Manchester, Newcastle, Portsmouth, Salford, Sheffield, Stoke-on-Trent, Sunderland, Wolverhampton, York; also to A.R. Sutcliffe for information about Birmingham.
5. The personal network included J. Hughes, who in 1934 moved from Liverpool, where he was Senior Architectural Assistant, to be Assistant Housing Director at Manchester. His appointment was hailed in the local press as a 'flats pointer' (*Manchester City News*, 17 March 1934). R.A.H. Livett, first City Architect and Housing Director of Leeds, appointed in 1934, had previously been Deputy Director of Housing at Manchester, and one of his assistants (J. Austen Bent, later City Architect of Bradford) had also previously worked in Manchester. L.H. Keay, City Architect of Liverpool, had previously held an appointment in Birmingham.
6. For costs see Ministry of Health *Annual Reports*; London County Council, *London Housing*, 1937; *City of Liverpool Housing*, 1937; *City of Manchester Housing*, 1939; The Building Centre Committee, *Housing: a European Survey*, Vol.I, 1936 (vol.II never appeared).
7. Council for Research on Housing Construction, Slum Clearance and Re-housing, *Report*, 1934 (reported in *Yorkshire Post*, 14 June 1934) gave different costs for flats of five and ten storeys. London's *Report by the Chairman of the Housing and Public Health Committee . . . of a visit to continental housing estates*, 1935, noted that ten-storey blocks cost 30 per cent more than five-storey blocks.
8. Ministry of Health, *Construction of Flats for the Working Classes*, Final Report of the Departmental Committee, HMSO, August, 1937, conclusions, pp.30ff.
9. *The British Building Industry: Four Studies in Response and Resistance to Change*, Cambridge University Press, 1966.
10. The Kennings estate is mentioned in *LCC Housing with Particular Reference to Postwar Housing Schemes*, 1928. For L.H. Keay's slightly regretful dalliance with unconventional methods see his lecture, 'Working-class flats: a suggested solution of the housing problem', at an exhibition of a competition of reinforced concrete flats organised by the Cement Marketing Co, *The Builder*, 5 April 1935. He did use reinforced concrete frame construction at Speke Road Gardens.
11. *Report on the Mopin System of Building Construction by the Building Research Station, Watford* (typewritten, 21 pages, n.d. but 1934). The features of the Mopin System that were either unusual or completely new at this time were cold rolled steel members, welding, vibration of concrete *in situ* and in prefabricated slabs, the sharing of the load between the steel frame, concrete filling and concrete facing, so as to make a monolithic structure. The sequence of construction eliminated scaffolding, shuttering and skilled labour for erection and permitted all-weather working. See R.B. White, *Prefabrication: A History of its Development in Great Britain*, National Building Studies Special Report 30, Ministry of Technology Building

Research Station, 1965, pp.97ff; *RIBA Journal*, 24 March 1934, pp.518–21; *RIBA Journal*, 14 April 1934, pp.575–7; *The National Builder*, June 1937, pp.379–82. For the results, social and technical, of using this innovating system, see my own book, *Model Estate*, Croom Helm, forthcoming.

12. Ascot Water Heaters Ltd, *Flats: Municipal and Private Enterprise*, London, 1938, pp.234–8. The Leeds Sweet Street flats (St Barnabas Garth), of which the foundations and part of the carcase were begun before September 1939 and which were finished after the war, were constructed in this system. Newcastle Corporation was asking Leeds about using the Mopin System again in the early 1950s and presumably received a negative reply.

13. Some of them actually were Peabody tenements, built with housing subsidies. Flats of 1926 in Hammersmith were built with only three hot water taps shared between 284 dwellings, and a communal bath house which could be used twice weekly: J. Fletcher, 'Kensington builds for the poor', *Architectural Review*, vol.LXXV, 1934. To appreciate the depths that even local authority flats of the 1930s could reach see L.E. White, *Tenement Town*, Jason Press, London, 1946.

14. There is a folk memory in Leeds (partly due to Charles Jenkinson's militancy) that only the catholics opposed moving working-class populations to the suburbs, but this is belied by the report on the deputations received by the Housing Sub-Committee on Friday 22 April 1932. The deputations came from the Church of England, the Roman Catholic Church, the Society of Friends and the Free Church Council.

15. *Leeds Weekly Citizen*, 16 February 1934.

16. For Birmingham see *Report to the Estates and Public Works and Town Planning Committees respectively of the deputation visiting Germany. Czechoslovakia and Austria in August 1930*; for London see f.n.7; for Leeds see *Decent Houses for All, being the minority report with some additional notes &c*, published by the *Leeds Weekly Citizen*, Leeds, 1933, appendix 21; for Liverpool see *Post and Mercury*, 24 July 1931; a delegation to German and other continental cities included L.H. Keay and the Housing Chairman, for Scotland see Department of Health for Scotland, *Working-class Housing on the Continent*, Edinburgh, HMSO, 1935. At the other critical points of flats development, around 1900 and again in 1954, the leading English cities sent deputations to key places – the earlier ones to German and other British cities, the later ones to the USA and France. Keay disparaged the Viennese flats in the 1930s, calling them back-to-back houses that would not be permitted by English bye-laws and he was much more influenced by Berlin estates. It may show how far the English flats development was really independent of continental example, that his estates so closely resembled those of Manchester and Leeds, who were much more consciously imitating Vienna. For US attitudes to Europe at this time see James Ford, *Slums and Housing with Special Reference to New York City*, 2 vols, Harv ard University Press, 1936.

17. Birmingham report, op.cit., p.70 (original italics).

18. At Quarry Hill the extra costs were for the estate laundry (£40), the Garchey refuse disposal system (£25–30); lifts (£28); the community hall, shops, gardens and equipped playgrounds (not estimated). The cost of the buildings only was £430 per flat: R.A.H. Livett, 'Housing in Leeds', *The Structural Engineer*, December 1936, pp.518ff; estate records.

19. It is fair to say that the delegation found that English houses made much more satisfactory dwellings than flats and advised flats only as a last resort.

20. The Ministry of Housing and Local Government again recommended window boxes in *Living in Flats*, 1952, p.16.

21. J.N. Tarn, *Working-Class Housing in 19th-Century Britain*, Architectural Association Paper No.7, London, 1971.
22. 'The architect's problem', in 'Slum', *Architects Journal*, special issues, 22 June 1933, p.844.
23. See John R.H. McDonald, *Modern Housing: A Review of Present Housing Requirements in Scotland, &c*, Glasgow, 1931, which found that flat roofs were more economical, gave better insulation, stability and lighting, and provided space for play.
24. *Green-belt Cities, the British Contribution*, Faber, 1946, p.44.
25. Elizabeth Denby, *Europe Rehoused*, Allen & Unwin, 1938, p.264. See also L.H. Keay, 'The redevelopment of central areas in Liverpool', *RIBA Journal*, 1939, pp.293ff, and 'Post-war housing', *RIBA Journal*, 1946, pp.259ff.
26. *op. cit.*, The Architectural Press, London, p.13.
27. Sir Hilton Young, addressing The Royal Sanitary Institute. The remark was followed by cries of 'NO!' *Yorkshire Post*, 14 June 1934.
28. *Yorkshire Post*, 2 March 1938.
29. *Some Social Aspects of Pre-war Tenements and of Post-war Flats*, Manchester University Settlement, Manchester and District Regional Survey Society no.12, 1932 (according to E.D. Simon the author was A. Trench). It was explicitly written for the general public who might be responsible for voting for new schemes of flats. Apart from being noticed by Simon it seems to have provoked no remark. At this time also the valuable work of the Merseyside Surveys was begun in Liverpool.
30. These might cost up to £1. In spite of the cost of electricity the departmental committee on the construction of flats found that a single ceiling light was marginally better than gas light, because it was cleaner. Critics of electrical fittings in flats argued that the extra cost would force working-class tenants back to oil lamps.
31. At Quarry Hill Flats one 10 amp plug was provided in the living room and one in the second bedroom (the first bedroom had a coal grate).
32. 'We found that these had been very rarely used; in one case on three occasions in five years, in another once only, and in the third, not at all,' Ministry of Housing and Local Government, *Living in Flats*, 1952, p.25.
33. Even five storeys were considered to be a marginal height at which lifts might be needed: Departmental Committee on the Construction of Flats, *Final Report*, 1937, para.43. The ten-storey flats approved by Liverpool City Council in 1930 were in a cruciform shape with lifts in the centre core; water tanks were to be on top of the lift towers and heating might be all-electric to eliminate flues: *Evening Express*, 30 May 1930; *Liverpool Echo*, 2 July 1930. These reports claimed that an even earlier scheme for ten-storey flats had been rejected by the Minister, who exacted a promise from the Council not to exceed five storeys in future.
34. The departmental committee on the construction of flats estimated that the cost for engineering work alone for a lift in a five–six storey block would be £800. In Manchester the Labour Party was campaigning for lifts in 1935 and the cost, it was said, would put 3s 6d per week on the rents: *Daily Dispatch*, 10 January 1935. A. Trench, *op. cit.*, claims to have seen lifts operating in a block of flats where tenants were provided with keys for a charge of 1s per week. 'It was said to be little used' (p.14). Liverpool intended to put a lift in a block of flats in 1938; 110 flats arranged round four sides of a courtyard would be served by one lift. Serious consideration was given to whether people from 'poor houses' could be trusted to operate a lift, but the cost of an attendant would have added shillings a week to the rent: City of Liverpool Housing Committee, *Report of the Director of Housing in regard to the*

installation of lifts in flats, July 1938.

35. J.H. Forshaw and Patrick Abercrombie, *The County of London Plan*, Macmillan, 1943; City of Liverpool Housing Committee, *Preliminary Report of the City Architect and Director of Housing on Housing and Rehousing*, December 1943; City of Leeds Housing Committee, *Post-war Housing Report*, April 1943; City of Manchester, *A Short History of Manchester Housing*, 1947, p.56. In Liverpool, after the completion of the estates of inter-war type, with five storeys, by 1950, the reluctance to use lifts led to a return to three-storey flats, until the first 'high-rise' blocks (in the modern sense) were begun in 1954.

36. Cf. the tone of Ministry of Housing and Local Government, *Living in Flats*, 1952.

Chapter 6 High Flats in Local Authority Housing in England and Wales since 1945

E.W. Cooney

*The problem of explaining the rise and decline of the high flat is not primarily a difficulty of pointing to possible causes. Anyone acquainted with recent history and the organisation of building could readily make suggestions. There is, for instance, evidence of enthusiasm among architects at one time and, later, a good deal of doubt and disillusionment. The disaster to Ronan Point was widely reported and so were its repercussions. They could not be overlooked in any plausible account of events. Public concern to economise in the use of supposedly scarce land has been evident. So has the belief that flats – and high flats in particular – were a means to that end. Land use planning has clearly been much more strongly applied since the Second World War. And so on. The basic problem is not simply to identify probable causes. It is to establish their sequence, comparative importance and interaction. That is what this essay attempts to do, at least to the extent of an exploration of the main positive features of an explanation. As with any exploration, it may also serve to sharpen awareness of what remains to be settled.

Official statistics show the rise and decline of the high flat[1] in the building activity of local authorities in England and Wales[2] since the 1950s (see Table 6.1). On the basis of tenders approved by the central government the proportion of dwellings in blocks of five storeys or more averaged 6.9 per cent a year from 1953 to 1959, rose to a peak in the mid-sixties with a maximum of 25.7 per cent in 1966 and had fallen back to 9.8 per cent by 1970. This cycle was on the one hand part of a wider movement which emphasised flats in local authority plans rather than houses (particularly the three-bedroom houses which had predominated in the early post-war years) and on the other hand embraced a shift towards an increasing proportion of very high blocks of fifteen or twenty storeys and more. In 1953 flats (and maisonettes) in blocks of all storey heights – but the great majority less than five storeys – were 23.3 per cent of all dwellings in tenders approved. The proportion rose to a maximum of 55.2 per cent in 1964 and, in contrast to high flats,

*I am grateful to Dr Michael Young and Mr Peter Willmott for opportunity to study the social implications and history of multi-storey housing at the Institute of Community Studies during 1960–62.

151

Table 6.1   The Rise and Decline of the High Flat: Tenders Approved
for Local Authorities and New Towns in England and
Wales by Storey Heights as Percentage of All Dwellings
Approved.

	5–14 (A)	15 & over (B)	A + B	No. of dwellings
1953 to 1959	6.4	0.5	6.9	971,678
1960 to 1964	12.3	7.0	19.3	595,403
1965	10.9	10.6	21.5	162,540
1966	15.3	10.4	25.7	172,557
1967	13.3	9.7	23.0	170,545
1968	14.0	5.9	19.9	154,308
1969	9.7	3.8	13.5	112,201
1970	8.0	1.8	9.8	98,080

Source: Department of the Environment, *Housing Statistics*, No.24,
February 1973, HMSO 1972, based on Tables 10 and 12,
pp.24–25.

remained not far below that level, falling only to 48.1 per cent in 1970.
The high blocks therefore show both the greatest increase and the
sharpest decline. This is most extreme in the case of the very high
blocks. Dwellings in buildings of fifteen storeys or over, for instance,
were 0.5 per cent of all dwellings built by local authorities between
1953 and 1959, reached a maximum of 10.6 per cent in 1965 and had
declined to 1.8 per cent by 1970. An increase in the proportion of
dwellings in blocks of flats of less than five storeys from 27.0 per cent
in 1967 to 38.3 per cent in 1970 offset to a large extent the effect of
the decline in the higher blocks, so that there is no indication of a
substantial departure from the policy of building a large proportion of
local authority dwellings in the form of flats and maisonettes. Finally,
it should be noted that the rise and decline of the high flat took place
not only in proportional terms but also in the context of a concurrent
increase and decrease in the total figures of all dwellings approved for
local authorities. The annual figures rose to a peak of 172,557 in 1966
and had declined to 98,080 by 1970.[3]

An episode of high-rise, multi-storey housing is therefore clearly visible in statistical terms. But high-rise housing is of course distinguishable from other forms not only by abstract reference to height but because it is associated with other real or alleged differences which have been thought important. Among these are aesthetic satisfaction, social and cultural implications, costs, technology and the organisation of building contracts, consequences for the use and economy of land and the policies of central and local government. It can also be viewed as an attempt at a major innovation. As such it can be expected to have presented all concerned in taking decisions about it — from potential tenants to ministers of housing — with exceptional difficulties. This follows from the fact that less information is available about an innovation than about a matter of tried experience. There is the further implication of a prospect of enhanced benefits if the innovation is successful and exceptional losses if it fails.[4]

What is the explanation of this episode? Why was the innovation attempted at that particular time and on such an extensive scale and then so greatly curtailed after a decade of activity? At this point it is important to consider the fact that each local authority and the district for which it was responsible has its own history and made its contribution to the overall course of events outlined in the figures. As Cullingworth observed in explaining the administrative framework of housing, the role of the Ministry of Housing in policy formulation was 'remarkably weak'.[5] The Ministry could 'encourage' effort in particular directions but a local authority might see its local problems differently. On the other hand the central authority had formal powers of control through such means as conditions attached to payment of subsidies.

At the end of 1971 there were 1,367 housing authorities in England and Wales and twenty-four New Towns to which the statistics also refer and there is nothing readily available to show which built high flats and which did not. In view of the great differences in population, resources and cirmumstances it can be assumed that there was great variation. For instance, few if any of the 469 rural districts can have given any thought to them. The inference of variation is supported by published regional figures which show, taking 1965 as an example, a concentration of high-flat building in Greater London and the West Midlands and, at the other extreme, negligible activity in East Anglia.[6] Whereas the rural districts had little reason to consider high flats many of the London boroughs, by contrast, constrained by shortage of land and not permitted to build outside their boundaries, increasingly turned to them. But it would not do to base a history simply on those authorities which did build high flats — supposing the information were available — since a balanced explanation would have to take account of negative decisions which may have been taken by some authorities which built no such flats, particularly those seemingly similarly situated to others which did so. An inductive approach therefore is faced with the task of adequately surveying the record of the large number of relevant authorities. The results of such a survey would be useful but in their absence much more limited information about particular authorities can be used in the framework of the alternative approach already indicated. That is, to interpret available information in the light of the descriptive hypothesis that the high flat was an innovation at the centre of a complex of decisions made by a variety of persons, individual or corporate, over a period of several decades in the light of a diversity of purposes and circumstances.

The explanation to be developed here can be summarised as follows. The process of innovation had its origin in an architectural ideal and the initiative in advocating and developing the high flat lay with architects. The process led in the end to a reality more or less remote from the original ideal and control lay less with architects and more with other interests and institutions such as building contractors and government. A number of stages can be distinguished and related at least approximately to the extent of high flat building.

1. Specification of a new solution to old problems. High-rise, multi-storey housing seen as the setting of a better life for city dwellers and a remedy for the persistent evils of unhealthy homes in squalid surroundings and the sprawl of cities over the countryside. An aspect of the Modern Movement of the inter-war years.

2. First examples of the new housing, mainly by authorities in London, 1945–50.
    (These stages are dominated by architects. The amount of building is small.)

3. Central government, some local authorities and sections of public opinion begin to look more closely at the new housing in connection with immediate problems and requirements, such as greater emphasis on slum clearance, growing scarcity of urban building land, heightened determination to check urban sprawl and conserve agricultural land and rural amenities and recognition of the suitability of tall blocks for smaller dwellings than the hitherto predominant three-bedroom house. With larger resources and wider support, high flats spread.

Broadly, this is the decade of the 1950s though some authorities act much earlier than others and the balance of considerations varies so that there is no more than a tendency in policy-making, not a common line.

4. Building contractors become more closely interested as they see the potential increase of demand and the possibilities of competitive advantage through new construction methods and new forms of contract. New relationships develop with the local authorities. The government encourages industrialised building. This is in the later 1950s and much of the 1960s. Building reaches its peak in the mid-sixties.

5. Experience leads to increasing aesthetic and social criticism, both professional and popular. This has to be assessed in the light of developments in high flats such as greater height, more intensive utilisation in some developments and new methods of construction. This is mainly in the 1960s (though high flats were never without their opponents).

6. Official concern about high costs and social implications with reappraisal of policy, especially in 1965–67. In 1968, adverse effects of the Ronan Point disaster. Rapid decline of the high flat.

Innovation is the outcome of decisions inspired by creative imagination. Of all the groups and interests in local authority housing architects were, by disposition and training, best able to visualise a new approach or to understand and respond to proposed innovations. While the elusiveness of ideological influences must be recognised there can be little doubt about the pervasive influence of the Modern Movement on the generation of architects who were coming to professional maturity in Britain in the inter-war years, or about the prominent part they played in post-war developments. That is not to say that no other conceptual basis existed for the innovation of high-rise housing by councils in this country. There was the empirical example of the high blocks built in European and American cities, including London, since the later nineteenth century by private enterprise for the middle classes. A policy of high-rise housing for large numbers of city dwellers could have derived from this example and may in fact in some instances have done so. Clarence Perry's study in 1939 of a 'more comprehensive housing policy' in American conditions shows schemes some of which bear at least a family likeness to products of the Modern Movement, but he refers neither to that movement nor to leading figures such as Gropius (by that time in the U.S.A.) or Le Corbusier.[7]

It is obvious, however, that in the English case example and inspiration came, for instance, from Highpoint One by the Tecton partnership in the 1930s rather than from mansion flats of the Edwardian era.[8] Apart from its place in the origins of new thinking about local authority housing the Modern Movement, as an ideology which was winning increasing allegiance, gave a thrust and coherence to the innovation. Architects knew, so to speak, where they wanted to go and what they were determined to leave behind. Without the support of a strong ideology it is not unlikely that housing design in this country would have continued far more along the well-established line of the sort of four- and five-storey blocks which figured so prominently, for example, in the work of the London County Council and were in essentials descended from the 'philanthropic' tenements of Victorian times. There is no occasion to rehearse here the history of the Modern Movement. It is sufficient to recognise that by the mid-1940s a new generation of architects in Britain included many who were broadly committed to its aims and methods; committed, that is, to the break with the past and, important in the present context of public authority housing design, imbued with an ethic which emphasised the obligations of architecture as a service to society and not simply to the individual client, whether single or collective. The social change they looked for came about so that, as Lords Esher and Llewellyn-Davies have observed, ' . . . in Britain the years 1940–60 saw a remarkable deployment of architects into new or greatly expanded fields . . . Much of this new deployment took its impetus from the social idealism of the period . . . '[9]

Le Corbusier indicated the nature of the break with the past succinctly: 'Principles of the architectural revolution: houses raised above the ground on columns, independent framework, the free plan, the free facade, roof-gardens.'[10] This was the architecture of towns to be planned on new lines. The vertical garden city of blocks of flats in ample open space was to supersede the horizontal garden cities favoured by public policy and opinion and in doing so provide more efficient living accommodation and check urban sprawl with its waste of time and resources. Gropius, probably the equal of Le Corbusier in influencing the rising generation of architects, taught the same lesson. During his years in Britain between 1934 and 1937 after leaving Germany, in partnership with E. Maxwell Fry, he projected 'an influential and prophetic' design of high flats in a park-like setting at Windsor which points towards the early post-war innovations.[11] The new perception of the relation of architects to society in the era of the

Welfare State was expressed in the Royal Institute of British Architects: 'It was pointed out that, with the coming of the post-war period, it was extremely likely that many architects would find themselves working more for the community at large than for the individual client or committee . . . ' In that situation, it was asked, where were they going to get their instructions? It would not do simply to take them from officials or committees. Understanding of social needs was required. Guidance, it was thought, could be found in sociology.[12] (A quarter of a century later the RIBA was calling public attention to its continuing concern in a newspaper advertisement in which the caption 'New Slums for Old' summed up the Institute's interpretation of a photograph showing a tower block of flats under construction behind a partly demolished street of old, terraced houses, some still occupied. The advertisement concluded: 'Building new slums is easy. Building new communities is difficult. But if society is to survive, that's what we must learn to do.')[13]

In the progress of an innovation there is usually evidence of the working of a 'demonstration effect', the achievements of the pioneers providing example and encouragement and so serving to diffuse the innovation more widely. In the case of local authority housing in this country one of the most influential sources of such a demonstration is to be found in the work of the Architects' Department of the London County Council from the time of its reorganisation in 1950, when it was given undivided responsibility for the design of housing (formerly under the supervision of the Valuer who was not an architect) and the way was open to an era of experiment and innovation.[14] Groups of designers led first by Robert H. Matthew and then by Leslie Martin as Chief Architect for housing, including high flats, some of which gained world-wide reputation. In this respect, the earliest examples probably made the greatest impression, partly because of their novelty and partly because of exceptionally favourable circumstances in some instances.

'A percentage of houses and ground-floor maisonettes with private gardens for larger families is now made possible in medium- and high-density schemes by providing the smaller dwellings in the form of flats or maisonettes in tall buildings.'[15]

Thus cautiously the London County Council outlined and accounted for the substantial change in policy which had begun about 1950. The innovation is presented conservatively as a means of doing more to meet the need for houses with private gardens which were widely preferred. (Successive social surveys showed that from 80 to 98 per cent of a cross-section of the working population would plump for a house rather than a flat if rents were the same.)[16] In resorting to mixed development the LCC was using a scheme discussed before the war[17] and recommended by the government in its *Housing Manual, 1949*.[18] But the social argument was not the only consideration. The case in favour of houses rather than flats had long been acknowledged and was no stronger just after the war than before. It is also the case that the number of houses made possible by mixed development at the relatively high densities worked to in London was small.[19] A wider view, counting not only houses but also maisonettes in four-storey blocks, gives of course a larger result. Experience of the early schemes showed that about a third of the dwellings could be in these two forms.[20] But resemblance of the maisonettes to houses was a matter of uncertainty.

Another source of readiness to experiment with mixtures of high and low buildings can be seen in the opinion among the new generation of architects that better-looking estates could be designed on that basis. The LCC made this point when it explained that the first opportunity to express post-war architectural thinking came with the redevelopment of extensive areas in the vicinity of Wimbledon Common and at Roehampton:

> 'The scale of operations called for mixed development, for really high domestic buildings to be used against the woodland background accorded by Wimbledon Common and Richmond Park. In place therefore of the relative monotony of the early post-war designs the first eleven-storey point blocks to be seen in England were introduced into this scheme and, subsequently, were provided in many different parts of London.'[20]

Subsequently high slab blocks were also built at Roehampton, akin in form though not in size and complexity of function to *l'Unité d'Habitation* then under construction by Le Corbusier at Marseilles.

The taste of eighteenth-century gentlemen favoured parklands of woods and grass such as Richmond; the new architecture encouraged belief that municipal housing could harmonise with such a background, rather than affront it, if it was contained in great towers. The result was a striking visual effect such as could not have been achieved by a uniform distribution of lower buildings.[22] It is all the clearer that aesthetic considerations weighed heavily in the decision to use high buildings since there can have been no question that they would be more expensive than low ones. As the Ministry of Housing later remarked, ' . . . money can be saved in tens of thousands of pounds by planning for only the minimum of high building, or often none at all'.[23]

These developments were widely noticed in the professional and technical press and in popular surveys.[24] Visitors were numerous.[25] Yet influential though London's example undoubtedly was there were other sources. Continental European experience was available for study, especially in Scandinavia, as Sheffield Corporation for instance acknowledged,[26] and at least one great city looked across the Atlantic for guidance. Liverpool in 1954 sent a deputation to the United States, particularly New York. Its report was considered by the Housing Committee and by the Council ' . . . and it was from the recommendations of that report that the city's ambitious programme of multi-storey development has resulted'.[27] Finally, autonomous development must not be overlooked, of which Leeds would appear to provide a notable example with its experimental Quarry Hill development just before the Second World War and a forward-looking study during that war which, while emphasising that no simple formula could meet all housing needs, called for 'boldness in the introduction of strong vertical development' with blocks of flats of eight or even ten storeys in central area redevelopment.[28]

The high flat having developed by the early 1950s from the status of a proposed innovation to an established form of which a small number of examples had been built, its history begins to make contact with a variety of problems with which public opinion and central and local government were concerned. Some of these were of longer standing than others but they tend to fall together in an analysis because it was in the 1950s, broadly speaking, that they came into effective relationship with the high flat at the level of policy and building.

High-rise housing was coming to be seen by increasing numbers of authorities and their professional advisers as capable of taking an important place in the programmes of slum clearance and urban renewal which were undertaken with increasing vigour, resources and support from the central government from 1953 onwards in terms of the White Paper, *Houses: The Next Step.*[29] The post-war drive to build new housing had been concentrated on the three-bedroom house which was generally regarded as the most suitable home for families with children and had the further virtue of conforming with customary expectations.[30] As early as 1949 the Ministry of Health had advised that a greater variety of housing would be needed than had been envisaged in its previous advice of 1944 to local authorities.[31] Traditional two-storey 'cottage' housing, built at suburban densities, was incompatible with the conditions of high density redevelopment of inner city areas where the cost of land was normally greater than on the periphery and the existing density of population to be re-housed also above the urban average. Awareness was spreading, too, that apart from questions of density there was a social and financial case for providing housing in greater diversity of sizes and arrangements in order to match the needs of households of different sizes, ages and resources. There was, in particular, a need for a higher proportion of one- and two-bedroom flats such as could be accommodated with comparative ease of design and construction and economy of cost in tall blocks.[32]

In the course of the 1950s an increasing number of authorities were facing shortages of building land within their boundaries. Particularly severely affected were some of the largest such as Birmingham, Liverpool and Manchester. If building was to continue it would have to be either at a greater distance from their centres, even in the areas of other authorities, or by means of more intensive exploitation of such land as remained or could be made available within their areas, or of course by some combination of both these measures. As will be seen, there was no uniformity of response to this difficulty but there is evidence that a number of councils resorted to high building as a means of carrying out development at densities greater than those they had been accustomed to. The course of obtaining extension of the city boundary to take in unbuilt land, a measure which had so greatly enlarged the areas of a number of the greater cities in the past, was less feasible than hitherto. It was unlikely to meet with the approval of a central government which was increasingly concerned to check urban sprawl, so that a strong force was added to the always likely opposition of the adjacent authorities. For instance, Liverpool's boundaries were extended seven times between 1895 and 1952 but then there was a check in 1952 with the failure to embrace Kirkby where the City was planning a large development.[33] Liverpool's view of its situation in the 1950s has been explained in an official review:

'Clearly it was in the interests of the City Council that, so far as possible, the overspill of population into areas beyond the surrounding green belt should be minimised.'[34]

Higher building was seen as one of the methods whereby higher densities could be obtained and yet 'reasonable living conditions' be provided. The height of blocks of dwellings could no longer be limited to five storeys, which had been the 'accepted maximum' in the inter-war period.[35]

Manchester, facing similar difficulties, had resolved the problem differently some years earlier in 1947 (when of course there were fewer examples of high flats to study in this country). The Council noted the recommendations in the Ministry's *Housing Manual* of 1944 that flats with lifts should be not less than five storeys high (for economy) and that families with children should so far as possible be on the lower floors. Remarking that compliance with the latter recommendation would not be possible in view of the urgency of the housing problem, they resolved that flats were to be avoided wherever possible and that in no case were they to be more than three storeys high.

'The general policy thus to be pursued is the erection of flats at a density of not more than thirty to the acre, not exceeding three floors in height and not possessing lifts.'[36]

As a corollary to this decision they stressed the urgency of the problem of achieving 'overspill' ' . . . 'Manchester's only solution is to build outside the present City boundaries.' This was seen as 'not surprising in view of the fact that housing at densities varying from forty to sixty to the acre in the decayed areas has to be replaced at the modern densities of twelve to fourteen houses to the acre or thirty flats to the acre'.[37] This policy reaffirmed recommendations against flat development made in 1943 by the principal officers concerned with housing.[38] Manchester's aversion to high flats seems to have been sustained. It was reiterated in 1967 in a study which, while affirming the merits and distinctive qualities of city life and criticising the inadequacies of 'the suburban semi' for urban living, stated among other 'precepts' that, while multi-level living was necessary, dwellings must not be put into ' "office-block" arrangements' and depicted no buildings higher than six-storey maisonette blocks in sample schemes.[39]

While Manchester resolved against high flats its close neighbour, Salford, did the opposite. Of the 8,462 dwellings built there between 1945 and 31 August 1968, 3,972 were in forty-seven blocks of flats. This drive for flats has been explained as a response to losses of population and rateable value so great as to threaten Salford's existence as an independent local authority.[40] If so, an authority threatened with such a fate could by the 1950s cite with some confidence the less parochial arguments which were increasingly justifying flats and, more particularly, high flats. Against such a background Salford, proposing the First Amendment to its Development Plan, put forward a large and complex scheme of comprehensive redevelopment in 1963 which included a mix of housing ranging from four-storey maisonettes to twenty-two-storey point blocks. Their advisers were Professor Sir Robert Matthew and Percy Johnson-Marshall, both of whom had been involved in the pioneering work of the London County Council.[41]

The example of Southampton illustrates what may well have been the most usual policy with regard to the related issues of city expansion and overspill, higher density and standards of accommodation and amenity, and subsequent resort to high blocks for housing. In November 1958 Hampshire County Council had made proposals for a Green Belt 'closely surrounding the town'. In this context an authoritative view of the City's situation, provided by the Chairman of the Town Planning Committee and a Senior Planning Officer in 1964, was that increase of population and 'internal land use pressure' would have the inevitable effect of increasing the density of certain parts of the town, giving rise to circumstances appropriate to tall blocks of flats.[42] This view was shared by the County Planning Officer who explained that 'as a general policy' development of land in Town Map areas should be at the maximum density commensurate with the provision of adequate amenity for the future residents of the town as a whole.[43] Similar considerations and pressures were evidently at work in neighbouring Portsmouth. Alderman Day is reported to have put the case for twelve-storey blocks in a central area:

'The chief consideration in Portsmouth, where we have so little land at our disposal, is to make sure of its economic use. We appreciate the difficulties. But we also appreciate that if too many people go outside the City boundary, Portsmouth will become a less economic unit.'[44]

The City went on to build numbers of high blocks in the 1960s. Its hesitation in the face of such a radical step is suggested by a critical comment several years earlier. Hampshire's Planning Officer is reported to have said that Portsmouth could probably have reduced its overspill problem had it built flats such as the eleven-storey blocks envisaged by its neighbour, Gosport. Portsmouth, he said, had decided on a compromise — and compromises were never satisfactory — of three to four storeys. The blocks were not really high enough to give residents a good view and caused the maximum inconvenience to the people in the lower flats.[45]

Sheffield's appraisal of multi-storey housing was undertaken fairly early and ranged widely and thoroughly over a number of considerations of which the shortage of land was one. A deputation whose members included the Leader of the Council and J.L. Womersley, City Architect, reported in March 1955 on a tour of some European countries which were known to have had greater experience of flats. The Grindleberg Hochhauser development in Hamburg, in the form of twelve slabs ten to fifteen storeys high, was an instance of the favourable impression made by Continental innovation, having '... immense visual advantages over the congested surrounding areas of older and much lower properties.' The report advised:

'In the circumstances now obtaining in Sheffield — land shortage, ever increasing distances between houses and work-places, immobility of heavy industry and the urgency of slum clearance — the deputation is convinced of the need to introduce schemes of multi-storey flats, particularly in the redevelopment areas, as a means of solving the housing problem and reducing the overspill.'[46]

They went on to recommend the Architect's plan for Park Hill, a high-rise development with remarkable features, particularly its street decks. Sheffield has also built numbers of high blocks of more conventional kinds.

Central government in the 1950s was increasingly concerned to promote slum clearance, prevent urban sprawl and conserve agricultural land and the amenities of the countryside. The advice in the White Paper of 1953 that greater emphasis should be put on slum clearance was shortly followed by increased government support for planning of green belts around the major conurbations and encouragement of housing development at higher densities than local authorities had generally been accustomed to consider. During the years between the Housing Subsidies Acts of 1956 and 1967 financial support from the central government was formulated so as to offset in varying degrees the extra costs to local authorities of high building, while at the same time the 'general needs' subsidy which had been particularly associated with the great drive to build houses was inoperative or low in that period.[47] As the Ministry noted in its *Report* for 1956, while the building of multi-storey flats was still infrequent, the new subsidy arrangements provided for the first time for the subsidy to increase

with the height of the block.[48] They can be seen to have been
exploring for some years before that the possibilities of building to
higher densities (though not necessarily to greater heights). Their
Report for 1950/51 to 1954 noted the problems of urban sprawl, the
wish to conserve agricultural land, the need to economise on
construction costs and the desire to obtain more compact development,
all of which had led to 'a tendency towards planning for somewhat
higher densities than before'.[49] *The Density of Residential Areas*,
1952, was intended to assist local authorities without, however, laying
down hard and fast rules. But the sharpening of concern is evident in
the Foreword by the Minister, Mr Harold Macmillan, in which he drew
attention to the heavy demand for land and emphasised: 'It is
important to save every acre that can be saved.'[51]

At about the same time, new impetus was given to the policy of
green belts. Until the middle 1950s only London had been the subject
of a formal proposal for a green belt. Mr Duncan Sandys, the Minister
in 1955, expressed his conviction in the House of Commons that
' ... we have a clear duty to do all we can to prevent the further
unrestricted sprawl of the great cities', and asked all local authorities
concerned to consider the establishment of clearly defined green belts
where that was desirable.[52] Here was another contrasting influence,
strengthening the case for authorities to review standards of density and
the possible contribution from high-rise housing. Overspill, as an
alternative, was not of course ruled out in central government policy
but definition of a proposed green belt implied that overspill would
probably be at a greater distance and to that extent might be less
attractive or even less feasible. Another aspect of government policy in
the 1950s which probably tended towards more intensive use of urban
land was the fact that no New Towns were established in England and
Wales (although those already in being were supported and a new
programme of extending established towns to receive people from the
conurbations was begun under the Town Development Act of 1952). In
this period the London County Council's proposal for a New Town at
Hook in Hampshire failed to win government support and was rejected
by that county's authority (schemes of town expansion being put
forward as an alternative). Planning of further New Towns was not
announced until 1960.[53] A larger programme of New Towns in the
1950s might have lessened the inclination of at least some local
authorities towards high-density housing. Manchester, for instance, in
1947 had noted the New Towns policy in connection with its strongly
stated arguments for building outside the City boundary.[54]

The Ministry's advice, by means of design manuals, planning bulletins, circulars, ministerial speeches and informal consultation, was not meant to encourage indiscriminate resort to multi-storey housing, but the growing emphasis on the importance of building to the highest density compatible with currently recognised standards of good housing is evident. Associated with that emphasis, but originating at an earlier time and in response to other concerns than that of land-use economy alone, was the concept of mixed development incorporating high-rise housing. The idea was elaborated in the manuals, culminating in *Flats and Houses 1958*, a work described by one of its principal originators as 'a study of design and economy in high density housing' which provided for the first time a rationale of mixed development.[55] In his Foreword the Minister, Mr Henry Brooke, while emphasising that 'I certainly do not mean it to encourage the use of higher densities or multi-storeyed buildings where they are not really necessary', pointed out that:

'Many local authorities ... are facing what to them are novel problems of building at higher densities: densities where houses will need to be intermingled with maisonettes or flats.'[56]

By these means the central government's concern in the 1950s and early 1960s was expressed to the accompaniment of increasingly detailed technical advice. A further strong expression of policy, accompanied by technical explanation and advice, came in 1962 in *Residential Areas. Higher Densities*.[57] Sir Keith Joseph, the Minister, pointed in his Foreword to the 'formidable problem' of providing at least six million more houses in the next twenty years and to the two 'inescapable consequences' of need to allocate more land for housing and use higher densities, 'especially in the pressure areas'. He asked all authorities to review their housing density policies in the light of the advice given in the bulletin. As before, indiscriminate resort to multi-storey housing was not envisaged. But by distinguishing a category of areas of special difficulty, the pressure areas, the bulletin pointed to circumstances in which development or redevelopment at unusually high densities might be justifiable.[58] Where building was to be carried out at high densities, above ninety persons per acre, it was recognised that tall blocks of flats would become necessary but need not predominate until densities of at least 140 persons per acre were reached.[59] Thus in certain parts of the major urban areas, and in some districts beyond their green belts, local authorities proposing schemes including high flats would be likely to find that they were acting in accord both with the spirit and the letter of the Ministry's advice. It was in the years following this bulletin that the boom in high flats reached its peak.

In the light of this record, should an affirmative answer be given to the question: Did the government at any time decide that the local authorities must build larger amounts of multi-storey housing? Given the difficulty of identifying decisions as clear-cut events, differing answers seem likely. It is probably more realistic to observe instead that there was a sequence of decisions on a variety of policy concerns which bore on multi-storey housing and, as part of this, an increasingly exact specification of conditions for such housing which arguably generated increasingly strong central government commitment to it.[60] With this in mind and in view of the complexity of relations between the central government and the numerous semi-autonomous local authorities, observable in political, administrative and technical aspects, assessment of the contribution of the central government to the increase in high flats can best take the form of an inferred tendency of the events reviewed. It can be seen that policies of planning and housing increasingly opened the way to a serious case for high-rise housing despite all the counter-arguments, that administration reinforced this, particularly with the subsidies, and that increasingly sophisticated technical advice enhanced the feasibility of the idea from the point of view of inexperienced local authorities. At the administrative and technical levels a further, late development took the form of an innovation, the National Building Agency, set up in 1964. Since this body was also closely connected with another innovation, industrialised (and, particularly, system) building and with the building contractors whose role in high-rise housing became increasingly important, it can best be considered with them.

The building industry in the early 1950s had little experience of high building for local authorities but it did of course possess the basic capacity to supply high buildings constructed with one or other of the principal structural innovations of the later nineteenth century, the steel frame or the reinforced concrete frame, and served by another innovation of the same era, the passenger lift. Such buildings of course cost substantially more for the same amount of accommodation than did traditional two-storey houses. So far as the construction of the latter was concerned A.W. Cleeve Barr observed in the later 1950s:

'Particularly in housing, building work is carried on today over wide areas of the country with hardly any advance on the same skills, materials and methods as were used over a hundred years ago.'[61]

But attention was turning increasingly to the possibility of 'industrialising' building, making it more like a factory industry in the hope of achieving the advantages associated with that system of production, especially progressive reduction of costs, uniformity of product, freedom from interruption by weather and lessened dependence on particular local labour supply conditions. The drive to industrialise the building process accompanied the advance of the high flat but was not concerned only with that form of building. However, the opportunity of offering local authorities patented systems of construction was likely to sharpen contractors' interest in high flats since a successful system could obviously bring large profits in the context of an expanding demand. Growth of confidence in the favourable prospects for industrialisation led to stronger support not only from contractors and local authorities but also from central government.

In the face of the great upsurge of work demanded from the industry the Government set up the National Building Agency to advise on improved methods, both in traditional and industrialised work, and offer its services to all concerned with building.[62] In the Agency can be seen another development tending to spread knowledge of new methods of erecting multi-storey buildings much larger than many authorities or their advisers had been accustomed to. This was so not because the Agency had a particular commitment to high building – industrialised methods and improvements in the productivity of traditional methods could be looked for in both high- and low-rise work – but because it was an authoritative body with professional and technical staff whose function was to make information and advice more readily available. It so happened that in the 1950s innovation went on rapidly in the development of patented systems of building with prefabricated, heavy components which were particularly suited to construction of tall blocks. Some systems were imported under licence from the Continent, others were developed independently in this country. While such systems were unlikely to prove cheaper than longer established methods – although there might be better prospects in the longer run – they did offer an immediate means of easing the bottleneck of shortage of skilled labour which, particularly in inner city districts (where high-rise building was most likely), was often a principal constraint on any large increase in housebuilding. Much more of the work of at least some kinds of system building could be carried out at a distance in factories located where labour was more easily available. This advantage of system building was, for instance, important in the decision to use such a system for the building of Ronan Point, whereas there was no expectation of lower cost.[63]

Another secondary innovation of this period which tended to change the terms on which local authorities took decisions about high blocks was the 'package deal' contract devised by some builders in which were offered not only the customary building work but also professional services of architectural design and engineering consultancy which had hitherto been provided separately. Again, the Ronan Point contract provides illustration. Specialised engineering advice relating to the system used was provided, as a condition of the contract, by an engineering consultancy firm which was a subsidiary of the contractors' parent company.[64] The advantage claimed for the package deal was that it reduced cost and gave better assurance of smooth, speedy work by involving all the specialist services required for a complex operation in consultation and decision-making from the outset rather than bringing in the contractor only after major decisions had been taken by the client and his professional advisers. From the point of view of local authorities as potential customers for tall blocks, particularly those built by new methods, the package deal had attractions, especially if they were looking only for small numbers of such buildings and had only small numbers of professional staff in their own service — as might of course be the case and was likely to be increasingly so, as the interest in high building spread from the larger pioneering authorities.

What caused the decline in the high flat which can be seen in the percentage figures from 1967 onwards? An explanation can be developed at three levels. First, by reference to particular contingencies such as the Ronan Point disaster and the state of the economy; next in terms of relations between central and local government; and finally in the light of evidence of a changing balance of considerations likely to influence decisions as experience and new information accumulated about consequences of innovation of high-rise housing in the public sector.

The partial collapse of Ronan Point, a twenty-two storey block belonging to the London borough of Newham, on the morning of 16 May 1968, was a sharp setback to high-rise housebuilding. As the Ministry remarked: 'Authorities with system-built high flats had to check their design and in some cases to strengthen them before passing them as completed.'[65] Similarly, the undertaking of further building was delayed by the need to re-check the designs. The Ministry considered that these difficulties contributed to the decline in 'public starts' and 'public completions' in the total of housing in 1968 compared with 1967. The *Report* of the Inquiry is concerned with an accident which not only was evidently closely limited in location and occurrence but is also unique in the history of high flats in this country. The explosion of leaking gas in the kitchen of one flat on the eighteenth floor blew out the external walls of the livingroom and bedroom and this structural failure developed progressively so that the whole of the south-east corner of the building collapsed from the top down to the level of the podium. Four residents were killed and seventeen injured. The disaster was unique but its consequences spread widely.

The Tribunal of Inquiry soon appreciated that the essential cause of the catastrophe was a defect in the design of the structure and they so informed the Minister several months before their final *Report*, anticipating a recommendation that owners of tall blocks built by 'system' methods should have them appraised for liability to progressive collapse and, wherever the danger existed, should have the gas turned off and should give consideration to strengthening of such blocks.[66] They noted that there were some 30,000 dwellings belonging to local authorities which had been built in tall blocks by various methods of system building. The accident had a disconcerting effect on local authorities, on their tenants and on public opinion generally, naturally causing anxiety and uncertainty about high flats as well as delays and disruption of building already described. However, considerable as the adverse effects of the collapse of Ronan Point clearly were they cannot be held to have been the original cause of the onset of decline in high flats since that had begun quite clearly at an earlier date. Ronan Point has its place therefore as a secondary explanation to which weight will be given according to views and judgements about the probable long-run response of local authorities and others, such as central government and building contractors, to such a contingency. It is scarcely plausible to hold that after Ronan Point there was little future for high flats. Not all high blocks were system-built and even for those that were remedies could be applied to existing structures and the weakness eliminated in subsequent designs, as the Tribunal pointed out.[67]

The prime significance of Ronan Point from the standpoint of this study is to be found in what the *Report* indicates and illustrates about the nature and the problems of innovation in building. Ronan Point's structure was an example of a recent innovation, being built up from large pre-cast concrete panels which formed the load-bearing walls and floors. According to the *Report* the organisation in terms of which this innovation was introduced was inadequate to appraise it, so that a fundamental weakness of design had gone unnoticed. In lay terms, the block had been designed too much in the manner of a house of cards, needing only an unacceptably small force to disrupt one part of the structure and bring down much of the rest. The censure delivered by the Tribunal ranged widely: 'In the broadest sense, it could be argued that the two major professions concerned – architects and structural engineers – have been found wanting, the former for their failure to call adequately upon the latter and the latter for failing to take much interest in system building generally.'[68] Particular sources of error were found in the procedure for assimilating innovations into the Building Regulations[69] and in the building contract, which led the client to dispense with direct employment of consulting engineers.[70] The problems of Ronan Point can be seen as aspects of the process of innovation. They illustrate how it enlarges not only the prospect of benefits but also the risk of failure and loss in a setting of abnormal uncertainty, the extent of which is not always readily perceivable by all concerned. They show, too, how the initiative in carrying forward an innovation can pass from one kind of centre to another – in this instance, from the architects to the building contractors – with unforeseen consequences.

Substantial though the Ronan Point disaster was in its impact on high-rise building, decline had already begun in the previous year. It coincided with the passing of the Housing Subsidies Act 1967 which legislated proposals of a Bill of November 1965, reducing financial support for high flats by abolishing the additional subsidy for each storey in excess of six and so ending an arrangement which had helped local authorities with the high cost of high blocks since 1956. According to Cullingworth, one reason given was that, owing to improvements in industrial methods, building costs for the taller blocks no longer increased proportionately with height as they had when the old scale was introduced and there was also a feeling that high building should not be indiscriminately encouraged.[71] The first reason may well have been over-optimistic. Analysis by Stone for the period 1953 to 1964, while showing that there had been 'some reasonable fall' in the difference in the prices of flatted blocks of different numbers of storeys as a result of increased experience in the design and construction of high blocks compared with low ones, gave no evidence that the movement was continuing. As he observed, in the absence of 'some revolutionary new method' the effect of increased experience was likely to decline.[72] If so, the second reason, restraint on high building, may have had a greater effect than officials had envisaged. Abolition of this subsidy took place in the context of a radical development in the system of assessing financial support for housing. The method of cost 'yardsticks', prepared by the Ministry's expert staff, was extended and strengthened and presented in tables which, while expressing a relationship between density and higher cost, specified no particular form of building but were accompanied by explanatory notes drawing attention to the high cost of high building and the possibilities of alternative patterns of housing layout.[73]

These two changes could have been expected to influence local authorities away from high-rise housing and towards schemes not exceeding six storeys, even in areas of relatively high density.[74] Subsequently there does seem to have been an increasing number of 'low-rise, high-density' schemes. In accounting for this change of emphasis one should not overlook the process of informal consultation between expert staffs of the Ministry and the local authorities, particularly with respect to proposals involving very high blocks. Another likely cause of the downturn is to be found in the reduction of the public sector programme decided on by the Government in the aftermath of devaluation of the pound in November 1967. As the Ministry explained, in January 1968 the Government decided to make reductions below the level previously planned in each of the years 1968 and 1969.[75] The decline then initiated continued, so that by 1970 public authority housing had fallen back and was below the level of 1960 in terms of tenders approved.[76] Expensive high building was still further disadvantaged.

While the Government was reducing the incentives and increasing the restraints on high building by means of financial and technical arrangements in the second half of the 1960s, the early part of that decade saw growth of criticism of high flats on social and aesthetic grounds and increasingly precise explanation of the grounds for scepticism towards the claim that high density housing was an important method of saving land and preventing urban sprawl. With regard to land, there was growing awareness that, as Stone has pointed out, ' . . . the savings in land likely to be secured by developing housing at high densities are not very significant in relation to land needs'.[77] Such criticism was expressed, for instance, by the economic geographer, Robin H. Best, in 1966 in *New Society* where it was likely to reach a variety of groups concerned with social policy.[78] The earlier, impressionistically based commitment to saving agricultural land in particular could be strongly questioned when it was seen that, whereas the cost of saving an acre of land by building at high density would be about £30,000 at the time of Stone's analysis, most of the land saved would be farmland worth about £200 per acre.[79] Such comment could undermine resistance to New Town development and, generally, to dispersal of people from the conurbations.

Architectural opinion about multi-storey housing became increasingly adverse during the 1960s. It is only possible here to indicate the change by pointing to the very favourable view generally taken of such places as the Roehampton Estates in the previous decade and then note several instances of criticism of the appearance and social implications of later high-rise housing. Kenneth Campbell, for example, with much experience of designing housing, defended the original concept of mixed development but recognised that the tall block had been misused. Among other criticisms, it had provided an opportunity for architects in 'the brutalist period' to produce 'large, grim and squalid monuments, rather than small ones', and the gross housing shortage led to 'inappropriate' families moving into tall blocks. The quality of the blocks had been impaired by over-riding concern to reduce costs and there was inadequacy in the architecture, planning and investment in the environment. The original purpose, to provide flexibility in the remainder of the housing scene, had been lost or blurred, the tall block had become 'an easy solution without professional advice or with inadequate professional services', and it had been the easiest way to 'sell' industrialised building. Moreover, it had become a prestige symbol.[80]

There is an early indication of the way in which things could begin to go wrong in the appraisal of a LCC estate by A.W. Cleeve Barr while working as an architect for that authority. The Loughborough Estate, completed in 1957, was, he wrote, 'unfortunately intersected by two major traffic streets . . . and dominated by a large railway viaduct . . . A large proportion of accommodation has been placed in tall blocks, which enables a buffer zone of grass and trees to be created between the railway and most of the housing.' Although the density was high, 'the principles of mixed development evolved at Roehampton have been methodically applied – 61 per cent of accommodation is in eleven-storey blocks, 31 per cent in four-storey maisonettes, mostly with gardens and 8 per cent in houses'.[81] The *Architectural Review*, which in the 1950s and earlier had played a prominent part in turning attention to high density and high-rise housing, both by its praise of the

work of the Modern Movement and by its attacks on the New Towns
and 'prairie planning',[82] now turned its criticism against the current
versions of high-rise, high density design, especially in the judgement by
Nicholas Taylor that: 'More slums are likely to be built in the next five
years than in the past twenty.'[83]

A little later Sir Hugh Wilson, during his year as President of the
Royal Institute of British Architects, wrote in *The Times* in the
aftermath of Ronan Point. Observing that the original idea of 'towers in
a park' had gone by the board, he described what had taken their place:

> 'Instead, very much taller blocks (some over thirty storeys high)
> often now rise from a sea of concrete and asphalt, are inserted on
> pocket handkerchief sites in areas of semi-industrial squalor, or in
> gaps in low density inter-war or post-war development, where the
> open space that brings the overall density down to acceptable
> standards is often in private gardens, inaccessible to the flat-dweller.
> The crude visual impact of many of these developments on our city
> skyline is already apparent. The social consequences will take longer
> to manifest themselves fully.'[84]

In fact, assessment of the social consequences of high flats (or any
other form of housing) takes not only time, as Sir Hugh suggested, but
is also a difficult and elusive task, the complexity of which has become
apparent during the past two decades or so. Throughout the history of
high flats there was a running fire of adverse, reasoned criticism of
them, particularly from the Town and Country Planning Association
which favoured continuing outward movement of people from the
congested cities to New Towns, avoidance of high densities and
provision of houses, rather than flats, for all who needed them. But it
was always open to advocates of high flats to claim not only that they
were putting forward something new but also something that was at the
least better than the older kinds of flats and even preferable to houses
for some families and generally conducive to a higher level of welfare
for the community as a whole. The outcome of a considerable amount
of research has been to show the difficulty of identifying positive
relationships between the built environment and particular behaviour
and states of mind of individuals or groups at the level of scientific
proof. A review of research concluded that study of the problem was in
a 'pre-paradigmatic stage:

> 'In most cases the recent findings seem to be of a mutually

contradictory kind. One can find a study to support any position and can quote in favour of any decision.'[85]

Throughout the shifting course of opinion, both expert and popular, about the social and aesthetic implications of high flats, one judgement appears to have been accepted from the outset and for long not challenged. That is, that a home in a high block was not well suited to the needs of families with small children. In practice such families were increasingly housed in high blocks and reports began to appear describing the ill-effects. Observations by social workers in London prompted an early enquiry, *Two to Five in High Flats*.[86] Later the National Society for Prevention of Cruelty to Children confirmed the unsatisfactory situation:

> 'There seems little doubt that families with small children living in high flats feel cut off from their fellows, and indeed are cut off from them, in a way that did not obtain when they were living at ground level.'

Children's play was adversely affected with injury to development. There was also 'some evidence to show that this kind of life contributes to the social isolation which is so common in modern cities, and under the impact of which many families break down.'[87] Such conclusions, deriving from systematic attempts to reach objective conclusions by means of social surveys, were likely to be influential, all the more as they were, as has been said, consistent with a long-established opinion. If, therefore, high flats were being provided in such numbers or in association with such management policies that families with young children were apparently living in notably unsuitable conditions, the case for continued building was very likely to be weakened. Such criticism recurred frequently in newspapers and journals in the 1960s.

Such were some of the criticisms which told against high flats on social grounds. An authoritative survey which produced results tending to deflect criticism from the high flat as such came too late, in 1972, to affect the decisions which led to the decline of the high flat. The Department of the Environment's *Design Bulletin 25*, reporting on reactions of residents to aspects of housing layout in estates ranging from high to low density and comprising houses and a variety of blocks of high and low flats in the sample, found that:

> 'Surprisingly, satisfaction with the estate was not determined by

such factors as density, building form, living on or off the ground and problems with children's play, but was closely related to the appearance of the estate and the way it was looked after.'[88]

Even so, two-fifths of the housewives with children under five were unhappy living off the ground in one or another of the variety of blocks involved. At the same time and, as the bulletin says, surprisingly, houses with gardens did not always emerge as the best solution.[89] The difficulty of predicting the social and psychological implications of new forms of housing will be evident.

This analysis of the complex history of high-rise housing by public authorities in England and Wales points pretty obviously to the conclusion that it was an innovation that failed. This follows not simply from the decline shown in the figures or from the increasing strength of criticism but is an implication of the fact that the problems with which the innovators of the high flat were concerned have not been resolved and persist strongly. The conurbations still have their slums, the green belts have been maintained, allocation of rural land for urban uses is as much a difficult, contentious matter as it ever was, problems associated with the overspill of population from cities have not ceased (nor, of course, have the benefits). It is not therefore plausible to interpret the rise and decline of the high flat in terms of an innovation to meet a limited emergency, on the analogy of a new weapon produced to meet the needs of a war and then abandoned with the peace. In housing and town planning the struggle continues, but now with little assistance from the high flat.

Viewing the high flat as an innovation and reflecting on the causes of its failure as a major element in local authority housing (which is not, of course, the same as saying that all who live in such flats are unhappy with their accommodation or surroundings), a number of comments can be made. In the first place, the conditions under which the innovation, like any other, had to be made were far from ideal from a decision-maker's standpoint. Not only did the fact of innovation itself imply an increase of uncertainty, and therefore risk, compared with that associated with an established form of housing, but uncertainty varied among the several factors which required evaluation. For instance, relative costs were known from the outset to be high and the technical and organisational determinants of any lessening of this disadvantage were fairly widely understood by expert advisers. Technical matters were in general well understood although later, secondary innovations such as some forms of system building raised the level of uncertainty there. By contrast, the sociological implications could be debated in the absence of experience or any firm theoretical basis for prediction. The aesthetic aspect, too, eluded resolution. Would the appearance of the new buildings come to be generally approved? Who could tell? It was open to architects and others to take an optimistic view. Some naturally did so. Such uncertainties, varying in degree over time, were in themselves likely to lead to a shifting balance of decisions. But there were also other, so to speak, external forces which had the same tendency to generate an unstable situation. One was inherent in the relationship between the central government and the local authorities. Its tentative, persuasive, rather than mandatory, character is evident. Government policy nudged the local authorities first in one direction, then, when experience suggested they had gone too far, it sought to draw them back. This alone would have produced fluctuation. Then there were contingencies such as the Ronan Point disaster and the financial crisis of the later 1960s. The failure of Ronan Point is, of course, just the kind of setback which is particularly likely to occur in connection with any innovation. If it had not occurred, the decline might have been less abrupt but would have still have taken place. Next, it can be seen that the policy considerations which determined high-rise housing tended to change over time in strength though probably not in their basis. The most important is clearly the desire to save land. This grew strongly under the Conservative administrations of the 1950s and 1960s. Its effect was to limit still further the land available to local authorities, particularly those in the conurbations, already becoming worried about the various unsatisfactory aspects of continuing overspill of their populations. It can scarcely be said that these difficulties have been overcome; simply that the high flat is no longer often seen as a means of grappling with them. Another factor which clearly formed part of the basis of the high flat 'boom' and has been assumed here without discussion of its wider setting in economic and financial terms is its 'uneconomic' character. As the subsidies imply, decisions to build high flats were not constrained by evidence of an effective demand capable of covering the full costs of any particular output contemplated by the innovators. The private sector showed no boom of comparable magnitude, despite the higher level of incomes of its customers. Finally, it can be seen how the initiative in promoting the innovation tended to pass from place to place. At the outset, architects were predominant, concerned with aesthetic and social considerations in particular. Later, a small number of local authorities set the pace, less convinced of the positive aesthetic and social merits of high flats than by the evidence of land shortage and its adverse effects on their activities and the lives of their citizens. In this they were joined by the central government, acting with increasing precision in a situation which nevertheless always precluded a quick, exact response. Lastly, there was the active contribution of the building and civil engineering contractors, responding to their awareness of a growing demand with innovations in methods both of construction and contracting and encouraged by the Government's support for industrialised building. This sequence illustrates a feature of any innovation; that its control may pass from hand to hand and the purposes it serves come to differ from those of its originators. So it was that in the middle 1960s many architects stood appalled while high blocks multiplied whose lineage could be traced to their profession's radical thinking of thirty and forty years previously. They were in the situation of the sorcerer's apprentice. The sorcerer himself is seen to be a complex figure.

Notes

1. The high flat can be defined in different ways. That used here follows an official definition given near the beginning of the period, from 1945 on, with which this essay is mainly concerned: '... high blocks of flats or maisonettes, with lifts, or five or more storeys.' Ministry of Health, *Housing Manual 1949*, HMSO, London, 1949, para.133.
2. Differences in the history of the flat in Scotland precluded adequate consideration of the high flat in this analysis. See below, pp.000–00.
3. All figures derived from Ministry of Housing and Local Government (henceforth MOHLG), *Housing Statistics*, No.1, 1966, HMSO, Table 7, p.13, and Department of the Environment, *Housing Statistics*, No.24. Feb. 1972, HMSO, Tables 10 and 12, pp.24–5.
4. The main source of the concept of innovation is the work of Joseph A. Schumpeter, especially *The Theory of Economic Development*, first published in German in 1911 and in English in 1934.
5. J.B. Cullingworth, *Housing and Local Government in England and Wales*, George Allen & Unwin, London, 1966, p.61.
6. *Housing Statistics*, No.1, 1966, Table 8, HMSO, 1966.
7. Clarence Arthur Perry, *Housing for the Machine Age*, Russell Sage Foundation, New York, 1939.
8. On Tecton see Anthony Jackson, *The Politics of Architecture*, Architectural Press, London, 1970, pp.44–9.
9. 'The Architect in 1988', *RIBA Journal*, Vol.LXXV, no.10, Oct. 1968.
10. *Concerning Town Planning*, Architectural Press, London, 1947, p.72.
11. Obituary, *The Times*, 7 July 1969. For illustration of the design see F.R.S. Yorke and Frederic Gibberd, *The Modern Flat*, Architectural Press, London, 2nd ed., 1948, p.13.
12. Architectural Science Board Study Group No.1, 'Sociology and Architecture', *RIBA Journal*, Third Series, Vol.LIII, July and August, 1946, p.443.
13. *The Times*, 6 April, 1970, p.3.
14. Jackson, *op. cit.*, p.185.

15. London County Council, *Development Plan, First Review*, London, 1960, p.88.
16. Peter Self, *Cities in Flood*, Faber, London, 1957, p.44.
17. Elizabeth Denby, *Europe Re-housed*, George Allen & Unwin, London, 1938, p.273.
18. HMSO, 1949, p.82, para.132.
19. No more than 4 per cent of homes built by the London County Council since 1945 were in the form of houses, according to data in LCC, *Housing Londoners*, 1961.
20. 'In the Alton scheme at Roehampton, with a density of 100 persons per acre, about 27 per cent of the 2,611 dwellings are either maisonettes in four-storey (two-tier) blocks or terrace houses each with a private garden.' LCC, *Development Plan, First Review*, p.88.
21. *Housing Londoners*, pp.2–3.
22. Nikolaus Pevsner, 'L.C.C. Housing and Picturesque Tradition', *Architectural Review*, Vol.CXXVI, no.750, July 1959, p.21.
23. MOHLG, *Flats and Houses 1958*, HMSO, 1958, p.61.
24. An example of the latter is G.E. Kidder Smith, *The New Architecture of Europe*, Penguin Books, 1962.
25. In 1961, for instance, the LCC arranged 120 tours most of which included visits to the Alton Estate, Roehampton. (Information given to the writer at County Hall.)
26. City of Sheffield Housing Deputation, *Multi-Storey Housing in Some European Countries*, 1955.
27. *Liverpool Builds 1945–1965*, 1967, p.42 (issued by the City's Public Relations Office and prepared by Ronald Bradbury, City Architect, in collaboration with other Chief Officers concerned with the building programme).
28. *Post War Housing Report*, p.10 (undated but the Housing Committee approved the Report on 25 May 1943 according to City of Leeds, *A Short History of Civic Housing*, 1954, p.51).
29. MOHLG, *Houses: The Next Step*, Cmd.8996, HMSO, 1953.
30. Of about two million dwellings built by local authorities between 1945 and 1960 three-quarters were in the form of houses and, of those, 70 per cent had three bedrooms whereas of the flats only 17 per cent had three bedrooms. Department of the Environment, *Housing Statistics*, No.24, Feb. 1972, Table 7, HMSO, 1972.
31. *Housing Manual 1949*, p.11.
32. A.W. Cleeve Barr, *Public Authority Housing*, Batsford, London, 1958, p.134.
33. *v.* map, Central Library.
34. *Liverpool Builds 1945–1965*, p.42.
35. *ibid.*,
36. Housing Committee, *A Short History of Manchester Housing*, 1947, pp.55–6.
37. *ibid.* p.78.
38. *Flats*, Joint Report of the Medical Officer of Health, the City Surveyor and the Director of Housing, May 1943.
39. Housing Committee, *Urban Renewal Manchester* , 1967.
40. M.E. Blunt and M.J.E. Goldsmith, *Housing Policy and Administration: A Case Study*, Occasional Papers in Politics, Salford University, July, 1969, p.13.
41. *City of Salford Development Plan, Amendment No.1*, Public Enquiry into Objections, 26 November 1963.
42. J.H.J. Matthews and R.J. Coles, 'The Planning of Southampton', in F.J. Monkhouse (ed.), *A Survey of Southampton and Its Region*, British

Association for the Advancement of Science, Southampton, 1964, pp.344—6.
43. A.D.G. Smart, 'The Hampshire Development Plan', *ibid.* p.160.
44. *Evening News*, Portsmouth, 9 March 1960, p.5.
45. *Evening News*, Portsmouth, 10 June 1958.
46. *Multi-Storey Housing in Some European Countries*, especially pp.6, 8 and 37.
47. On housing subsidies generally see J.B. Cullingworth, *op. cit.* and N.P. Hepworth, *The Finance of Local Government*, George Allen & Unwin, London, 1970.
48. *Report of the Ministry of Housing and Local Government for the Year 1956*, Cmnd. 193, HMSO, 1957, p.10.
49. *Report of the Ministry of Housing and Local Gove rnment for the Period 1950/51 to 1954*, HMSO, Cmd.9559, p.87.
50. *ibid.*
51. MOHLG, *The Density of Residential Areas*, HMSO, 1952.
52. MOHLG, *The Green Belts*, HMSO, 1962, p.4.
53. MOHLG, *Report . . . 1960*, HMSO, 1961, p.78.
54. Housing Committee, *A Short History of Manchester Housing*, 1947, p.56.
55. Report of interview with Alec Bellamy, Under-Secretary, Housing Directorate, Department of the Environment, *Building*, 28 April 1972.
56. MOHLG, *op. cit.* p.v.
57. MOHLG, *Residential Areas. Higher Densities*, Planning Bulletin 2, HMSO, 1962.
58. *ibid.*, p.6.
59. *ibid.* p.5.
60. *cf.* P.H. Levin, 'On Decisions and Decision Making', *Public Administration*, Vol.L, Spring 1972.
61. *op. cit.* p.125.
62. Ministry of Public Building and Works, *A National Building Agency*, Cmnd.2228, HMSO, 1963.
63. MOHLG, *Collapse of Flats at Ronan Point, Canning Town, Report of the Inquiry*, HMSO, 1968, p.6. (henceforward *Ronan Point)*.
64. *ibid.* pp.6—7.
65. MOHLG, *Report . . . 1967 and 1968*, Cmnd.4009, HMSO 1969, p.3.
66. *Ronan Point*, Appendix IV, pp.69—70.
67. *Ronan Point*, pp.63—4.
68. *Ronan Point*, p.53.
69. *Ronan Point*, Ch.7.
70. *Ronan Point*, p.7.
71. Cullingworth, *op. cit.* p.164.
72. P.A. Stone, *Urban Development in Britain: Standards, Costs and Resources 1964—2004*, Cambridge University Press, London, 1970, pp.122—3.
73. N.P. Hepworth, *op. cit.* pp.172—5.
74. That this was the effect of the yardstick was stated by Kenneth Campbell, Principal Housing Architect, Greater London Council, in his Bossom Gift Lecture, 1969, *Building*, Vol.CCXVII, No.6583, p.118.
75. MOHLG, *Report . . . 1967 and 1968*, Cmnd.4009, HMSO 1969, p.2.
76. Department of the Environment, *Housing Statistics*, No.24, February 1972, Table 4, HMSO, London, 1972.
77. *op. cit.* p.296.
78. Robin H. Best, 'Against High Density' *New Society*, Vol.VIII, No.217, 24 November 1966.
79. *op. cit.* p.294.
80. Campbell, *loc. cit.*
81. *op. cit.* p.167.

82. Especially *Architectural Review*, Vol.CXIV, No.679, July, 1953.

83. Nicholas Taylor, 'The Failure of "Housing" ', *The Architectural Review*, Vol.CXLII, No.849, November 1967, pp.341–2 and 359.

84. 'Britain's failure to make use of its architects', *The Times*, 29 November 1968.

85. Amos Rapoport, 'Some observations regarding man-environment studies', *Architectural Research and Teaching*, Vol.II, no.1, November 1971.

86. J. Maizels, *Two to Five in High Flats*, Housing Centre Trust, London, 1961.

87. Arthur Morton in Foreword to W.F.R. Stewart, *Children in Flats: A Family Study*, London, 1970.

88. Department of the Environment, *The Estate Outside the Dwelling*, HMSO, 1972, p.2.

89. *ibid.* p.2.

Chapter 7 A Century of Flats in Birmingham 1875-1973

Anthony Sutcliffe

'There is a Birmingham prejudice against flats, and it is not confined to any one class. It springs, we believe, from something deep in the civic life. Indeed, it is probably one expression of the independence of character which has done so much for Birmingham.'

Birmingham Gazette, editorial, 24 May 1930.

*'No, we have no flats and no cellars,' Joseph Chamberlain told a Royal Commission in 1884, '(...) the habits of the people are to have separate houses'.[1] No one could have disputed the general validity of this statement, which was to remain true until the later 1920s. But from that time onwards Birmingham began to adopt the flat, with such effect that in the early 1960s flats made up the great majority of dwellings built in the city. By 1966 purpose-built and converted flats accounted for 10.9 per cent of Birmingham's total of homes.[2] How and why did this change occur? And what changes took place in popular and official attitudes to flats in the city?

Nineteenth-century Birmingham, like most English provincial towns, managed to accommodate its rapidly expanding population in small, self-contained houses. Nevertheless, the town's employment structure and the limitations of its transport system produced markedly higher densities in the central areas than on the outskirts. The highest densities were to be found in the central core of back-to-back houses, of which some 50,000 were built between the 1780s and 1876, when the Council banned their construction.[3] In the middle decades of the nineteenth century the back-to-backs probably housed up to two-thirds of the population of Birmingham and their modernity, convenience and cheapness recommended them to all classes of manual worker. But as the town's growth continued into the second half of the century, the ageing stock of back-to-backs corresponded less and less with the

*I wish to thank Dr Jennifer Tann and Mr Peter Aspinall for their generous advice and aid in the preparation of this paper. I am further indebted to the Corporation of Birmingham for granting access to the minutes of the Improvement Committee, and to the City Architect's Department which, in the person of Mr J.C. Harkness. went to considerable trouble to select the illustrations and kindly gave permission for their publication.

aspirations of the more prosperous sections of the working class. Many moved out to the spreading suburbs of terraced bye-law housing, contributing to a fall in the population of the central wards from the 1870s.[4] Yet the back-to-backs still had an important function to perform as a reserve of cheap, high-density housing for lower-paid workers, many of whom were employed in the small-scale, labour-intensive industries which increasingly typified the inner areas as mechanised industry developed along the canals and railways outside the centre. Moreover, by the end of the century the decline in the population of the central wards was being slowed by a sharp rise in the cost of more modern housing elsewhere in the city. From 1911 it remained stable at about 125,000, out of a total city population of 525,000 at that time.

This stabilisation of population set the seal on the slow transformation of Birmingham's back-to-backs from modern, efficient housing into hard-core slum. All who could afford to live elsewhere, or whose employment would allow them to move, had now left. Those who remained were condemned to perpetual residence in housing conditions which the middle classes now came increasingly to regard as detrimental to health, morals and education. It was not, however, until the 1920s and 1930s that the municipality accepted a responsibility to demolish this housing and reaccommodate its residents. Until this time, the exodus from the central areas and later the structural soundness of many of the back-to-back houses had reassured the Council that no radical intervention was necessary. Thus the large-scale reconstruction of residential accommodation in the central areas, which, it was agreed, would require extensive flat-building, had been postponed. Indeed, a strong middle-class distrust and a working-class dislike of flats had contributed to that postponement.

In Birmingham, as in most provincial towns, private investors and builders showed virtually no interest in flats during the nineteenth century. Middle-class apartments were unknown, for access to the centre was easy, especially from the leafy avenues of the Calthorpe Estate, Edgbaston, which restrictive covenants maintained as Birmingham's most desirable residential area only a mile from the Town Hall. Nor were working-class housing conditions bad enough to stimulate the building of tenements by model dwellings companies. A two-storey block of four 'Prince Albert' tenements was erected at Small Heath in 1855, but it was not imitated and soon fell into obscurity.[5] In the 1860s a town-centre vicar tried repeatedly, but in vain, to stimulate interest in building model dwellings and lodging houses in his parish.[6]

In the following decade even the reservation of sites by the Council for model dwellings failed to encourage the foundation of a Birmingham dwellings company.[7] Not until August 1883 was such a company incorporated, in the shape of the Birmingham Artizans' Dwellings Co. Ltd. and this, the brainchild of a group of prominent Conservatives, was a nine-days' wonder.[8] Two years later the Improvement Committee was gloomily complaining that 'there does not appear to be any probability of such a Company being formed in Birmingham'.[9] In these circumstances the Council was the only potential builder of flats in the town.

The Council made no positive intervention in housing until 1875 when, under the mayoralty of Joseph Chamberlain, some ninety-three acres of the central area were affected by an ambitious renewal project, the Birmingham Improvement Scheme.[10] As the scheme's prime mover, Chamberlain wanted to emulate the Glasgow Improvement Trust (1866) by extending the commercial area and improving housing in one of the town's most congested central quarters. The former objective, however, gradually came to outweigh the latter.[11] The Artisans' and Labourers' Dwellings Improvement Act 1875, under which the scheme was executed, required the Corporation to ensure that all residents displaced were rehoused *within* the cleared area, but the wording of the Act did not oblige the Corporation to provide the housing itself – indeed, it discouraged it.[12] At first, however, Chamberlain and the other Liberal leaders had few doubts that the required housing would be provided in one way or another. Nor did they hesitate to advocate flats; Chamberlain told the Council:

'The [Improvement] Committee will also no doubt erect buildings which will be in flats or storeys, much higher at all events than buildings have hitherto been built in Birmingham. The time is coming, as I believe, when that must be done, if the poor are to be housed in close proximity to their work, and for a reasonable rent.'[13]

Both he and Councillor White, chairman of the Improvement Committee, assured the Council that modern tenement dwellings, in London, Glasgow and even Paris, had a good health record and Chamberlain urged the committee to make a point of visiting Glasgow.[14]

However, visits to Glasgow and London in April and May 1877 did more to persuade the Improvement Committee of the social and financial drawbacks of flats. The Council was told that the deputation were 'not of the opinion that the [flat] system could be readily adapted as a general rule to the requirements and habits of a population like that with which the Borough Improvement Committee has to deal'.[15] Although the committee still sought, and obtained, the Council's unanimous support in principle for an *experimental* block of flats, more significant by far was its decision to let the first rehousing site for 'Artisans' Dwellings in open Terraces', rather than for a 'block of Artisans dwellings' as had originally been agreed.[16] Even this more conventional proposal failed to arouse effective interest among Birmingham builders and when Joseph Chamberlain renewed his advocacy of the flat system before the Council in June 1878, he did so in more cautious terms:

'... it is no doubt possible on that system to give a better kind of accommodation for less money than in any other way. It may be that our Birmingham artisans will not take to this system; if so, after the experiment has been tried, it is not likely to be repeated.'[17]

As time passed, the possibility of such an experiment receded. A depression in trade restricted bids even for commercial sites and interest among builders and speculators in taking on a housing site was derisory. In consequence, surprisingly few households were actually displaced — only 137 by December 1881 — and the Improvement Committee began to repair many of the houses it had acquired. Moreover, only a quarter of those dishoused accepted the committee's offer of another tenancy within the area.[18] The Improvement Committee therefore rejected the contention of its Conservative critics that it had a duty to provide housing itself and its case was reinforced in June 1884 by the report of a special Artisans' Dwellings Inquiry Committee.[19] The report based its argument on the general availability of low-rent housing, even in the central areas, but reinforced it by references to the drawbacks of flats: 'such a system was not adapted to the English workman, who preferred a separate dwelling.'[20] The committee was not against a small-scale private experiment with two-storey flats, whose virtues in Edinburgh had been described to it by H.G. Reid.[21] But the report placed much greater emphasis on the desirability of requiring the tramway companies to provide cheap fares to cater for working-class ambitions to live in the suburbs, which several working-class witnesses had stressed during the inquiry.

This report convinced not only the Council but the Local Government Board, which greatly relaxed its rehousing demands. Yet the

Improvement Committee chairman, Alderman Richard Chamberlain (Joseph's brother), who had been convalescing during the inquiry, was still convinced of the need for new housing in the town centre. Early in 1885 the committee asked the manager of the Improvement Scheme to report on the possible erection of flats and received a very enthusiastic reply.[23] The manager contended that the demand for 'the superior accommodation' offered by block dwellings was increasing among the better class of artisan in London. He admitted that working-class witnesses at the 1884 inquiry had generally stated that Birmingham workers were averse to flats, but he maintained that if the experiment were tried, numbers of 'respectable working men' would soon come to appreciate 'complete, comfortable and healthy homes within a short distance of their work'. The manager appended a plan for a four-storey municipal block of twenty-four flats, which he wanted to see sited in a central position, free from all 'objectionable' surroundings.

These proposals were put to the Council, with only minor modifications, in June 1885.[24] The attack on them was led by the Conservatives, who took this golden opportunity to please their middle-class supporters by arguing that municipal building was unnecessary and expensive, and their working-class followers by pointing to local people's known dislike of flats and the exclusion of the very poor by high rents.[25] This last was in fact one of the scheme's major weaknesses, for in designing flats which might appeal to the prosperous artisans without whose approval flats could never be expected to spread to the very poor who most needed them, the rents had been set at a level, 5s 6d per week, equal to those of many suburban houses. It was in vain that several Liberal speakers echoed Richard Chamberlain's confidence that flats were healthy and convenient and that having been a success in other towns, they would succeed in Birmingham. Nor did Alderman White's vision of countryside eaten up by 'sprawling', jerry-built suburbs, unless more people were allowed to live happily in the centre, excite much sympathy. So, with numbers dwindling after a long debate, the Conservatives obtained enough backbench Liberal support to defeat the scheme by twenty-three votes to sixteen.

The Improvement Committee accepted this vote as a fair reflection of opinion in the town. Richard Chamberlain resigned the chairmanship in 1886 and by 1889 several members were said to have abandoned their earlier advocacy of flats.[26] The committee again discussed several possible flat schemes early in 1889, but never took them to the Council.[27] Later in that year the committee at last overcame the Council's objections to the *principle* of municipal building, but the 104 dwellings which it provided in the Improvement Area in the early 1890s were in the form of terraced houses.[28] Paradoxically, however, the very success of these cottages, which were quickly let at rents between 5s and 7s 6d, strengthened the case for an experiment with flats. It indicated a buoyant demand for good housing in the town centre and reinforced concern about the needs of the numerous workers who could not afford such high rents, but who were being displaced by a steady rate of attrition among the older and cheaper central houses. Similar conclusions could be drawn from a sharp fall in the number of vacant older houses in the Improvement Area in the later 1880s.[29] Poor housing conditions in the central areas were emphasised in the 1890s not only by SDF municipal candidates like John Haddon, but by Dr Hill, the MOH, who pressed hard for further improvement schemes.

In 1894 the Improvement Committee went to the Council with proposals for the demolition of two small areas of back-to-back houses, about two acres in all, under Pt.I of the 1890 Housing Act.[30] Only one area was approved, but by January 1897 a patent lack of interest by private enterprise in erecting replacement housing, required by the Local Government Board, had persuaded the committee to present a scheme for municipal dwellings.[31] The area concerned, in Milk Street, off Digbeth, was in a highly unattractive industrial quarter and the committee determined to build at rents low enough for labourers. After enquiries in a number of towns, the committee proposed a scheme for sixty-four two-bedroom dwellings in the form of 'dual houses', a euphemism for two-storey balcony access flats, which the manager had admired in Dublin as 'a medium between complete houses and huge flats'.[32] By making no charge for ground rent and including shared sculleries, the committee was able to keep rents down to 4s 3d for the lower dwellings and 3s 9d for the upper. 'Your Committee are aware,' the Council was told, 'that being a class of dwelling with which many are unacquainted, the plans have not met with unanimous favour; but the result of their long consideration has been to show that it is absolutely impossible to erect, without loss to the ratepayer, dwellings within the City suitable for the labouring classes at the rents above-mentioned, unless upon either this method or the Flat system.'

Opposition to these proposals was led by the Health Committee chairman, Alderman William Cook. Cook had seconded Richard Chamberlain's flats motion in 1885, but now he objected to certain design defects of the proposed flats and to their location in a congested area. Other speakers expressed more general criticisms of the flats principle and no one supported the proposals. So the Improvement

Committee withdrew its scheme. A period of deadlock was resolved by the appointment of a joint sub-committee composed of members of the two committees. Its discussions fully vindicated the Improvement Committee's attitude and, after visits to flats in Liverpool, Manchester and Bristol, it easily obtained the Council's approval, in July 1898, for plans for four terraces of two-storey 'tenements' which did not differ substantially from those originally proposed.[33]

The Milk Street dwellings were completed in 1901 and quickly occupied, by skilled workers as well as labourers.[34] But they did not set a precedent. In the meantime, the Health Committee had grown increasingly concerned about the 'inadequacy of the total supply' of housing in the city and in July 1900 it asked the Council to let it build a suburban estate of cheap municipal houses before any more demolitions were undertaken in the central areas.[35] The Council approved this proposal by forty-six to eight votes, a majority which accurately reflected the level of public concern over the housing question. The Trades Council, major mouthpiece of the skilled working classes, was delighted. It had been strongly opposed to the Milk Street

Plate XV. Milk Street dwellings, Birmingham, erected in 1901. Photograph taken in 1965, shortly before demolition. These were Birmingham's first municipal flats. (By permission of City Architect's Dept., Birmingham).

flats and had recently been campaigning with the Birmingham Socialist Centre for the building of municipal houses 'to suit various classes of working men' in 'the outlying districts of the City'.[36] The Health Committee's detailed housing proposals, in June 1901, included two four-storey blocks of flats on a central site, the product of further visits to flats in London and Manchester, but much more emphasis was placed on a suburban cottage estate planned for Bordesley Green:

> 'Your Committee recognise that there are a large number of persons to whom it is important that they should live near the centre of the City...With the increase of travelling facilities however, the necessity for men to live quite close to their work will become less and less pressing, and your Committee believe that the erection of low-rented dwellings within the City, but outside the older and more crowded central districts, with cheap and frequent tramway service or other means of travelling, will be one of the most important factors in solving the difficulties connected with such central insanitary areas.'[37]

Neither the flats nor the cottages were ever built. The Council, fearing a confusion of policies, decided to delegate all housing responsibilities to a new Housing Committee.[38] Its chairman, Councillor J.S. Nettlefold, favoured a new strategy, based on the 'patching' of central slum houses and a long-term movement of population to low-density suburban housing built by private enterprise but town-planned by the Corporation.[39] The city-centre flats proposals were an early victim of this new approach. A rearguard action in March 1902, led by the chairmen of the Health and Estates Committees, forced the Housing Committee to present detailed plans for the flats. This, however, merely invited Nettlefold to play the devil's advocate, a task which he performed with appropriate incompetence when he introduced the plans in June 1902.[40] His committee, he said, was 'entirely opposed' to the flats because they would need a big municipal subsidy and because there was no 'immediate' shortage of small houses in the city. Moreover, he said he had been assured that private capital was prepared to undertake 'an experimental trial of flats' if only the Council would hold its hand. These arguments, which the Council approved by twenty-six to eighteen votes, were reinforced in October 1903 by the results of a Housing Committee inquiry, which quoted a number of slum residents and housing experts to indicate the unpopularity and undesirability of flats in Birmingham.[41] Later, in

August 1905, a Housing Committee delegation returned from Germany full of praise for German town planning, but further convinced of the drawbacks of flat life.[42]

Nor did the private flat experiment to which Nettlefold had alluded in 1902 enhance the reputation of flats in the city. Two developments were undertaken, both in 1903, by Homes Ltd, a small housing society founded in 1902, mainly on the initiative of the Kenrick family of industrialists, and by Cregoe Colmore, of the Birmingham landowning family.[43] Homes Ltd built two four-storey blocks, containing sixty tenements, in Palmer Street, not far from Milk Street. Twenty-eight of them were one-room flats letting at only 3s per week, but this economy was achieved at the expense of sculleries, each one of which was shared by the occupants of seven flats (though each flat also had a sink in the living room). The remaining flats, of two and three rooms, had one scullery for every eight dwellings.[44] This spartan arrangement no doubt contributed to the flats' unpopularity; they were never more than one-third or one-half occupied until the First World War and Homes Ltd undertook no further housing of any kind.[45] Colmore's four-storey block of twenty-three flats, in Hospital Street, was much more comfortable, but rents were higher, at 3s 9d to 4s 3d for two rooms, and 5s 3d for three rooms. Colmore expected a return of only 3½ per cent and set out with the intention of building more flats if he achieved it.[46] But this experiment, too, was never repeated. The rents were undoubtedly low, at a time when private enterprise had ceased to build houses for less than 5s 6d anywhere in the city, but even 3s to 4s could still command an older three-room back-to-back house in the central areas.[47] In fact, it took the serious overall housing shortage created by the First World War to drive people into the Palmer Street dwellings.

The failure of Birmingham's first model dwellings and the continued absence of middle-class apartments meant that there were no concrete alternatives to oppose to Nettlefold's suburban solution. The standard for fine housing continued to be set by Edgbaston and George Cadbury's Bournville, and this sylvan ideal, municipalised by the Council's enthusiastic ventures into suburban planning, obscured the survival of the central slums.[48] Even when a special housing inquiry committee admitted in October 1914 that Nettlefold's methods had *reduced* the supply of cheap housing, owing mainly to closures by frustrated landlords, and that 'a large proportion of the poor in Birmingham' were still living in housing detrimental to their health and morals, it was unwilling to propose what it saw as the only feasible solution – the clearance of large areas of central Birmingham and the construction of at least 50,000 municipal dwellings there to replace the back-to-backs.[49] It cited expense as the main obstacle, but the inevitable inclusion of flats in any such undertaking was a secondary drawback. The committee had been to see Liverpool's latest flats, but concluded that they did not represent 'the ideal type for working people', lacking as they did 'those bright and cheerful surroundings which add so much to the amenities of life, but which as yet are unobtainable in the midst of a crowded industrial town'. Consequently, the report went on, 'the Committee feel that it would be a retrograde step to perpetutate the settling of families on the old sites, and that the efforts of the Council should rather be directed towards inducing them to move into the other areas still awaiting development.' In the meantime, the necessary improvement of central housing could best be achieved by a continuation of present policies, supplemented by a planning scheme to co-ordinate the gradual rebuilding of the central areas by private enterprise.

Within a few years of this report, the biggest obstacle to slum clearance was removed by the Government's decision to subsidise municipal housing. Meanwhile, a further deterioration of the central slums during the war strengthened the case for total clearance. During the early 1920s, however, the massive overall housing deficiency forced a *deceleration* in the pre-war rate of closure of slum houses.[50] Discussions on clearance began in 1923, but the problem of replacement housing prevented action. The Public Works and Town Planning Committee, now responsible for housing, was prepared to countenance flats. It had the support of the City Surveyor, Herbert H. Humphries, who was convinced that flats were needed, at least as temporary clearance accommodation. It faced, on the other hand, the opposition of the MOH, Dr Robertson. Robertson, a pre-war ally of Nettlefold, was now a convert to the principle of total clearance, but his earlier Glasgow experience kept him a sworn enemy of flats.[51]

By February 1925 the Public Works Committee, still convinced that the bulk of slum residents would be unable to move to the outer suburbs, had decided to take the bull by the horns.[52] It proposed an experimental block of flats of one to three bedrooms, to be built in connection with a pilot clearance scheme. Dr Robertson was horrified and with the support of the Health Committee sent a letter to all council members warning them of the evils of flats.[53] Flats, he maintained, always produced 'stunted growth, malnutrition and rickets' among young children, and he ended with a powerful restatement of the suburban ideal: 'The will to go into the suburbs is strong in the

Birmingham people.' This unprecedented initiative contributed to the extraordinary ill-humour of the Council's debate, which ended in ten minutes of total uproar. However, the objections of the Labour minority, who made most of the noise, were more to rough handling by the chair than to the flats scheme itself.[54] The committee was happy to promise that children would not be housed on the upper floors and Labour did not implement its threat, made in the heat of the moment, to reopen the whole issue at the next meeting.

In fact, the first serious objections to the detailed plans were made by the Minister of Health, former Birmingham alderman Neville Chamberlain. He refused to countenance the absence of bathrooms, rejecting the committee's argument that only such economies could make the flats cheap enough for slumdwellers.[55] In October 1925 the committee gave way and included the bathrooms, but they failed to still Labour's growing suspicions of the scheme's utilitarian design, which culminated in a vain attempt to persuade the Council to rescind

Plate XVI. Garrison Lane flats, Birmingham, erected in 1927. The mansard roof was probably a deliberate attempt to disguise the height of the flats and forestall 'barracky' criticisms. The railed gardens were an addition in the early 1930s after the previously open area around the flats had been churned up by fans taking short cuts to the Birmingham City football ground, visible in the distance. (By permission of City Architect's Dept., Birmingham).

its authority for the flats.[56] A further change of plan came when the committee decided that the housing shortage was still too serious for any clearance to be carried out. They therefore decided to build the flats, 180 of them, in three-storey blocks, on a vacant site in Garrison Lane, near the Birmingham City football ground.

The Garrison Lane flats, completed in 1927, were not unattractive in aspect; the locals nicknamed them 'The Mansions' at first. But the name soon changed to 'The Barracks' when they were occupied. Rents of 11s per week upwards did not deter tenants in such a serious housing shortage, but when combined with the flats' small size, the absence of communal amenities, and the rapid deterioration of the area around the flats, they aroused bitter complaints. Nor was the Public Works Committee any happier, for to avoid even higher rents the flats had to be let at a loss. In short, the Garrison Lane experiment was an almost total failure, which weakened the case for further flat developments.

Garrison Lane even contributed to a partial return to patching in the later 1920s. When the Council designated as its first post-war improvement area, in October 1926, eleven acres of back-to-back housing in and near New Summer Street, the press assumed that clearance would ensue.[57] The area had first been represented in 1898 and 'improved' by Nettlefold's methods; no one dreamed that the same mistake could be made again. Yet, after two years' prevarication, the Estates Committee went to the Council with a reconditioning scheme.[58] A desire to cause the minimum of disturbance to property owners had contributed to this decision, as had Neville Chamberlain's interest in reconditioning, but underlying it all was the rehousing problem. People in the New Summer Street area had immediately let it be known that they were opposed to clearance unless houses were provided at low rents in the immediate neighbourhood.[59] Flats of the Garrison Lane type were obviously too expensive and by March 1928 the Estates Committee was thinking of buying small houses in the central areas to relocate such people.[60] From here it was but a short step to keeping as many slumdwellers as possible in their original houses, especially as patching was given a good name after 1926 by the reconditioning work carried out by COPEC, the Conference of Politics, Economics and Citizenship Home Improvement Society, founded by Birmingham social reformers in 1925.

The Council's acceptance of these patching proposals was a step into the past, yet it indicated a fair measure of agreement that a generous supply of cheap housing was needed in the central areas. This partial rejection of the suburban ideal was reinforced from 1929 by a growing recognition of the social, economic and aesthetic drawbacks of Birmingham's sprawling suburbs and by a developing awareness that the reserves of building land within the boundaries would soon be expended.[61] In short, it came to be agreed in the 1930s by those who governed the city that Birmingham was already big enough and that those whom slum clearance would consign to the outer suburbs were the least willing and able to live in them. Moreover, for the first time Birmingham was producing a positive alternative to the now-tarnished suburban ideal, in the shape of private blocks of luxury flats near the city centre. The first of a swelling tide of such developments appeared, principally in Edgbaston and Moseley, in the late 1920s. Not only did they indicate that some at least of those with freedom of choice were prepared to sacrifice space for a convenient location, they also demonstrated that flats were not inimical to a high standard of accommodation.[62] Thus the 1930s saw the terms of the debate swing positively in favour of flats.

The first step towards a recasting of municipal policies occurred when Neville Chamberlain rejected the New Summer Street scheme because so few houses would actually be acquired.[63] The Unionists still maintained, against united Labour protests, that reconditioning would be enough, but the Estates Committee decided to await further legislation, which the Government had now promised.[64] By the time this materialised, in the shape of the Labour Government's 1930 Housing Act, a renewed public campaign for clearance had swung even Unionist opinion against reconditioning. The Act's encouragement of large-scale clearance, and its special subsidies for flats, decided the issue. By May 1930 it was being rumoured in the press that a majority of the Estates and Public Works Committees were in favour of building flats, and in August a deputation from the two committees visited flats in London and a number of Continental cities, including Berlin, Hamburg, Munich and Vienna. While awaiting the deputation's report, the Council approved a five-year programme to demolish 4,700 slum houses and build 7,000 replacements.[65]

The deputation reported to the Council in March 1931.[66] Its conclusions were very similar to those of the Glasgow deputation of 1877:

'Notwithstanding all we have seen, we are unanimously of the opinion that the most satisfactory system for housing the people, provided the requisite land and other facilities are available, is that which prevails in Birmingham at the present time ... All the towns we visited, without exception, acquiesced in this view.'[67]

It maintained, however, that the drawbacks of flats could be compensated by the inclusion of 'the necessary amenities . . . within the scope of the scheme' and ended with a proposal that the Council should build an experimental 'model colony of flats or tenement buildings up to a thousand dwellings'. Only a development of this size, it thought, could support the amenities, by which it understood shops, play-grounds, nurseries and social facilities. Only one member, Councillor W.J. Dalton (Unionist), chairman of the Estates Committee, differed; he presented a minority report calling for scattered small blocks of flats without amenities.

The deputation approached the Council with some confidence, but the four-and-a-half hour debate which ensued revealed the persistence of strong prejudice against flats among many members of both the Labour and Unionist groups. A majority of speakers opposed the flats. A motion to reject the proposal out of hand was turned down, but the Council refused to sanction such a potentially expensive scheme without further study and referred it to the Estates Committee for a detailed report. Particularly influential was Alderman Grey (Unionist), chairman of the Finance Committee, who pointed out that if the necessary amenities were provided, the flats would be too expensive for the very poor people whom it was hoped to rehouse.[68]

The Estates Committee reported in September 1931.[69] It rejected the flat colony as too expensive and because a sufficiently large site was not available. Also turned down was its chairman's own proposal for small blocks without amenities – probably influential here were the continuing complaints from Garrison Lane.[70] Finally, it opted for redevelopment with small houses and 'maisonettes', the latter being yet another euphemism for two-storey cottage flats, a few of which had been built in the suburbs in the 1920s as low-rent accommodation.[71] It admitted that if the Government subsidy and land costs were taken into account, small blocks of flats were cheaper than either small houses or maisonettes. It felt, however, that financial arguments were not sufficiently cogent to overrule the deputation's opinion, and what it considered to be the general feeling of the Council, that as far as possible each family should have a separate house and garden.

The Finance Committee was even more aghast at these proposals than it had been in March. The total annual cost to the rates of rehousing 7,000 families in flats was estimated at £40,225, but with maisonettes it was £59,354 and with maisonettes and houses, £67,775.

The committee therefore warned that it was financially impracticable to erect houses or maisonettes on expensive land in the central areas. It wanted to see the Council's share of the cost limited to its statutory contribution, which worked out at £23,796 per annum, but it agreed to wait five years before passing final judgement. The Labour group's reaction was not unanimous, for it contained several confirmed opponents of flats and debates at Borough Labour Party meetings had confirmed that a majority of the rank-and-file were still against multi-storey housing.[72] Some Labour members, and notably those three who had been on the Continental delegation, tried to keep the 'flat colony' proposals alive, but in vain. Finally, the Council gave general approval to the Estates Committee proposals.

The task of converting the confusion of this long debate into consistent action fell to a young Unionist councillor, Theodore Pritchett, who became chairman of the Estates Committee in November 1931. With his first major report, in April 1932, Pritchett persuaded the Council to build 180 maisonettes on a five and a half acre central area site.[73] He also presented alternative plans for flats, but stated that his committee believed that the higher standard of amenity secured by the maisonettes outweighed the flats' higher densities, the rents being almost identical. The Finance Committee was pleased to hear that the actual cost would be much lower than that forecast in 1931 and that only the Council's statutory contribution was needed. This development with two-storey flats seemed an acceptable compromise and the Council rejected two minority amendments, one (Councillor Dalton's) calling for high-density flats and the other for small houses.

Work began on the maisonettes forthwith and others began to be erected on many of the smaller sites which the clearance programme now began to make available. But, inevitably, they could house only a minority of those displaced, many of whom found themselves moved into vacant slum houses within the central areas when they were unable to move to the suburbs. This problem was of particular concern to Labour members and did much to overcome their misgivings about flats. So in January 1934 Pritchett accepted an amendment, proposed jointly by a Unionist and a Labour member, calling for a report on the possibility of building a block of flats. In April Pritchett returned with a plan for 240 flats in four-storey blocks on a five-acre clearance area at Emily Street. Owing to the continued fall in building costs, the inclusive cost of flats was now less than of maisonettes. So, for the first time, the Council was able to judge a flat proposal purely on its merits as accommodation.[74]

Labour took steps to ascertain working-class opinion before the debate. A Borough Labour Party meeting came to no decision, but a majority of speakers criticised the flats. Meetings of Emily Street residents organised by Labour and Unionist councillors also produced criticisms, though the indications were that at least half of them wanted to be rehoused on the site. Middle-class opinion, on the other hand, was now much less opposed to working-class flats than in the 1920s, with the influential *Birmingham Post* a strong advocate of them. This distinction was reflected in the forty-eight to forty-five vote which rejected the flats and decided in favour of maisonettes after a five-hour debate in April 1934. Both groups were split but nineteen out of twenty-three Labour members voted for maisonettes; well over half the Unionists voted for flats.[75]

A similar decision in 1885 had been accepted as final. Not this one. The pro-flat lobby immediately claimed that the vote was not fully binding as one-third of the Council had been absent, and the *Post* was confident that it would be reconsidered.[76] In the following months the growing rehousing problem, persuasion from a pro-flat Minister of Health and a further shift of middle-class opinion away from the suburban ideal, built up further pressure for a higher-density solution. By August 1935 the *Mail* was suggesting that a majority of the Council were now 'converted' to flats and it was no surprise when Pritchett brought the Emily Street flats plan back to the Council in October 1935. His excuse for reopening the matter was that the flats, if built of concrete, would help to meet the overall housing shortage at a time when few bricklayers were available. But he emphasised that the basic issue had not changed:

'On the last occasion the Council refused to swallow the pill. I am not covering it with more jam. I simply say that if you want to get the better of the housing shortage you must have these flats.'[77]

The pill, this time, was swallowed. Pritchett promised that the best possible design would be selected by an open competition and although there was some opposition in the debate, notably from women members, the proposals went through without difficulty. From this day onwards, little was to restrain the advance of the flat in Birmingham until the mid-1960s. The significance of this watershed was emphasised by the failure to reverse the movement of the Emily Street scheme, which was in many respects as unsuccessful as Garrison Lane. The competition adjudicator, Louis de Soissons, selected a balcony-access solution by a London firm, G. Grey Wornum and Anthony C. Tripe.[78] Although the swingeing attack on it by the general secretary of MARS (Modern Architectural Research Group) was not entirely justified, the design's merits lay primarily in its high density (44.35 dwellings per acre) and economy, rather than in original planning or attractive appearance.[79] Moreover, the layout was modified in response to such criticisms.[80] However, these academic attacks were largely confirmed by the first tenants, with whom the Emily Street flats were instantly unpopular. Yet instead of reversing the flat tide, the Emily Street experience merely contributed to a great improvement in the design of early post-war flats.

That the City Council no longer looked back was due not only to the realities of the rehousing situation, but also to the consistent pro-flat influence of the new City Surveyor and Engineer, Herbert Manzoni, appointed in 1935. Much of the indecision of the early 1930s had resulted from the lack of a strong lead by the paid officers. But Manzoni, a trained architect whose greatest ambition was to redevelop Birmingham's slums on modern lines, was not afraid to mould public opinion by speeches and articles and to exercise a positive influence on

Plate XVII. St Martin's (Emily Street) flats, Birmingham, nearing completion in March 1939. Planting this time is an integral part of the scheme. Note the distinctive brick-like appearance of the 'clothed concrete' system. (By permission of City Architect's Dept., Birmingham).

the committees with which he worked. Some eyebrows were raised at first; officers were expected to execute policy, not to define it.[81] Within a year or two, however, Manzoni's creative role was recognised and valued. As a strong supporter of flats, he brought an unprecedented consistency to slum rehousing policies.

Although the principle of flats was now accepted, their location could still arouse controversy. With overspill from the clearance areas still occurring, the Estates Committee hit on the idea of building at least two massive flatted estates, with full amenities, in the seedier parts of the inner middle-class suburbs, about two miles from the centre. The committee claimed that such impressive developments, which were similar to the experimental 'colony' recommended in 1930, would *improve* the districts around them. Local owner-occupiers took the opposite view and behind-the-scenes pressure on Unionist council members by newly-formed residents' associations led to the rescinding, in June 1938, of an earlier decision to press ahead with the flats.[82] The ins-and-outs of this piquant episode unfortunately cannot be described here, but its major long-term effect was to strengthen the case for high-density redevelopment within the clearance areas. In December 1937 the Council had designated its first large-scale redevelopment area under the 1936 Housing Act, 267 acres in Duddeston and Nechells. Manzoni made clear that he wanted to see the population rehoused as far as possible within the area.[83] The very size of the area made this an acceptable as well as a feasible solution, for it offered the opportunity of forming extensive and convenient housing sites and of creating a pleasant environment, which previous flat undertakings had sadly lacked. With Pritchett warning that a new boundary extension was now essential, pressure for a total reappraisal of the City's housing and town planning policies was increasing, and many calls for higher central densities were made during the 1938 local election campaign.

This, then, was the atmosphere in which a majority of the Council welcomed a five-year clearance and rehousing programme, presented by the Public Works Committee in December 1938. It planned 10,000 houses on the outskirts, but 7,500 flats and the same number of maisonettes in the central areas. Many members of the Labour group were unhappy at the prospect of very high central densities, especially after the Unionist cave-in to electoral pressure over the inner-suburban flats, but Manzoni was perfectly confident. He told a Duddeston meeting that at least 5,000 of the 7,000 dwellings in the redevelopment area could be rebuilt there. With the latest figures showing that only 14 per cent of those to be displaced were prepared to move to the suburbs, the case for more central flats seemed watertight.[84] So, despite some Labour protests, two further flats schemes were approved in the early months of 1939, one of them six storeys high.

The war, of course, interrupted these plans. But it did not undermine Birmingham's general acceptance of the flat. In the atmosphere of lively public participation which marked the war years, the Council welcomed advice and received plenty. Even the Bournville Village Trust, oracle of the suburban tradition, accepted the need for a proportion of central flats in its *When We Build Again* (1941). However, it produced evidence of the continuing unpopularity of flats with working-class people. On the other hand, the Birmingham and Five Counties Architectural Association wanted to see a number of flats built on suburban estates.[85] The Borough Labour Party remained suspicious of flats; the Communists wanted to see even more flats than had been planned before the war.[86]

Within the City Council, the war years saw a strengthening of Unionist resolve to clear the slums. Plans for four more big redevelopment areas were drawn up and densities were set extremely high. The Duddeston and Nechells scheme, announced in 1943, envisaged a net density of forty-two dwellings to the acre, with a very high proportion of flats.[87] Labour protested, but their opposition was mainly tactical. Councillor W.S. Lewis, the group leader and a pre-war supporter of flats, presided over the elaboration of the high-density schemes from 1943 as the first-ever Labour chairman of the Public Works Committee. He, his Labour colleagues, and working people in general, were increasingly enthused by Manzoni's spectacular redevelopment proposals. So when the Unionists lost overall control of the Council in November 1945, Labour made no attempt to reject the major features of the wartime plans. Moreover, with Labour now actively shaping policy, opposition to flats rapidly waned within the Borough Labour Party.

In the redevelopment areas themselves, little more was heard of the pre-war aversion to flats. On the whole, slumdwellers appear to have been impressed by the post-war flat plans, in which the lessons of Garrison Lane and Emily Street seemed to have been fully learned. Particularly influential here were the plans for five twelve-storey towers at Duddeston and Nechells, which began to take shape from 1948 and were approved by the Council with only five dissentients in 1950. The Public Works Committee leaned over backwards to make them the ultimate in comfort, convenience and safety. In the end they became the most expensive municipal dwellings ever built in Birmingham and were never repeated, but they were supremely successful in dispelling the old Emily Street image.

With flats thus firmly established as a major instrument of central area redevelopment, the story which began with the Improvement Scheme in 1875 is complete. Yet meanwhile, in the early 1950s, the flat was about to take on a new role as a major means of *suburban* housing in a city whose physical growth was now restricted by Government design and, for a time, by municipal consent.

The exhaustion of vacant building land, foreseen in the 1930s, again became a major worry in the late 1940s. Overspill from the central redevelopment areas estimated, despite the flats, at 50 per cent, added to a big overall housing deficiency. With the Government unwilling to designate a new town for Birmingham under the 1946 Act and a general recognition on both sides of the Council that the city was already big enough, there was little alternative but to raise densities on suburban estates. As early as February 1945 the Council had agreed to include a small number of three-storey flats in suburban schemes, but its object was mainly to provide visual variety.[88] It was left to the Unionists, who regained control of the Council in 1949, to take the crucial steps towards suburban flats. Despite the major shifts in policy since the 1930s, the Unionists were still more strongly opposed than Labour to boundary extensions and less worried about the possible deterioration in housing standards which flats might bring.[89]

One of the Unionists' first actions was to speed up the building rate by bringing into the city a number of national building firms using non-traditional methods. Their success accentuated the land problem, but their ability to build, cheaply, much larger structures than two-storey houses suggested a solution.[90] So, in the summer of 1951, the House Building Committee announced that one-fifth of the dwellings in its 1952 programme would be flats. Most were to be in the central areas, but the rest would be in the suburbs. In fact, the House Building Committee even believed that suburban flats would be less objectionable to tenants than those in the centre.[91] Labour was worried about the planned increase in the proportion of two-bedroom dwellings, but not about flats as such. Indeed, when Labour took control again, in 1952, they were as enthusiastic about suburban flats as the Unionists.

Part of the explanation why suburban flats were such an easy pill to swallow lay in the appointment, in 1952, of A.G. Sheppard Fidler as Birmingham's first-ever City Architect. Sheppard Fidler was a faithful apostle of mixed development for both central and suburban housing.

His advocacy of the high standards of design and environment, as well as the higher densities, which mixed development allowed, finally dispelled Labour's remaining doubts. As the first local authority to build suburban flats, Birmingham was unable for a time to obtain the full expensive-site and flats subsidies, but once this matter was resolved in the City's favour in 1953, there was no further obstacle to the onward march of the flat throughout the city.[92] The proportion of municipal dwellings completed in buildings of three storeys or more rose from 3.69 per cent in 1951 to three-quarters in 1957. In the later 1950s, 30 per cent of new flat dwellings were in tall blocks, with the balance in four-storey maisonettes (the meaning of 'maisonette' had once again changed, to mean a dwelling occupying part of two floors in a building of three or more storeys).

Little had been heard since the early 1950s of the Birmingham citizen's 'natural aversion' to flats, for the press, officials and members of both party groups had been doing their best to promote them. But towards the end of the decade it emerged once again, based this time on experience rather than prejudice. Of course, much discontent sprang

Plate XVIII. Twelve-storey towers in Duddeston and Nechells redevelopment area, Birmingham, in 1954. The nearest block has just been occupied. These prestige flats mark a major step forward on earlier flat designs in Birmingham, but they proved so expensive that they were never repeated. (By permission of City Architect's Dept., Birmingham).

from the perennial defects of new housing estates, but most of it crystallised around the flats, especially in the suburbs, where tenants really resented the lack of a garden. Tenant grouses were increasingly voiced within the Borough Labour Party and were supported by a new reaction of informed opinion against flats. An outspoken newspaper article in 1957 by Dr David Eversley, lecturer and honorary secretary of the Midlands New Towns Society, caused a stir.[93] The Labour leaders were infuriated, but a further blow came when John P. Macey, the Housing Manager, admitted that at least 80 per cent of Birmingham flatdwellers disliked their homes.[94] In fact, the Labour leaders had already asked the House Building Committee, in February 1958, to slow down the building of tall blocks. Shortly after, they decided to seek a boundary extension.

Hindsight distinguishes the year 1958 as the beginning of the end of Birmingham's brief dalliance with the suburban flat. But building land outside the boundaries was not granted until 1964, and for a while the proportion of flats built rose even further, reaching a peak of 84.86 per cent in 1961. Even as late as 1965 the proportion was as high as 77.08 per cent, but thereafter the easing of the land problem and subsidy changes sharply reduced it. As early as November 1964 plans were announced for a suburban estate with a high proportion of two-storey houses and the City Architect's Department soon developed a rare skill in designing high-density, low-rise layouts. Plans for the Chelmsley Wood out-city estate, finalised in 1965, put only 10 to 15 per cent of dwellings in multi-storey blocks, with the rest in small houses. This proportion was maintained in developments approved by the Conservatives (they had dropped the name 'Unionist' in 1953) after they came to power in 1966. With the overall housing shortage virtually solved by the later 1960s, prospective municipal tenants became harder to please; by 1968 the Housing Management Department was having considerable difficulty in filling flats in the north-eastern suburbs.[95] The occasional tall block was still built in connection with redevelopment schemes, but as the emphasis switched from clearance to rehabilitation pressure was reduced even in the inner areas. Low blocks of flats or maisonettes, now recognised as highly unpopular with tenants owing to the absence of lifts, hardly came into the picture.

Would this reduction in flat-building prove long-lasting? The municipal flat had now done its job of replacing the back-to-back house in a city whose further growth had been viewed as undesirable by the Council and/or Westminster since the 1930s. With Birmingham's population in decline and a modicum of land becoming available outside the boundaries, it was arguable that the flat would no longer be needed to meet any future housing deficiency. Yet Birmingham still needed more flats for its middle classes, as pressure on private building land and the proportion of tertiary employments increased and traffic congestion put a premium on accessibility to the centre. The first post-war private flats appear to have been erected after building controls were relaxed in 1954. Like the pre-war private flats, they were built to rent, but the real boom occurred from the later 1950s when building societies recognised the need and began to grant mortgages on flats in the city.[96] A further boost came with the inclusion of a high proportion of flats, including several multi-storey blocks, in the Calthorpe Estate's development plan, announced in 1958. Most of the high blocks were abandoned in the mid-1960s, but the three-storey block of private flats had become a familiar feature of the Birmingham scene by the early 1970s. Housing associations continued to build them even after the Corporation had ceased to do so. With much of the best residential land used for municipal housing, private flats were to be found even in the distant, fashionable suburbs. The conversion of older houses into flats also proceeded apace. As only a minority of dwellings created in Birmingham were private, the high proportion of flats among them could not rapidly increase the proportion of flats in the city. But with every prospect of a bigger role for private and housing-society building in the 1970s, a further spread of the flat looked on the cards. Separate houses still accommodated the great majority of the population, but the flat was making an essential contribution to the adequate housing of all classes in Britain's second-biggest city – without any visible effects on the local 'independence of character'.

Notes

1. Royal Commission on the Housing of the Working Classes 1884, *First Report*, B.P.P. 1884–5, C.4402–I, XXX, p.443.
2. Calculated from *Sample Census 1966, England and Wales, Warwickshire County Report*, table 5.
3. The origins of the Birmingham back-to-back house are touched on in S.D. Chapman (ed.), *The History of Working-Class Housing*, David and Charles, Newton Abbot, 1971, pp.221–46. For examples, see Bournville Village Trust, *When We Build Again,* Birmingham, 1941.
4. For population changes, see *Victoria County History of Warwickshire*, Vol.VII, pp.4–25.
5. See Douglas Hickman, *Birmingham* (City Buildings Series), Studio Vista, London, 1970, p.39.
6. See *Builder*, no. 1341, 17 October 1868, pp. 768–9.

7. One such call is made in Frank R. Heath, *Artisans' Dwellings and the Birmingham Improvement Scheme*, Birmingham, 1876.

8. *Builder*, no.2118, 8 September 1883, p.334; P.R.O., B.T.31/3218/18782.

9. *Council*, 2 June 1885, p.338.

10. See J.T. Bunce, *History of the Corporation of Birmingham*, Vol.II, Birmingham, 1885, pp.455–506.

11. For Glasgow's influence, see Borough of Birmingham, *A Short History of the Passing of the Birmingham (Corporation) Gas Act . . .*, Birmingham, 1875, pp.84–5.

12. Local Government Board's Provisional Orders Confirmation (Artisans and Labourers Dwellings) Act, 1876, p.7, para.7 (B.P.P., 1876 [287] IV).

13. Borough of Birmingham, *Proceedings on the Adoption by the Council of a Scheme for the Improvement of the Boroughs . . .*, 6 October 1875, p.25.

14. *Ibid.*, p.22.

15. *Council*, 1 May 1877, pp.321–2; 13 November 1877, pp.50–52.

16. *Council*, 5 December 1876, p.111; 13 November 1877, p.49.

17. Borough of Birmingham, *The Progress of the Birmingham Improvement Scheme . . .*, 11 June 1878, pp.17–18.

18. Borough of Birmingham, *Report of the Health Committee . . .*, 5 March 1878, p.15; *Council*, 5 March 1878, p.227; 20 December 1881, p.133.

19. *Council*, 3 June 1884, pp.376–95. Conservative campaigning on this issue is described in C.M. Green, 'The growth of Conservatism in Birmingham, 1873–1891' (Birmingham University B.A. dissertation, 1971), esp. p.34.

20. Here the report echoed the strong objections to flats of the M.O.H., Dr Hill (see e.g. *Report on the Health of the Borough of Birmingham for the Year 1884*, p.57).

21. See above, p.101.

22. For similar concessions made by the Board to the Metropolitan Board of Works, see London County Council, *The Housing Question in London*, London, 1900, pp.8–12.

23. Improvement Sub-Committee minutes, 10 March 1885.

24. *Council*, 2 June 1885, pp.336–66.

25. The Conservatives' growing success in appealing both to the middle classes and to the poorer sections of the working class is described in Green, 'Growth of Conservatism', esp.pp.26–8, 51–6.

26. *Birmingham Mail*, 28 February 1889.

27. Improvement Committee minutes, 13 February 1889.

28. *Council*, 2 July 1889, pp.361–6; 3 February 1891, pp.205–10.

29. *Council*, 5 February 1889, p.130.

30. *Council*, 1 May 1894, pp.320–4, 336–41.

31. *Council*, 5 January 1897, pp.141–5; *Birmingham Post*, 6 January 1897.

32. Improvement Sub-Committee minutes, 10 April 1896; Improvement Committee minutes, 11 November 1896.

33. *Council*, 26 July 1898, pp.670–75; *Birmingham Post*, 22 July 1898. For a plan and description, see Sydney Perks, *Residential Flats of All Classes*, London, 1905, pp.92–3.

34. *Council*, 18 June 1901, pp.570–72.

35. *Council*, 2 May 1899, pp.365–6; 5 December 1899, pp.93, 130; 31 July 1900, pp.627–40; J.A. Fallows, *The Housing of the Poor*, Birmingham, 1899.

36. Birmingham Trades Council, *Annual Report*, 1896–7, p.5; 1897–8, p.4; 1899–1900, p.9; letter in *Birmingham Post*, 5 January 1897; *Council*, 26 July 1898, p.673; 5 December 1899, p.93. The pro- and anti-flat arguments are encapsulated in *The Housing of the Labouring Classes*, Birmingham, 1901, the proceedings of a public debate on flats held in March 1901 (Birmingham

Reference Library 156537).
37. *Council*, 8 June 1901, pp.529–62.
38. *Council*, 18 June 1901, pp.572–4.
39. The best statement of his policies in his *Practical Housing*, Garden City Press, Letchworth, 1908. The Birmingham Socialists' general support for suburbanisation is best expressed by J.A. Fallows, *The Housing Question*, Birmingham, 1902, and J.A. Fallows and Fred Hughes, *The Housing Question in Birmingham*, Birmingham, 1905.
40. City of Birmingham, *Housing Committee Report*, 3 June 1902.
41. *Housing Committee Report*, 20 October 1903.
42. *Council*, 24 October 1905, pp.700–705; 3 July 1906, pp.498–605.
43. Both are described, with plans, in Perks, *Residential Flats*, pp.90–93. For the Kenricks, see R.A. Church, *Kenricks in Hardware: A Family Business, 1791–1966* David and Charles, Newton Abbot, 1969.
44. *Housing Committee Report*, 20 October 1903, p.5; text of Nettlefold's speech, attached, p.6.
45. *Birmingham Post*, 3 February 1925; Homes Ltd, *Report and Accounts . . . 1911* (Birmingham Reference Library 481610).
46. *Housing Committee Report*, 20 October 1903, appendix, pp.43–4.
47. In 1902, 670 houses rented at less than 4s a week were vacant within three miles of the centre, and most of these would have been situated within the central areas (*Housing Committee Report*, 3 June 1902, p.9; 20 October 1903, p.3).
48. See Asa Briggs, *History of Birmingham*, Vol.II, OUP, London, 1952, passim.
49. *Council*, 27 October 1914, pp.733–50. The proportion of the population living in overcrowded dwellings had fallen from 14.27 per cent in 1891 to 10.32 per cent in 1901, but in the following decade it declined only marginally, to 10.1 per cent. Landlords' reasons for closing their houses rather than bringing them up to the standards required by the Housing Committee are set out in Birmingham and District Trades and Property Association, *Objections to the Housing and Town-Planning Bill . . .*, Birmingham, 1908.
50. See e.g. *Birmingham Gazette*, 4 November 1920.
51. See his *Report* for 1918, pp.85–8.
52. *Council*, 3 February 1925, pp.128–48.
53. *Birmingham Post*, 3 February 1925.
54. *Birmingham Post*, 4 February 1925.
55. *Council*, 20 October 1925, p.694; *Birmingham Gazette, Birmingham Despatch*, 13 August 1925.
56. *Council*, 1 December 1925, p.40.
57. *Council*, 19 October 1926, pp.736–41; *Birmingham Mail*, 13 October 1926; *Birmingham Gazette*, 2 February 1927, editorial.
58. *Council*, 5 February 1929, pp.185–6.
59. *Birmingham Gazette*, 18 October 1926.
60. *Birmingham Mail*, 29 March 1928.
61. See e.g. *Birmingham Mail*, 5 June 1929, editorial; *Birmingham Gazette*, 8 July 1929; *Birmingham Post*, 19 September 1929. The best official statement of this view is *Council*, 31 March 1931, p.334.
62. See e.g. *Birmingham Mail*, 1 April 1931, editorial. For the best-known of these developments, Viceroy Close, see *Architectural Review*, Vol.LXXXIV, July 1938, pp.66–7.
63. *Birmingham Gazette*, 6 February 1929.
64. *Council*, 30 July 1929, p.750.

65. *Council*, 9 December 1930, pp.69–70.
66. *Council*, 31 March 1931, pp.331–85; City of Birmingham, *Report . . . of the Deputation Visiting Germany, Czecho-Slovakia and Austria in August, 1930, for the Purpose of Studying the System of Tenement or Flat Dwellings Erected in Various Towns*, 1930.
67. *Report*, p.70.
68. *Birmingham Post*, 1 April 1931; *Town Crier*, 3 April 1931.
69. *Council*, 22 September 1931, pp.783–801.
70. *Council*, 28 July 1931, p.662; *Birmingham Despatch*, 23 February 1931.
71. See *Birmingham Post*, 24 February 1927.
72. See e.g. *Town Crier*, 17 April 1931; 7 August 1931.
73. *Council*, 12 April 1932, pp.350–60.
74. *Birmingham Post*, 10 January 1934; *Council*, 10 April 1934, pp.318–33.
75. *Town Crier*, 16 March 1934; *Birmingham Post*, 10 January 1934, editorial; 17 March 1934, editorial.
76. *Birmingham Despatch*, 11 April 1934; *Birmingham Post*, 11 April 1934, editorial.
77. *Birmingham Mail*, 3 August 1935; *Council*, 15 October 1935, pp.892–4; *Birmingham Gazette*, 11 October 1935.
78. *Council*, 8 December 1936, pp.53–62. The prize-winning designs are described in *Architect and Building News*, Vol.CXLVII, 28 August 1936, pp.246–52.
79. See letter in *Birmingham Post*, 14 September 1936.
80. For the final arrangement, see *Architects' Journal*, Vol.XCII, 26 December 1940, pp.509–11.
81. See e.g. *Birmingham Post*, 21 November 1936, editorial. For Manzoni's first public advocacy of flats,.see report of a lecture in *Birmingham Gazette*, 21 November 1936.
82. *Council*, 28 June 1938, p.656; *Birmingham Mail*, 28 June 1938.
83. *Council*, 14 December 1937, pp.125–33; *Birmingham Mail*, 4 December 1937.
84. *Birmingham Post*, 25 January 1939; *Birmingham Despatch*, 20 June 1939.
85. 'Extract from a memorandum on the planning of a typical housing development in the outer area of the city', *Architect and Building News*, Vol.CLXXIX, 29 September 1944, pp.195–8.
86. *Homes for the People! Labour's Policy for Birmingham's Needs*, 1945, p.10; Phyllis Stevens, *The Housing Problem: A Plan for Birmingham*, 1943, p.11; Birmingham Communist Party, *Homes for Birmingham*, 1945, p.6.
87. See *Ideal Home*, February 1944.
88. *Council*, 6 February 1945, p.117.
89. See e.g. speech by Ald. Pritchett, *Birmingham Gazette*, 15 June 1949; *Birmingham Post*, 2 November 1949, editorial; speech by Pritchett in *Birmingham Mail*, 13 December 1949.
90. See e.g. 'The first six-storey no fines flats', *Municipal Journal*, Vol.LXI, no.3141, 1 May 1953, pp.889–90.
91. *Your Business*, no.55, August 1951, p.1; *Birmingham Gazette*, 4 January 1951.
92. *Birmingham Gazette*, 22 May 1953; 28 July 1953.
93. *Birmingham Mail*, 20 March 1957.
94. John P. Macey, 'Problems of flat life', paper read at the Public Works and Municipal Services Congress, 12 November 1958.
95. *Birmingham Mail*, 19 January 1968.
96. *Birmingham Mail*, 18 July 1960.

Chapter 8 Multi-dwelling Building in Scotland 1750–1970: A study based on housing in the Clyde Valley

Roger Smith

Multi-Dwelling Buildings in Contemporary Scotland

Previous essays have shown that multi-dwelling building in England before the 1950s was rare.[1] On the whole the Englishman returned after the Second World War to 'a cottage type dwelling'. The demobilised Scottish soldier, on the other hand, returned more likely than not to a tenement. Within the context of urban housing throughout Western Europe the preponderance of multi-dwelling building in Scotland was far from remarkable. It was English housing that was a deviation. The 1966 Sample Census confirmed the wide differential in this matter between England and Scotland. In that year only 8 per cent of all dwellings in England and Wales had been originally designed to share a common building.[2] The Scottish figure was 51 per cent.[3]

A major factor responsible for this difference was the extensive volume of tenements that had been erected in Scotland during the nineteenth century. This was at a time when urban working-class accommodation in England was predominantly in the form of back-to-back court dwellings and bye-law terraced houses.[4] But whereas by 1966 most of the English back-to-back houses had been cleared, many of the early nineteenth-century tenements remained and so swelled the Scottish census figures for multi-dwelling building.

During the inter-war period there was something of a reaction to building tenements in Scotland. In the private market those who could afford to were buying bungalows on the outskirts of towns and cities whilst the local authorities, by now having become major providers of accommodation, were laying out municipal estates influenced by the English garden suburbs. But whereas in England municipal and private estates of the period were dominated by cottages, in Scotland the tenements, although now of a different design, still continued to be built. There were still, therefore, proportionately more multi-dwelling buildings being erected north of the border.

From the late 1950s onwards, however, the ratio of multi-dwelling buildings being erected in the two countries narrowed. This was partly because proportionately more cottage-type dwellings were being built

207

in Scotland and partly because more flats were being built in England and Wales. The number of approvals granted by the central government to local authorities for housing tenders submitted demonstrates this point.[5] Between 1960 and 1966 52 per cent of all approvals in England and Wales were for flats.[6] In Scotland the figure was somewhat higher at 59 per cent.[7] But whereas between 1967 and 1970 the English and Welsh figure had remained approximately the same (50 per cent) the Scottish one had fallen to 45 per cent.[8] The novel situation had thus arisen in which Scottish local authorities were building *pro rata* less flats than their English counterparts.

The 1960s was the period when high-rise blocks of flats came into vogue and during the first half of the decade they found equal favour in Scotland and England. Between 1960 and 1966 21 per cent of English and Welsh local authority approvals were for dwellings in blocks of five or more storeys.[9] In Scotland the figure was 20 per cent.[10] During the following four years, however, this situation changed a little. The proportion of dwellings approved in blocks of five or more storeys in Scotland remained the same but in England and Wales it had fallen to 18 per cent.[11] Thus by 1970 Scottish local authorities were tending to build either cottages or tower blocks whilst English local authorities were much more willing to compromise between these two extremes and provide low-rise flats.

Yet these post-1960 dwellings made up only a minor proportion of the total housing stocks of the two countries at the time of the census. Much more representative were those housing types built before 1939 and which consequently accentuated the basic national differences. But there is another point. The discussion has so far been restricted to local authority building. There is unfortunately no readily available data on the proportion of flats built by private developers. It can be argued, however, with a high degree of confidence that in both England and Scotland a very substantial proportion of private post-war dwellings were cottages. As, therefore, a higher proportion of local authority housing was built in Scotland (85 per cent of all post-war development up to 1970, compared with 54 per cent in England and Wales)[12] it is reasonable to assume that this would skew the proportion of cottages even further in favour of England.

But what of the distribution of multi-dwelling buildings in Scotland in 1966? According to Table 8.1 they dominated the country's four cities with Glasgow having the highest proportion (only a little under 90 per cent). Aberdeen had the lowest figure although even here it was nearly 60 per cent. These are especially noteworthy when comparisons

Table 8.1   Houses in Purpose Built Multi-Dwelling Buildings in the
              Major Cities of Scotland and England 1966.

	Total No. Dwellings	No. in Multi- Dwelling Buildings	Percentage of Dwellings Sharing Building to All Dwellings
Scotland			
Glasgow	322,440	282,190	87.5
Aberdeen	60,250	35,310	58.6
Dundee	63,780	41,990	65.8
Edinburgh	157,240	107,680	68.5
England			
Birmingham	325,320	30,810	9.5
Greater London	2,346,750	557,330	23.8
Leeds	174,410	19,220	11.0
Sheffield	169,800	15,160	8.9
Liverpool	200,310	24,040	12.0
Manchester	192,760	17,320	9.0

Source: General Register Office, Edinburgh, *Sample Census 1966,
          Scotland, County Reports, Aberdeen etc.; Dundee etc.;
          Edinburgh etc.; Glasgow etc.;* all H.M.S.O., Edinburgh,
          1967, all Table 5; General Register Office, *Sample Census
          1966, England and Wales County Reports, Greater London,
          Warwickshire, Yorkshire, Lancashire,* all H.M.S.O., London,
          1967, all Table 5.

are made with the larger English cities. Less than 24 per cent of housing in Greater London, for example, shared a building whilst in Sheffield the figure was less than 9 per cent.

The large-scale building of tenements in Scotland during the nineteenth century was undertaken to accommodate workers drawn into the central belt as it grew into prominence as one of the world's major industrial regions and Figure 8.1 shows that the East Central and to a much greater extent the West Central Region contained the highest proportions of homes in multi-dwelling buildings. This much might have been expected. More remarkable is the high proportion of such dwellings in the less industrialised parts. The Crofting Counties, which contain some of the least populous districts in Europe, had a higher proportion of multi-dwelling buildings than the major provincial towns of England. And the North East and the Borders had a higher proportion than Greater London.

A number of important questions arise from this sketch of multi-dwelling building in Scotland. Why was the tenement such a popular building form in the nineteenth century? What provoked the reaction against it and why was that reaction not more extensive? Is it possible to see the building of flats after 1945 as the continuation of an older tradition? Rather than attempting to provide answers by undertaking a superficial inquiry into the housing history of the whole of Scotland, a more detailed study will be made of Glasgow and its surrounds. Glasgow has been selected because it highlights why tenement building on a large scale was undertaken during the nineteenth century. And, because the social problems that were created as a result were of such magnitude, it is here that the reaction to the tenements in the 1920s and 1930s was most pronounced. Again Glasgow makes an illuminating study of those factors which were responsible for the building of flats, especially in tower and slab blocks, during the post-war period. But in discussing events after 1945 it has also been decided to draw upon the experiences of the new towns of East Kilbride and Cumbernauld. Both were linked with Glasgow. And because they had no pre-war history the extent to which flats were built in them can be used to gauge the degree to which 'anti-tenement' attitudes had taken root after 1945.

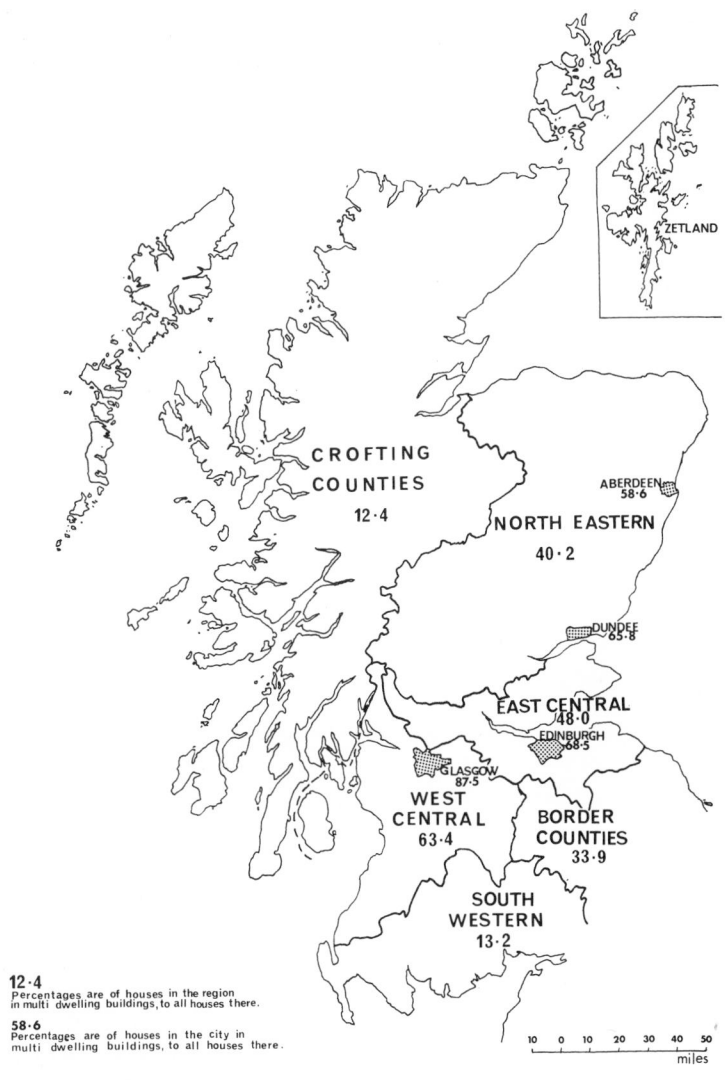

CROFTING
COUNTIES
12·4

NORTH EASTERN
40·2

ABERDEEN
58·6

DUNDEE
65·8

EAST CENTRAL
48·0

EDINBURGH
68·5

GLASGOW
87·5

WEST
CENTRAL
63·4

BORDER
COUNTIES
33·9

SOUTH
WESTERN
13·2

ZETLAND

12·4
Percentages are of houses in the region
in multi dwelling buildings, to all houses there.

58·6
Percentages are of houses in the city in
multi dwelling buildings, to all houses there.

10 0 10 20 30 40 50
                        miles

8.1 Houses in multi-dwelling buildings by Scottish regions, 1966.

The Origins of Scottish Tenements and Their Adoption in the Clyde Valley

Relatively little is known about the origins of the tenements in Scotland. It is, however, generally assumed that they first appeared in Edinburgh during the sixteenth century.[13] A defensive settlement was established from a very early date on the Castle Rock, an ideal strategic point controlling a major route to the Highlands.[14] The rock made a virtually impregnable defensive position because of the escarpments that surrounded it. This topography, however, created problems when in the thirteenth century King David I wanted to lay out a market town to adjoin the castle and thereby attract Scottish and foreign merchants.[15] The only possible site was a relatively narrow ridge stretching out to the east from the rock. Immediately adjoining the northern side of that ridge was Nor'loch, a swampy area at the bottom of a steep cliff. This was mirrored on the south side by a second loch, Cowgate. A third loch, Holyrood, lying to the east, brought the ridge to an end. Initially there was sufficient room for an elongated settlement to establish itself, like a tail attached to the castle. But the city's prosperity and corresponding population growth created a land shortage. Until the Hanoverian peace it was unsafe to build extensive satellite settlements away from the castle and the protective walls of the parent city. This meant that Edinburgh had to grow upwards. Perhaps drawing on the experience of France this is what began to happen in the sixteenth century,[16] and the original wooden two- and three-storey dwellings were replaced by stone buildings rising frequently to seven or eight storeys and exceptionally to thirteen.

There were, however, also sound commercial reasons for building tenements in Edinburgh. Under Scottish law the seller of land had the right to demand an annual fee (feu duty) from the purchaser. As this feu was fixed in perpetuity the seller would, of course, insist on obtaining the maximum he could. Consequently the purchaser and the developer would be equally anxious to maximise their returns by constructing as many dwellings per acre as possible. The tenement was an ideal way of doing this.[17] These newer tenements were built very closely together and the main street itself was consequently narrow. Even narrower were the lanes leading off. David Buchanan, a citizen of Edinburgh with a wide knowledge of the Continent, writing between 1642 and 1652, commented that, 'I am not sure that you will find anywhere so many dwellings and such a multitude of people in so small space as in this city of·ours'.[18]

It should not however be thought that during the first half of the eighteenth century the Edinburgh tenements were unique in Scotland. On a smaller scale, both in terms of height and numbers, they could be found in towns such as Stirling, another settlement guarding a major thoroughfare. But paradoxically, tenement building did not become established in the Clyde Valley until the 1780s at a time when the wealthier classes of Edinburgh had decided to forsake them in favour of elegant terraced houses, now provided in a new town which was being laid out to the north of the older settlement on land opened up after the construction of a bridge over Nor'loch.[19]

This is not the place to examine the growth of Glasgow from the small academic and ecclesiastical community that it was in the sixteenth century to the important mercantile centre, with a commanding share of the American tobacco trade, that it had become by the middle of the eighteenth century.[20] Neither is this the place to analyse the effect of the trade in providing capital for and otherwise stimulating those industrial enterprises which were taking root during that period. Suffice it to note that by the 1780s Glasgow had a flourishing linen industry. Then from 1792 onwards, as steam replaced water power, spinning factories, previously located in surrounding rural areas, began to be established in the town. This early factory system was reinforced in 1801 when Glasgow's first steam-powered weaving looms were set in motion.

This industrial revolution that was generated in Glasgow, as well as in many of the other towns of the region, created a substantial demand for labour which began to pour in from rural areas in the central belt as well as from the Highlands and Islands and Ireland. It was to accommodate these newcomers that the tenements were first built in any numbers in the western parts of the country. But why tenements? Why not the back-to-back dwellings that were being built in England? A simple answer is probably that for the Scottish builder tenements were more profitable. The cost of building a stone dwelling in a tenement, seemingly, was no greater than building a comparable cottage of brick.[21] On the other hand, tenement building enabled more houses per acre to be built; an important factor because of the feu system.

Even so, without supplies of local stone the tenements could not have been built. Neither could they have been built had there been no precedent for them on the other side of the country. The Edinburgh tenements served as models providing basic pools of experience from which the builders in the west could draw. In addition, because of the early experiences of Edinburgh and the other towns in the east,

Scottish law had accommodated itself to this type of building in a way that English law had not. In Scotland it was possible to purchase an individual flat even if it was off the ground.

Initially the tenements in Glasgow adjoined roads and were provided with some land at the rear ('back greens'). During the first four decades of the nineteenth century the textile industry continued to prosper but so did the newly emerging engineering and shipbuilding industries. As a result the population of the burgh increased threefold to 256,000. The built-up area of Glasgow consequently expanded to the south across the Clyde into the Gorbals as well as to the east and west. But in addition there was the building of the notorious 'backjams' or 'backlands'.[22] These were tenements erected in the back greens. From this point onwards the majority of citizens were now denied fresh air and sunlight and compelled to live at densities in excess of 1,000 persons per acre. The classic Glasgow slum had been formed.

The early tenements of Glasgow, unlike those in Edinburgh, tended to have only four storeys, although higher ones could be found. The tenement blocks usually stretched the length of a street and a series of dark passages led from the front of the tenements to an enclosed spiral staircase at the rear (see Fig. 8.2). These stairs then wound up to an inverted T-shaped corridor on each of the floors. There were two two-roomed dwellings in each of the right-angles formed by the T and two more two-roomed dwellings opposite them. Then at the two ends of the bar of the T were two one-roomed dwellings. In other words each floor contained eight dwellings, four with two rooms and four with only one. A major structural problem was that, because the passages contained no outside wall, no light even at midday and practically no fresh air could penetrate.[23]

Yet as early as the 1860s, Glasgow Corporation, perhaps the most enlightened in Britain at that time, began its fight to improve the city's housing environment. In 1866 the Glasgow Improvement Act was passed setting up a Housing Trust with powers to demolish properties in eighty-eight acres of slums and replace them with more wholesome dwellings.[24] Eventually, supplemented by further Improvement Acts in 1871 and 1897, this task was accomplished. But the 1,646 dwellings that were erected to replace those that were demolished were tenements, although redesigned to enable a little fresh air and sunlight to enter the passages and built at somewhat lower densities. There were also a number of bye-laws passed in Glasgow from 1866 onwards that, to an extent, regulated for the better the design and distribution of the tenements.[25] Thus during the period 1851–1911, when ship-building

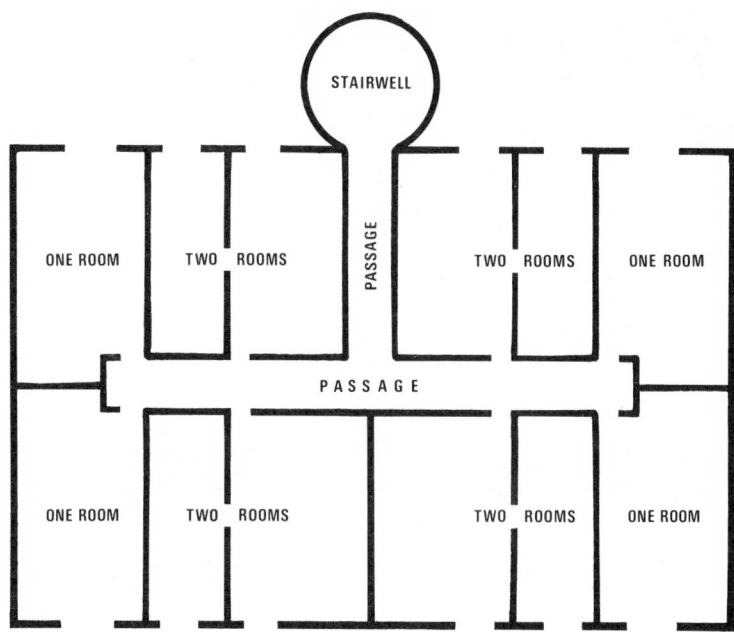

8.2 Sketch plan of an early nineteenth-century Scottish tenement.

and other major engineering enterprises were growing apace and during which time the city's population had risen to 784,000, there was a small but undoubted improvement in Glasgow's housing environment.

The tenement was not, of course, an exclusively working-class form of accommodation. During the seventeenth and eighteenth centuries the wealthier classes in Edinburgh frequently shared them with some of the poorest, although the New Town effectively brought that tradition to an end. The late eighteenth and early nineteenth centuries also witnessed attempts in Glasgow to build a 'new town' of elegant terraced houses for the wealthy of the city. Land in the Gorbals was originally laid out for that purpose but the inability of the developers to exclude industry dissuaded the rich from settling there and subsequently the area was given over to working-class tenements.[26] Much more successful was the building of elegant terraces and circuses to the west of the older settlement. These, however, were dwellings exclusively for the wealthy merchants and entrepreneurs. They were certainly beyond the means of the lower bourgeoisie, a social class that was growing as the city's industries began to demand an increasing number of lawyers,

Plate XIX. Frontages of late nineteenth-century tenements, MacLellan Street, Tradeston, Glasgow.

accountants and managers. For these people a superior type of tenement was built. Externally these tenements resembled those for the working classes that were being built in Maryhill. But internally all similarities ended and the superior dwellings frequently had seven rooms including bathrooms, toilets, extensive halls, etc.

Despite the change of design during the nineteenth century the evils associated with this type of housing were still very evident at the outbreak of the Great War. This was a point which was emphasised in the *Report of the Royal Commission on Housing in Scotland*, issued in 1917. Most of the Glasgow 'backlands' still stood and 'even in a hot dry summer', the Commissioners commented, '(such tenements) remain damp and unwholesome'.[27] A by no means untypical street was 'known as "The Coffin Close", so bad is its repute — narrow stairs and dark twisting lobbies, with no light and absolutely no air'.[28] The majority of the Commissioners also voiced their disapproval of single-roomed dwellings, which housed 105,000 Glaswegians and which were still being built. The most poignant attack on them came from

James Russell, previously the city's Medical Officer of Health, when he claimed that:

> 'Of all the children who die in Glasgow before they complete their fifth year, 32 per cent die in houses of one apartment, and not 2 per cent in houses of five apartments and upwards. There they die, and their little bodies are laid on a table or on the dresser so as to be somewhat out of the way of their brothers and sisters, who play and sleep and eat in their ghastly company. From beginning to rapid-ending, the lives of these children are short parts in a continuous tragedy.'[29]

In terms of the scale of its housing problem it was clear that Glasgow was unique in Scotland, but the *Report* also demonstrates that tenements and the social disorders that arose from them were distributed throughout the country. In describing the typical Scottish town the Commissioners suggested that the outskirts were 'marked by an irregular row of small cottages along the side of the highway, gradually rising in height from one to two or three storeys, and eventually, as we approach the centre of the town, to the typical four storey tenement'. The Commissioners then noted the general congestion and lack of air and sunlight in the central areas. 'This condition,' it was commented, 'which is to be found from Dumfries in the South to Lerwick in the far North, is a good example of the similarity or even identity, . . . which marks the housing problem in the towns of Scotland.'[30]

Glasgow Housing 1919—1947

By the beginning of the twentieth century the lower middle classes of Glasgow were beginning to leave their tenements for bungalows and cottages in the suburbs. An early example of this reaction to what was by now traditional Glasgow housing was the founding of a garden suburb at Westerton.[31] Financed on co-ownership principles, the plans were drawn up by Raymond Unwin. Yet Westerton was developed on a limited scale and quantitatively a much more significant indication of the move away from tenements was the growing volume of cottages built outside the municipal limits during the inter-war years.

But there was also a reaction to the tenements on the part of the Glasgow Corporation, encouraged partly by the findings of the Royal

Commission. Even so the Commissioners made no outright condemnation of the tenements although the tenement concept was heavily criticised. It was put that, compared with cottages, even in the best tenements parents could not supervise their children properly, the stairs were frequently filthy, outbreaks of fire were more dangerous and there was greater difficulty in policing.[32] The Commissioners, therefore, recommended that the single-roomed house should no longer be built and in order to allow the free passage of fresh air and the penetration of sunlight to all parts of the building a maximum height was suggested of three storeys. It was further recommended that the tenements were to be built in free-standing blocks. Open spaces should be interspersed amongst the buildings.[33]

The Royal Commission Report was issued at a time which was ripe for recasting older attitudes. The Great War slogan of 'Homes fit for Heroes' was still untarnished and the ideas of Ebenezer Howard and Raymond Unwin were becoming influential. And then, especially on Clydeside, there was the impact of the growing Labour Movement with its insistence on improving housing conditions. The ideal of cottage-type dwellings with gardens was beginning to take root in the region. Means to achieve at least a part of this ideal were provided in a series of Housing Acts, beginning in 1919, which enabled the Exchequer to subsidise municipal housing schemes.[34] But if Glasgow was to achieve

Plate XX. Two-storey flats built in the 1930s, Barrhead Road, Pollok, Glasgow.

anything in the housing field after 1918 it needed more land. This it obtained and between 1926 and 1938 some 20,500 acres were added to the city leaving it with a total of just under 40,000 acres.[35]

To what extent, then, was the new housing ideal achieved during the inter-war period? Certainly none of the type of tenements that had been built before 1914 were erected between the wars, although it will be seen from Table 8.2 that of the 52,000 municipal houses that were built between 1919 and 1946 just over half were flats. They were, however, only three storeys high and their design would have met, on the whole, with the approval of those who had sat on the Royal Commission. Densities were relatively low and plenty of open spaces were left. The notable figure in the table is, however, the 17 per cent of cottage-type dwellings. In comparison with municipal housing in England at that time this may seem a derisory figure. However, bearing in mind Scottish housing traditions such a figure is remarkably high. In addition there were the 'four in a block' houses which, being two-storey cottage flats in blocks of four, had far more in common with the twentieth-century English 'semi' than with the nineteenth-century Scottish tenement.

Attempts by Glasgow to absorb garden-suburb thinking were most successful in the early and mid-1920s. It was then that the Mosspark, Knightswood and Carntyne Estates were laid out at net densities of no greater than twelve houses to the acre.[36]

Figure 8.3 shows that the proportion of flats built by Glasgow Corporation rose especially during the first half of the 1930s. This was partly because many of the dwellings built then were on cleared sites and it was considered desirable to rehouse in flats in order to reduce decantation from those areas. And whereas in the 1920s municipal house-building had been directed to a general need, which meant that the more prosperous of the working classes were being offered cottages at rents somewhat above what would be paid for flats, during the 1930s municipal building was now aimed more specifically at helping those living in overcrowded conditions. As these were often the poorest sections of the community it was thought prudent to offer the cheaper forms of accommodation, namely flats. Typical of the Glasgow housing estates of the 1930s was Blackhill with 74 per cent of its housing in flats and only 4 per cent in cottages. Even so there was a dramatic contrast to the older housing.

Between 1919 and 1939 the Glasgow Corporation demolished some 15,000 unfit houses.[37] Yet the problems of the tenements largely remained. Overcrowding, it is true, fell a little partly because of a

Table 8.2   Municipal Flat Building in Glasgow 1919–1946

(a) Whole of Glasgow

	Act under which Built	% Municipal Houses built as:-			Total No. Municipal Houses Built
		Cottages	4 in Block	Flats	
	1919	46.9	38.0	15.1	4,690
	1923	14.6	13.3	72.1	9,026
	1924	14.9	46.0	39.1	21,586
	1930–35*	7.6	19.5	72.9	11,731
	1938	24.2	25.2	50.6	4,551
	Total	16.9	31.7	51.4	51,584
(b) Selected Estates					
1 Mosspark	1919	67.4	32.6	—	1,510
2 Knightswood	1923) 1924)	42.9	57.1	—	6,056
3 Carntyne	1924	26.7	72.2	1.1	2,924
4 Blackhill	1930–35	3.6	22.4	74.0	1,324

N.B. excluding 99   1-apartment dwellings built as hostels.

Source: Based on figures in, A.G. Jury, *Housing Centenary, A Review of Municipal Housing in Glasgow from 1866–1966. The Corporation of the City of Glasgow Housing Committee, 1966,* Tables VI, VII, VIII, IX, X.

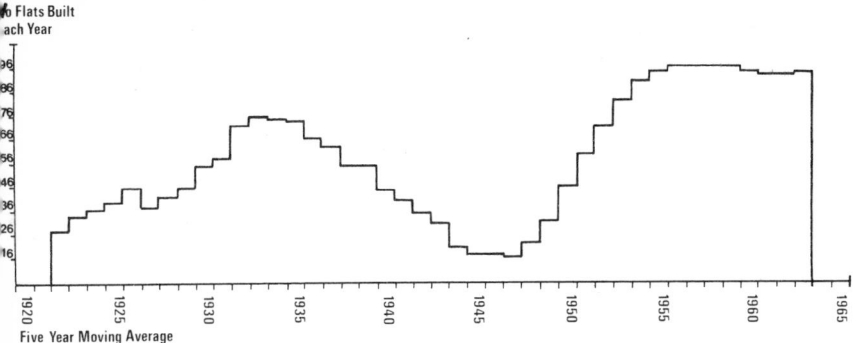

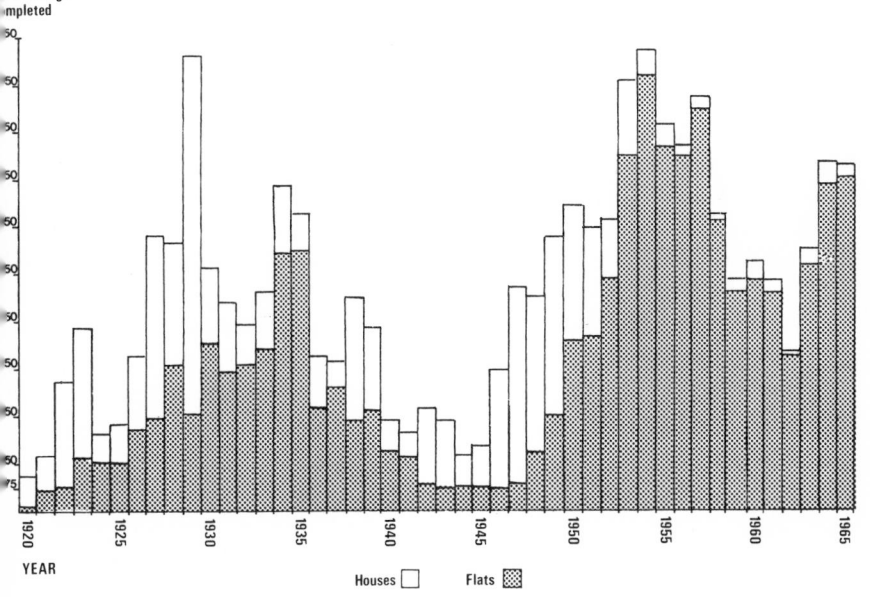

8.3 Flats in Glasgow, 1920–1965.

movement out to the new municipal estates and partly because of a movement away from the country as the region's industrial structure collapsed. But whilst the depression may have indirectly eased congestion the poverty and degradation it brought in its wake added considerably to the strain of living in the tenements.[38] In 1942, therefore, Glasgow Corporation's attention was again redirected to the question of slum clearance in a preliminary report on post-war planning prepared by the Town Clerk.[39] A significant point to emerge from the report was that the low-density developments undertaken during the inter-war period had been too prodigal of land. In order to undertake rehousing schemes in the central areas it would be necessary to transfer a substantial volume of population to the outer reaches of the city. There was, however, relatively little virgin land left there and a further boundary extension was regarded as unrealistic. The building of new towns was also felt by the Corporation to be undesirable and impracticable. Consequently it was reluctantly agreed that post-war municipal estates would have to be built at densities higher than those previously adopted.

Meanwhile the wartime Secretary of State for Scotland, Thomas Johnston, had convened an advisory planning committee made up of representatives of all the local authorities in the Clyde Valley region. Subsequently a small full-time technical committee, headed by Sir Patrick Abercrombie, was appointed to prepare a regional plan. A major concern of this technical committee was with the enormous congestion that still remained in Glasgow where in the mid-1940s over 700,000 persons lived in less than three square miles.[40] Using the more detailed work undertaken by Robert Bruce, the city's Municipal Engineer, Abercrombie and his team came to the conclusion that Glasgow should be redeveloped at net densities in the central areas of 120 persons per acre, ninety per acre in the intermediate zone and sixty per acre in the outer parts. If these figures were to be obtained 500,000 would have to leave the central areas. It was where they were to be resettled that provoked a major disagreement between Glasgow and the Regional Planners.

The Clyde Valley by this time had become one of the most congested regions in Europe. Glasgow had a population in excess of one million and the other towns in the region, despite the effects of the inter-war depression, were physically expanding. Abercrombie was anxious to prevent these towns from merging with each other and with Glasgow. He therefore recommended a green belt to envelop the whole of the region, thereby containing the physical growth of these towns which were held within it.[41] Furthermore Abercrombie wanted the green belt to encroach over Glasgow's boundaries. This was partly because he believed that the city was already too large, partly to keep open land between it and its neighbouring towns and partly to preserve areas of high scenic value. By denying Glasgow land upon which to build Abercrombie found that there was room within the city to accommodate only 250,000 of those to be displaced from the central areas. The rest would have to be rehoused outside Glasgow. For them Abercrombie recommended the designation of four new towns to be set within the green belt.

Glasgow Corporation objected to the proposed encroachment of the green belt over the city boundaries and the designation of new towns.[42] Without such a policy, it was argued, Glasgow would have sufficient land within its boundaries to undertake all the rehousing that was needed. However, for reasons that are too complex to enter into here, the Scottish Office, the central department responsible for housing and town and country planning in Scotland, decided in the face of bitter opposition from Glasgow to accept Abercrombie's recommendations on the green belt and new towns and accordingly East Kilbride was designated in 1947.[43] The effects of this conflict were to have a profound effect on multi-dwelling building in Glasgow. The Scottish Office remained determined to preserve the green belt and was anxious that Glasgow should lose a substantial proportion of its population through overspill schemes. Glasgow, on the other hand, agreed to overspill only reluctantly and attempted to build upwards in an attempt to accommodate as many of its population as possible.

Glasgow Housing 1947–1971

Flat-building after 1945 by Glasgow Corporation fell into two periods. During much of the 1950s a very high proportion of new municipal houses were flats in blocks of three and four storeys. The second period, which extended throughout the 1960s, witnessed the building of flats in tower and slab blocks. Certainly had the assumptions of either Abercrombie or Bruce held good the three- and four-storey block would not have dominated the housing of the 1950s. It is true that the redevelopment of the central areas of Glasgow at 120 net persons to the acre would have meant building a substantial proportion of 'new tenements' there.[44] But on the outskirts of the city, where both planners wanted to see net densities of no more than sixty persons per acre, there would have been room for a substantial number of cottages. This point was demonstrated in the *Clyde Valley Plan* which gave detailed specimen layouts for the Vale of Leven which with only a minimum of alteration could equally have been used in Glasgow.[45] However the Bruce plan was unworkable once the Scottish Office had decided to implement Abercrombie's green belt recommendations. Densities of sixty persons to the acre on the outskirts of Glasgow could only be obtained under these circumstances provided that the Scottish Office also built new towns. A start was made with the designation of East Kilbride which was built under the 1946 New Towns Act (i.e. the Treasury would provide the necessary finance through loans). During the early post-war years the Scottish Office intended that at least two more new towns should be provided in the Clyde Valley in order to realise the recommendations in the Regional Plan. However by the early 1950s it was decided after some years of uncertainty that, on grounds of economy, the 1946 Act would have to be shelved.

This put Glasgow in a great dilemma because the situation had arisen whereby the Scottish Office had denied the city building land for housing, whilst at the same time refusing to provide it with overspill towns. To add to Glasgow's problems much valuable building land had been used up immediately after the war by low-density housing developments. If the city was to provide any dwellings during those years it had to use non-traditional materials. For technical reasons, this necessitated low-density building.

By the early 1950s Glasgow Corporation reacted to the pressing need for accommodation by preparing housing estates on what land remained on the outskirts at densities well in excess of the sixty to the acre that had been originally thought desirable. But even by doing this the Corporation realised that it would not be able to rehouse all those in need. Somewhat under 50,000 municipal houses were built under the 1946, 1950 and 1952 Housing Acts, i.e. between 1946 and *circa* 1957 (see Table 8.3), and nearly three-quarters of them were flats. This contrasts with the 50 per cent figure during the inter-war period. Some of the early post-war developments, as at Pollok for example, still had a relatively high proportion of cottages (for reasons mentioned above) and the 'four in a block' flats continued to be built. But later schemes, such as Easterhouse, contained, almost exclusively, rows of three- and four-storey flats. Indeed Easterhouse is one of the most notorious examples of an estate planned solely to provide the maximum number of houses and with very little attention given to the provision of services.

Table 8.3   Municipal Flat Building in Glasgow Under 1946/1950/ 1952 Housing Acts.

Percentages

Major Estates	Cottages	4 in a Block	Flats	Total
Castlemilk	5.5	–	94.5	7,726
Easterhouse	.6	–	99.4	3,163
Pollok	28.7	14.3	57.0	4,514
Glasgow	19.4	9.5	71.1	49,013

Source: Based on figures in, A.G. Jury, *Housing Centenary, A Review of Municipal Housing in Glasgow from 1866–1966.* The Corporation of the City of Glasgow Housing Committee, 1966, Table XI.

In view of the chronic land shortage which had resulted in 'a return to the tenement type of development and average densities of up to 100 persons per acre ... contrasting sharply with the density of Knightswood, for example, which is under fifty persons per acre'[46] it might be asked why Glasgow was not one of the first post-war cities to build high-rise flats. Why did Glasgow lag behind some of the London boroughs, Birmingham and Coventry? A major factor was finance. High-rise flats were twice as expensive to build as cottage-type dwellings and they were also costly to run. And until 1957 there were no additional Government subsidies given to cover the extra cost. Glasgow was by no means a prosperous city and it argued that it could not afford the extra expense. It is true that at about this time a handful of experimental and prestigious tower blocks were built in the city but these were isolated examples; Glasgow had not yet been seduced by the glossy propaganda for high-rise living that was dominating the architectural press.

Glasgow's drive to build a substantial number of tower blocks did not begin until the late 1950s and early 1960s and this change of policy was closely associated with its plans to undertake an ambitious slum clearance scheme.[47] Up to 1954 Glasgow's primary housing concern had been to provide accommodation for the overcrowded and those on the general waiting lists. It was not until then that firm proposals were

Plate XXI. Four-storey flats built in the 1950s, Monymusk Place, Drumchapel, Glasgow. Note the similarity to the tenements in Plate XIX.

made to clear some of the worst slums in Hutchesontown and part of the Gorbals. The choice lay between slum clearance and Comprehensive Development Area powers. The Corporation decided to seek permission from the Secretary of State to pursue the latter course. This was given in 1957. Meanwhile in that year a report had been prepared delineating twenty-eight other areas in need of urgent treatment. In 1960 it was announced that permission to designate them all as C.D.A.s would be sought. In total they contained 118,500 houses, 80,700 of which were to be demolished as soon as possible.[48] Because of the high densities in the C.D.A.s less than half of those displaced by these schemes could be rehoused in the areas from which they had come. This problem only exacerbated the already acute land shortage in the city. Unless something was done quickly, all house building in Glasgow would have to cease as would the clearance schemes. Realising that this was likely to happen Glasgow Corporation, the Scottish Office and the Treasury agreed that the city should, after all, have a second 'overspill' town.

Cumbernauld was accordingly designated in 1956. The Treasury appeared adamant, however, that no more towns would be designated within the near future under the New Towns Act. For Glasgow, as well as the Scottish Office, this was something of a blow because two new towns were not enough to absorb all the overspill necessary before the city's housing problems could be solved. As a means to resolve this dilemma, therefore, a two-pronged approach was devised by the Scottish Office. The necessary legislation was embodied in the 1957

Housing and Town Development (Scotland) Act.[49] Scotland had not been included in the 1952 Town Development Act which had enabled English cities with congestion problems to make arrangements for their excess populations to be settled in other local authorities with land surplus to their own requirements. Under the 1957 Act Glasgow could make similar overspill arrangements. This it was hoped would compensate for the lack of more new towns.

The second prong of the new approach embodied in the Act was the provision of substantial subsidies to encourage the building of multistorey blocks of flats. The subsidy consisted of what was then the normal £24 for sixty years plus two-thirds of the extra cost incurred by building high when compared with that of building a cottage-type dwelling. The Scottish Office, confronted with the chronic land shortage that was facing many of the towns and cities of the country, but especially Glasgow, had decided to go for high-rise development as a means to push up residential densities. In many respects this appears to have been a panic reaction to a pressing problem, caused by the failure to implement a workable and substantial overspill policy for Glasgow during the late 1940s and early 1950s. Indeed there was some opposition to the building of high-rise flats from the planners within the Scottish Department of Health (responsible until 1962 for planning in the country). Certainly Robert Grieve, Chief Planner in the Scottish Office between 1960 and 1964, was critical of efforts to achieve net densities in excess of 120 persons per acre in the central areas of Glasgow when he wrote:

'Glasgow knows – and increasingly other towns will know – that the prospects of central reconstruction are in direct ratio to the success of these wider policies of planning. The dangerously simple expedient of higher and higher densities does not bear examination.'[50]

It is true that the Scottish Office in the late 1950s did have to put constraints on Glasgow in order to prevent it from building tower blocks at very high densities indeed. Nevertheless Glasgow was given permission to build high-rise flats resulting in densities greater than Abercrombie, Bruce, or Grieve would have approved.

As early as 1956 a small joint working party of officials from Glasgow and the Scottish Office was set up to consider the possibility of building multi-storey blocks within the city. The Housing Department of Glasgow Corporation was therefore able to take advantage of the new thinking to plan for high-density development in the new Hutchesontown/Gorbals C.D.A. In order to obtain a net residential density of 164 persons per acre there, of the 3,154 proposed dwellings, 1,800 were to be in twenty-five high-rise blocks and the rest in two-, three-, and four-storey buildings.[51] Designs for the multi-storey blocks were submitted by architects as eminent as Sir Basil Spence and Sir Robert Matthew.

It would be wrong, however, to interpret the building of high-rise flats in Glasgow as simply a response to the failure at a national level to formulate and implement a wide-ranging and sensitive overspill policy during the 1950s. By the end of the 1930s the Glasgow Housing Committee had become, in the hands of a Labour administration, the most powerful and prestigeous committee in the local authority. Because of this the primary goal of the Glasgow administration — a goal which was to dominate the city's politics during the post-war period — was to build the highest-possible number of dwellings a year.

During the 1950s Glasgow was able to fulfil that ambition through building low-rise flats on the outskirts of the city and between 1951 and 1960 on average 4,627 dwellings per year were completed. But obviously such a rate could not continue once land on the outer periphery had been utilised. Consequently high-rise blocks of flats were seen as a means to keep up the building rate. With the new system-building techniques major building contractors could erect these blocks with great speed. Completion rates could thus retain some of their former impetus and between 1961 and 1970 output was still impressive at 3,451 dwellings per year.

Originally the upper storeys of the high-rise flats were to be reserved for childless couples, but this soon became an impossibility as the Glasgow Corporation attempted to build as many high-rise blocks as it could in the C.D.A.s (see Appendix). Then it was decided to amend the original policy even further and to build these tall blocks on the outskirts of the city, thereby pushing net densities there well above the 100 persons per acre level.

But was this obsession with high-rise blocks necessary during the 1960s? Arguably not because of the large numbers of people leaving the city during that decade. By 1971 Glasgow's population was 897,000, having fallen from 1,090,000 in 1951. This was partially the result of the post-1957 overspill scheme which, although it did not live up completely to expectations was, nonetheless, one of the most successful in Britain.[52] Much more significant, however, was the exceptionally high proportion of Glaswegians who left the city without official

Plate XXII. Hutchesontown-Gorbals redevelopment, Glasgow. Area B (1962) foreground, shows 17-storey blocks by Robert Matthew, Johnson-Marshall and Partners. Area C (1965) background, has slab blocks each of which contain 400 crossover maisonettes, designed by Sir Basil Spence, Glover and Ferguson.

encouragement. This exodus eased pressure on accommodation within the municipal limits far more than had been anticipated in the late 1950s. If this was the case, why did the Scottish Office allow Glasgow to continue with its policy of building high-rise blocks of flats? Until the relevant documents are released one can only speculate. However during the 1960s there were successively three Chief Planners in the Scottish Office. Under such circumstances its technical staff was not as rigorous in examining Glasgow's proposals as it had been during the 1950s and early 1960s. Consequently the city had a greater opportunity to go its own way.

But what was the scale of this high-rise building? By 1971 there were 208 tower blocks in Glasgow containing 20,836 flats. This, as will be seen from Table 8.4, amounted to nearly 40 per cent of all dwellings built by Glasgow since 1957. Although there are no published figures available the remaining dwellings were predominantly low-rise flats. From the table it will be seen that by 1971 somewhat under half the high-rise blocks built throughout Glasgow had between twenty and twenty-four storeys and contained consequently over half of all

Table 8.4   Dwellings in Tower and Slab Blocks in Glasgow 1971.

No. Tower and Slab Blocks

No. Storeys	Glasgow No.	%	C.D.A.s No.	%	Glasgow excluding C.D.A.s No.	%
8–14	60	28.8	12	15.6	48	36.6
15–19	35	16.8	15	19.5	20	15.3
20–24	90	43.3	37	48.0	53	40.4
25–29	15	7.2	11	14.3	4	3.1
30–	8	3.9	2	2.6	6	4.6
Total	208	100.0	77	100.0	131	100.0

Houses in Tower and Slab Blocks

No. Storeys	Glasgow No.	%	C.D.A.s No.	%	Glasgow excluding C.D.A.s No.	%
8–14	2,359	11.3	640	7.0	1,719	14.7
15–19	3,248	15.6	1,214	13.2	2,034	17.5
20–24	11,763	56.5	5,381	58.6	6,382	54.7
25–29	2,398	11.5	1,592	17.4	806	6.9
30–	1,068	5.1	348	3.8	720	6.2
Total	20,836	100.0	9,175	100.0	11,661	100.0

Source: Based on figures in A.G. Jury, *Housing Centenary, A Review of Municipal Housing in Glasgow from 1866–1966.* The Corporation of the City of Glasgow, 1966, pp.49–54.

multi-storey flats. A slightly higher proportion of high-rise blocks had under twenty storeys but they, of course, held only a relatively small proportion of high-rise flats (just over one quarter). Only about one-tenth of the blocks had more than twenty-four storeys but they contained 17 per cent of all high-rise flats. Comparative figures show, as might have been expected, that the C.D.A.s contained a substantially higher proportion of blocks with twenty and more storeys than the rest of Glasgow but, perhaps more unexpectedly, a lower proportion of blocks with thirty or more storeys.

Flats in the New Towns

Having analysed some of the factors which were responsible for the high proportion of flats in Glasgow, attention can now be focused on East Kilbride and Cumbernauld. First, then, East Kilbride. Although it has sometimes erroneously been described as a 'garden city', its first detailed Master Plan, completed in 1950, did owe a great deal to the low-density concepts that had been explored at Letchworth and later Welwyn Garden City.[53] For Sir Patrick Dollan, the first chairman of the Development Corporation (the statutory body empowered to build the town), East Kilbride was to be designed to contrast as sharply as possible with the housing environment of central Glasgow. This meant providing as many cottage-type dwellings as possible. By the mid-1940s Dollan, a former Lord Provost of Glasgow, had come to hate the notion of flats and ideally would have wanted none in his town. This was not, however, practicable. East Kilbride had been designated as part of a regional strategy to help to ease congestion in Glasgow and North Lanarkshire. If it was to play its role adequately it would have to absorb 40–45,000 immigrants. However, extensive sites were not available in the hilly terrain of the Clyde Valley. Consequently it was argued that if a new town was to be built in the vicinity of East Kilbride, and if it was to have a full complement of industries and services, only 1,900 acres would be available for the 12,000 houses it was estimated a population of 45,000 persons would need. Because the amount of land was severely restricted in East Kilbride net residential densities would have to be up to forty persons per acre.[54] This meant that one-third of the dwellings had to be in the form of low-rise flats. A compromise between the Garden City ideal as it had developed in England during the 1930s and the traditional Scottish attitude to urban housing had been reached. Nonetheless this still meant much lower net

Table 8.5   Houses Built by East Kilbride Development Corporation
1950–1971.

Year ending March	No. Houses Built per Year	No. Flats Built per Year	% Flats to all Houses Built per Year	% Flats to all Houses; Accumulated Totals
1950	68	24	35	35
1951	178	–	–	10
1952	97	–	–	7
1953	458	33	7	7
1954	1,008	228	23	16
1955	1,011	378	37	23
1956	1,012	457	45	29
1957	759	241	32	30
1958	712	153	22	29
1959	961	326	34	29
1960	1,057	601	57	33
1961	919	514	56	36
1962	478	281	59	37
1963	571	248	43	38
1964	832	250	30	37
1965	1,345	609	45	38
1966	1,101	494	45	38
1967	1,486	809	54	40
1968	1,433	861	60	42
1969	1,200	407	34	41
1970	948	434	46	42
1971	545	226	45	42

Source: Figures provided by East Kilbride Development Corporation

densities for East Kilbride than those recommended for the outskirts of Glasgow.

Table 8.5 shows the percentages of flats built in East Kilbride annually between 1950 and 1971. It will be seen that up to March 1953 only a very small percentage of them had been built. The policy decided upon was to provide as many cottage-type dwellings as possible, initially to accommodate the young families who were expected to make up the first immigrants; later, flats would be provided for couples after their families had grown up and left home. From the mid-1950s onwards, however, pressure was brought to bear on the Development Corporation by the Scottish Office to increase the proportion of flats in the town. It was during these years, it will be remembered, that the Scottish Office and Glasgow Corporation were attempting to encourage a substantial volume of the population to leave the city. As part of this strategy East Kilbride was to take more Glaswegians than was originally intended and its target population was to be raised to 50,000, although no provision was made to increase the town's built-up area. This meant that housing densities would have to be increased by providing substantially more than one-third of the dwellings as flats.[55] Dollan tried to resist this and, although he gained some short-term concessions, in the long run he was unable to resist the dictates of central government. The effect of this in terms of flats can be seen with the increasing volume of them being built in the new town, although by 1960 they still made up only one-third of all completed dwellings.

The late 1950s and early 1960s, however, mark a turning point in the history of East Kilbride. The Development Corporation now became anxious to play a more direct role in taking Glasgow families. For the first time in 1959 East Kilbride reached a formal agreement with Glasgow, in accordance with the 1957 Town Development Act, to take overspill families nominated by the City.[56] Up to that date East Kilbride had taken only those who had already found work in the town and the Development Corporation was not too concerned where they had come from, although a high proportion did in fact come from Glasgow. During the early 1960s the target population was also increased by stages to 82,000 (i.e. the town was to hold more than twice what had been originally intended).[57] This was a clear response to increasing pressure for overspill outlets once the clearance schemes in Glasgow had got underway. However, these increases in the target population were accompanied by proposals for the extension of the planned built-up area by developing land which in the 1940s had been thought too difficult to build on. Nonetheless the proportion of low-rise flats also had to be raised and Table 8.5 shows that by 1971 the proportion of them that had been built had risen to 42 per cent. The shortage of building land in Glasgow, which had partly resulted in its building an extremely large proportion of high-rise flats in the mid- and late-1960s, had repercussions on East Kilbride. Nonetheless for all its desire to contribute to easing the housing problems of the region, the Development Corporation could still see the need for and the desirability of building cottages. Even so the Development Corporation could also see virtue in high-rise blocks and set about building twelve of them.

The Development Corporation had first given serious thought to the provision of high-rise flats in 1962, at a time when they were held in high esteem by central and local government.[58] In the case of East Kilbride, however, the Scottish Office advised caution and warned that it would not be prepared to meet the extra costs involved. A turning point came in 1965 when a market research exercise showed, contrary to many expectations, that there was a demand for high-quality flats in tower blocks even at rents three times those charged for their low-rise equivalents.[59] As a result, by 1971 1,068 dwellings had been built in high-rise blocks, nine of fifteen storeys and three of sixteen, nineteen and twenty storeys.

It had always been the ambition of the Development Corporation to create a heterogeneous social structure in the new town and the provision of luxury flats was seen as a means to this end. They were to be used to attract young middle-class couples without children. Once these couples started their families it was then hoped that they would take a house or a low-rise flat in the town. Thus, whereas in Glasgow the high-rise flats were seen predominantly as a means of accommo-dating the working classes displaced in clearance schemes, in East Kilbride they were to provide an 'urbane' atmosphere for the young executive.

Cumbernauld was designed within an entirely different climate of planning thought to that which had existed when East Kilbride was founded. Gone were the low-density ideals of the 1930s and 1940s. This was partly a fashionable reaction, especially amongst the architec-tural profession, to what by then had become a form of conventional wisdom. But, as in the case of Glasgow, there were more pragmatic reasons for adopting a newer planning philosophy. The Cumbernauld area was chosen in preference to other potential sites in the region because, it was argued, it would create only the minimum disturbance to agriculture. The site was small (4,150 acres, compared with 10,200 acres at East Kilbride) and on very hilly terrain.[60] It was consequently an ideal location for exploring high density concepts within the context of a new town. The original target population for Cumbernauld was set at 50,000, and the original area allocated for housing was 587 acres, i.e. net residential densities would have to be in the order of eighty-six persons to the acre. On the basis of these figures Cumbernauld has gained the reputation of being a high-density settlement, although when compared with the redeveloped parts of central Glasgow as well as with some of the recently-built outer areas, its reputation becomes somewhat over-shadowed. But certainly its density was considerably higher than in other new towns built before it and indeed since. Yet what did this mean in terms of the proportion of flats? They were to play a relatively insignificant role although for different reasons and without the crusading zeal of East Kilbride. At East Kilbride cottages with gardens were seen as an integral part of low-density planning. At Cumbernauld, Hugh Wilson, the town's Chief Architect/Planner, argued that compactness and urbanity could be achieved by building terraced houses. Thus it was noted in the First Addendum to the Preliminary Planning Proposals that:

'Consideration of the land forms, foundation problems, sunlight standards, methods of access to housing arising out of the communications system of the town and the need to provide the maximum privacy and convenience for the inhabitant leads to the conclusion that the general pattern of housing should be of houses on the ground.'[61]

Unfortunately the Cumbernauld Development Corporation has not published figures showing the number of flats it has built, but according to the 1966 Sample Census, 35 per cent of all dwellings in the Cumbernauld District shared blocks.[62] Clearly the intention of the original planning proposals have in this respect been adhered to more satisfactorily than at East Kilbride. But as at East Kilbride, Cumbernauld Development Corporation also thought it desirable to build luxury flats in multi-storey blocks for childless couples. To date, eleven twelve-storey blocks have been completed and one of twenty storeys.

Conclusion

The most significant point to emerge from the first section of this chapter was the very high proportion of dwellings sharing common buildings in all parts of contemporary Scotland compared to England and Wales. Part of this was the inheritance of the nineteenth century which bequeathed to Scotland a substantial volume of tenements. And they themselves derived from a much older tradition that had its Scottish origins in the seventeenth century. It was the inability of Edinburgh to expand outwards that created the tradition. But a land shortage was not the reason why the tenement took root in the Clyde Valley, or indeed elsewhere in the country, during the eighteenth and nineteenth centuries. The Clyde Valley, it is true, is surrounded by mountains, steep hills and the sea, which restrict its potential building area far more than in most English regions. Even so that did not appear to have been a significant factor during the nineteenth century. A much more convincing explanation of the popularity of the tenements in those years is that in relation to the demand they were the most economical form of accommodation to provide. But the high residential densities that resulted created massive social problems, so much so that once the local authorities were given Exchequer grants to help them build council houses, there was a sharp reaction to building tenements. Seeds of Garden City thinking were beginning to grow in Scotland. Nevertheless, it has been shown that in the case of Glasgow, and Glasgow was by no means unique in this respect, when costs made it necessary modified versions of the tenements were again built. In these instances there was a very real continuation of an older tradition and many of the municipal flats built in the 1920s and 1930s were in a direct lineal descent from the tenements of the 1860s and 1870s.

Throughout most of the twentieth century private developers, not experiencing the same constraints as local authorities in acquiring land, and no doubt sensing public taste in these matters, have concentrated on building cottages. But it will be remembered that during the second half of the 1960s 55 per cent of local authority approvals in Scotland were also for cottages. During those years, therefore, the case of Glasgow was untypical. More typical was the case of the new towns of East Kilbride and Cumbernauld, whose Development Corporations continued to affirm that ideally they wanted to build as few flats as possible.

The older housing traditions in Glasgow were returned to during the 1950s with a vengeance, due to a combination of factors. The city was facing a growing land shortage, which was exacerbated by the central administration's insistence on enveloping the Clyde Valley in a green belt whilst simultaneously refusing to provide overspill outlets. Then when the central administration did concede that the land shortage would prevent Glasgow from implementing a necessary and massive slum clearance scheme, almost as a panic measure, a new town was provided and the city was enabled to make overspill agreements with other local authorities. But the Scottish Office feared that these measures would not be sufficient and Glasgow was encouraged to increase the residential densities of subsequent housing schemes by building high-rise blocks of flats. This was a satisfactory outcome as far as Glasgow was concerned because the city was still reluctant to lose population and the building of tower blocks enabled the Corporation to retain a high annual housing output.

In many respects Glasgow was unique amongst the other cities and industrial burghs of the country. Glasgow had the largest population as well as the largest social problems to deal with. It was also the only Scottish local authority empowered to export population under the 1957 Act. Yet elements of all the factors which were responsible for tenements being built in Glasgow in the 1940s and tower blocks of flats in the 1960s were present in other cities and burghs, but especially those in the central belt.

Throughout the 1960s, however, it was realised that there were many disadvantages, some would have argued evils, associated with high-rise living. Recently, in an address on 'alienation', Jimmy Reid, one of the leaders in the Upper Clyde Shipyard 'work-in', has noted that:

'When you think of some of the high-rise flats around us, it can hardly be an accident that they are as near as one could get to an architectural representation of a filing cabinet.'[63]

In 1969 a Research and Development Group of the Ministry of Housing supported the view that living off the ground was least satisfactory for families with children. A year later the National Society for the Prevention of Cruelty to Children reported that life in high-rise flats could produce difficulties in children. In the same year the Working Party on Community Problems appointed by the Corporation of Glasgow and the Secretary of State concluded that grave social problems could arise through living in multi-storey flats.[64] The Scottish Office then began to have doubts about the advisability of encouraging the building of tower blocks and the Exchequer subsidies were changed. The 1957 Housing Act was modified by the 1962 Housing (Scotland) Act, which for administrative convenience, more than anything else, fixed the multi-storey subsidy at £40 per flat per annum extending over a sixty-year period. In addition a subsidy of £60 per acre was paid on each site where development costs were over £4,000 per acre. £34 was made available for each £1,000 extra on site costs.[65] However, by the 1967 Housing (Financial Provisions etc.) Scotland Act, although the additional subsidies for expensive sites remained the same, the multi-storey subsidy was reduced to £30.[66] In view of inflation and the increased rates of interest, effectively this act drastically reduced the financial incentive to build high.

Such was the mounting pressure during the late 1960s and early 1970s against high-rise building that Glasgow decided to erect no more high-rise blocks. East Kilbride and Cumbernauld have also taken this decision. In the case of Glasgow, the Corporation may revert to building proportionately more low-rise flats, perhaps another modified version of the tenement. Alternatively the Corporation could return to the housing of the 1920s and once more provide a substantial volume of cottage-type dwellings. In very recent years an increasing number of Scots have become owner-occupiers and to do this they have left the cities and industrial towns and have moved to commuter settlements. This has lowered the demand for municipal property in the towns and cities and so has reduced some of the pressure to build high-rise blocks. If this trend of 'automatic decentralisation' continues then arguably cottage-type dwellings will appear in increasing numbers beyond the city and municipal boundaries as well as inside. The nineteenth- and twentieth-century tenements as well as the flats in the tower blocks will continue to dominate the housing environment of Scotland for many years to come. But perhaps the tide is beginning to turn and traditional multi-dwelling building in Scotland is on the wane. The anti-tenement feeling generated at the beginning of this century may at last have become effective.

Appendix 8.1   Housing Types Planned for Comprehensive Development Areas up to 1969.

Comprehensive Development Areas	Date of Written Report	Grand Total of all Dwellings Planned to be Built	No Houses in Tower/Slab Blocks	No Tower/ Slab Blocks	Comments
Hutchesontown/ Part Gorbals	1956	3,154	1,800	25	14 tower blocks containing 72 houses; 11 slab 72 houses; 2,3,4 storey devel. containing 1,354 houses.
Pollokshaws	1957	2,222	1,264	18	17 tower blocks containing 1,224 houses; 1 slab 40 houses; 2,3,4 storey devel. 948 houses.
Anderston Cross	1959	1,165	819	7	7 multi storey slab blocks containing 819 houses; 2,3,4 storey devel. 346 houses.
Townhead	1962	2,000	2,000	4	Also included no. of slab blocks 6–9 storeys high.
Cowcaddens	1963	600	Figures not given	Figures not given	Houses for childless households partly in multi storey blocks.
Woodside	1963	1,985	Figures not given	Figures not given	In form of tower, slab and terrace blocks, some as maisonettes.
Royston	1964	1,398	Figures not given	Figures not given	Houses in form of tower, slab and terrace blocks.
Lauriston/Gorbals	1965	3,000	Figures not given	Figures not given	In form of tower and slab blocks.
Govan	1969	3,500	Figures not given	Figures not given	In form of walk-up flats and maisonettes and additional point blocks and maisonette integrated with commercial devel.

Source: Corporation of the City of Glasgow, *Comprehensive Development Areas Written Reports*, 1956–1969

Notes

1. I should like to thank Sir Robert Grieve, of Glasgow University, and Mr I.R. Patterson, of Glasgow Corporation, for their advice on key aspects of this paper. I am also grateful for the help given by Mrs Norma Wilson in preparing the Maps and Charts. Thanks are also due to Miss Elizabeth Mitchell for her comments after very thorough reading of a preliminary draft. Remaining defects in fact, interpretation and style are of course my sole responsibility.

2. Based on, General Register Office, Sample Census 1966, *England and Wales, Housing Tables, Part I*, H.M.S.O., London, 1968, Table 6.

3. Based on, General Register Office, Edinburgh, Sample Census 1966, Scotland, *Housing Tables*, H.M.S.O., Edinburgh, 1968, Table 6.

4. For a general history of working-class housing in Britain during the nineteenth century see, S.D. Chapman (ed.), *The History of Working Class Housing: A Symposium*, David and Charles, Newton Abbot, 1971.

5. Surprisingly, it is no easy matter to compare the building of flats in England with those in Scotland during the post-war period. No figures seem to be readily available on the numbers started, under construction or completed. Such statistics are not given in the *Housing Returns for Scotland* (issued up to 1962 by the Department of Health for Scotland and thereafter by the Scottish Development Department). The only recourse, therefore, is to use the figures based on the approvals granted by the central government to tenders submitted by local authorities, new towns, or Scottish Special Housing Association. Those for Scotland for 1960 onwards are available in Ministry of Housing and Local Government, Scottish Development Department and Welsh Office, *Housing Statistics Great Britain* (published by H.M.S.O., London) first issued in 1966. Comparable English statistics, going back to 1953, are also available from this source.

6. *Housing Statistics, Great Britain*, No.8, January 1968, Table 9.

7. Ibid., Table 10.

8. *Housing Statistics, Great Britain*, No.24, February 1970, Tables 10 and 11.

9. For figures see, *Housing Statistics, Great Britain*, No.8, January 1968, Table 9. Strictly speaking a multi-storey block of flats in Scotland (a definition used in order to assess Government grants) is one with six or more storeys (see, Scottish Development Department, *Report for 1962*, Cmnd.2004, H.M.S.O., Edinburgh, 1963, p.31). Unfortunately such is the breakdown of the figures in the *Housing Statistics* that it is not possible to calculate the number of houses in blocks with six or more storeys for England. Consequently the nearest alternative is used (i.e. blocks with five or more storeys) in order to note the comparison.

10. *Housing Statistics, Great Britain*, No.8, January 1968, Table 10.

11. *Housing Statistics, Great Britain*, No.18, February 1972, Tables 10 and 11.

12. *Housing Statistics, Great Britain*, No.20, February 1971, Table 2.

13. The Royal Commission on the Ancient Monuments of Scotland, *The City of Edinburgh*, H.M.S.O., Edinburgh, 1951, p.xlviii.

14. One of the best and perhaps most colourful histories of Edinburgh Castle is still, James Grant, *Memorials of the Castle of Edinburgh*, William Blackwood, London, 1850, although for a study of its relationship with the burgh see also, M. Wood, 'Growth of the City to the Sixteenth Century' in *Studies in the Development of Edinburgh*, published for the Institute of Public Administration, Edinburgh and East of Scotland Regional Group, William Hodge, London, 1939.

15. For general description of the founding of burghs in Scotland and their association with castles see, William Croft Dickinson, *Scotland from Earliest*

Times to 1603, Thomas Nelson, London, 1961, Chap. XII.

16. Some, however, have argued that the tenement arrived in Scotland from Central Europe via Holland; see C.A. Oakley, *The Second City*, Blackie and Sons, London, 1946, p.47.

17. This point is made in, *Statistical Account of Scotland*, Vol.I, Blackwood, Edinburgh, 1845, p.644.

18. David Buchanan, 'A Description of Edinburgh', translated by P. Hume Brown, in P. Hume Brown (ed.), *Scotland before 1700 from Contemporary Documents*, David Douglas, Edinburgh, 1893, p.314.

19. For an extensive study of the origins and development of Edinburgh's new town see, A.J. Youngson, *The Making of Classical Edinburgh*, University Press, Edinburgh, 1967.

20. Accounts of the economic history of Glasgow are contained in Henry Hamilton, *An Economic History of Scotland in the Eighteenth Century*, Clarendon Press, Oxford, 1963; and R.H. Campbell, *Scotland Since 1707*, Blackwell, Oxford, 1965.

21. Figures demonstrating this point for the second half of the nineteenth century are given in, Robert Baird, 'Housing', in *The Scottish Economy*, ed. A.K. Cairncross, University Press, Cambridge, 1954, p.201.

22. See, Robert Baird, 'Housing', in *The Third Statistical Account of Scotland. Vol.V, The City of Glasgow*, ed. J. Cunnison and B.S. Gilfillan, Collins, Glasgow, 1958.

23. For a description of these conditions see, *Report of the Royal Commission on the Housing of the Industrial Population of Scotland*, Cd. 8731, H.M.S.O., Edinburgh, 1918, Chap.VIII.

24. For an account of this see, John Butt, 'Working Class Housing in Glasgow 1851–1914', in *History of Working Class Housing*, and C.M. Allan, 'The Genesis of British Urban Redevelopment with Special Reference to Glasgow', *Economic History Review*, 2nd series, Vol.XVIII, No.3, Dec. 1965.

25. e.g. 1866 and 1890 Police Acts; Police Board Acts of 1873 and 1877, etc.

26. J.R. Kellett, 'Property Speculators and the Building of Glasgow, 1780–1830', *Scottish Journal of Political Economy*, Vol.VIII, 1961.

27. *Roy. Com. on Hsing the Ind. Pop.*, para.466.

28. *Ibid.*

29. *Ibid.*, paras. 643, 644. These quotations were taken from Russell's paper, 'Life in one Room', in *Public Health Administration in Glasgow*, ed. A.K. Chalmers, Glasgow, 1905.

30. *Roy. Com. on Hsing the Ind. Pop.*, para.345.

31. *Roy. Com. on Hsing the Ind. Pop.*, paras. 1778, 1788.

32. The pros and cons of tenements are set out in *ibid.*, para.480.

33. *Ibid.*, para.537. Some of the Commissioners did, however, accept that there was still a place for the one-roomed house.

34. For a study of the various Housing Acts see, R.D. Cramond, *Housing Policy in Scotland 1919–1964*, University of Glasgow Social and Economic Studies, Research Paper No.1, Oliver and Boyd, Edinburgh, 1966.

35. J.B.S. Gilfillan, 'The Site and its Development', *Third Statistical Account, Glasgow*, pp.43–4.

36. For a decription of these inter-war estates see, G.M. Morton, 'The Layout of Glasgow Corporation Housing Schemes 1919–39', Project Essay, submitted as part of the requirements for the Diploma in Town and Regional Planning awarded by Glasgow University, 1968.

37. A.G. Jury, *Housing Centenary, A Review of Municipal Housing in Glasgow from 1866–1966*, The Corporation of the City of Glasgow, 1966, p.61.

38. This has been very vividly described in the well-known novel, by A. McArthur

and H. Kingsley Long, *No Mean City*, Corgi Edition, London, 1961.

39. Town Clerk, *Memorandum on the Preliminary Problems Associated with the Post-war Planning of Glasgow*, Corporation of the City of Glasgow, 1943.

40. Sir Patrick Abercrombie and Robert H. Matthew, *The Clyde Valley Regional Plan 1946*, H.M.S.O., Edinburgh, 1949, para.28.

41. For the green belt concept see, *ibid.*, Chap.3.

43. Its objections were voiced at a public inquiry into the designation of East Kilbride; see, 'Notes of the Proceedings at the Public Local Inquiry before Professor T.A. Taylor', typescript, 1947.

43. For an examination of this whole issue see Roger Smith, 'The Origins of Scottish New Towns Policy and the Founding of East Kilbride', to be published during 1974 in *Public Administration*.

44. Robert Bruce, *First Planning Report to Highways and Planning Committee of the Corporation of the City of Glasgow*, Corporation of the City of Glasgow, 1945, p.59.

45. *Clyde Valley Plan*, esp. Chaps. 7 and 8, and Diagrams 178 and 179.

46. Jury, *loc. cit.*, p.37.

47. T. Hart, *The Comprehensive Development Area*, University of Glasgow Social and Economic Studies, Occasional Paper No.9, Oliver and Boyd, Edinburgh, 1967.

48. The Corporation of the City of Glasgow, *The First Quinquennial Review of the Development Plan 1960. The Survey Report*, Glasgow, 1960, Chap.13, p.4.

49. Acts of Parliament, 5 & 6 Eliz LI 1957 (Public), Housing and Town Development (Scotland) Act, Chap.38.

50. Robert Grieve, 'Planning in Scotland: A Review', *Golden Jubilee Conference of the Scottish National Housing and Town Planning Council*, Peebles, March 1962, p.29.

51. Corporation of City of Glasgow, *Hutchesontown/Part Gorbals Comprehensive Development Area 1956, Written Statement*, Glasgow, 1956, p.4.

52. Elspeth Farmer and Roger Smith, *Glasgow Overspill, 1943–1971*, Urban and Regional Studies Discussion Paper No.6, University of Glasgow, 1972, pp.11–23.

53. East Kilbride Development Corporation, 'Master Plan – Explanation of Proposals', typescript, Nov. 1950.

54. *Ibid.*, para. 53.

55. *Eighth Report of the East Kilbride Development Corporation for period ending 31st March 1955*, House of Commons Paper 39, 1954–55, H.M.S.O., Edinburgh, para.23.

56. *Twelfth Report of E.K.D.C. 31st March 1960*, H.C. Paper 268, 1959–60, H.M.S.O., Edinburgh, 1960, paras, 7, 8.

57. *Sixteenth Report of E.K.D.C. 31st March 1964*, H.C. Paper 309, 1963–64, H.M.S.O., Edinburgh, 1964, para.146.

58. *East Kilbride Development Corporation Minutes*, 22/11/1962, para.2.

59. *Eighteenth Report of E.K.D.C. 31st March 1966*, H.C. Paper 114, 1966–67, H.M.S.O., Edinburgh, 1966, para.20; *Nineteenth Report of E.K.D.C. 31st March 1967*, H.C. Paper 597, 1966–67, H.M.S.O., Edinburgh, 1967, para.21.

60. Department of Health for Scotland, *Draft New Town (Cumbernauld) Designation Order 1955*, H.M.S.O., Edinburgh, 1955, para.9.

61. Cumbernauld New Town, 'Preliminary Planning Proposals, First Addendum Report', 1959 (typescript), p.8.

62. General Register Office Edinburgh, *Sample Census 1966. County Report Dunbartonshire and Renfrewshire*, H.M.S.O., Edinburgh, 1967, Table 5.

63. James Reid. *Alienation*, Rectorial Address delivered in the University of

Glasgow 1972, University of Glasgow, Glasgow, 1972, p.10.
64. Para.9.
65. Acts of Parliament, 10 & 11 Eliz II 1962 (Public), Chap.28, Pt.1, para.5.
66. Acts of Parliament, 15 & 16 Eliz II 1967 (Public 1), Chap.20, Pt.1, para.4.

Index

Abercrombie, Sir Patrick 222-3
Adams and Kelly (architects) 92
Allen, Matthew 27, 34
amenities 133-4, 146, 194
Architect, The 100, 102
architects 25, 34, 36; and working class
    housing 100-102; attitude to flats
    140; influence on flat design 136-9;
    opinion on high flats changes 172;
    their advocacy of high flats 154,
    176; *see also names of specific
    architects*
Architectural Review 172-3
architecture 17, 28, 99-101; Modern
    Movement in 136-9, 154, 155-7;
    neo-Georgian style 138; quality of
    in London 37-8
artisans *see* working class
Artisans' and Labourers' Dwellings Act
    (1875) 74
Ashpitel, Arthur 29
Aspinall, James 64
Association for Improving the
    Dwellings of the Industrious
    classes (Liverpool branch) 65

back to back houses 13, 14, 46, 74,
    96, 181
Baltimore 10-11
Barr, A.W. Cleeve 166-7, 172
Barrow in Furness 90
Belgium 5
Berlin 9
Best, Robin 171-2
Birkenhead 55-63; Brougham Street
    61; Dock Cottages 56-7, 89; Morpeth
    Buildings 59; Mr. Hughes' develop-
    ment 61; Scotch Flats 61
Birmingham 97, 123, 102, 181-206;
    Artisans' Dwellings Inquiry Com-
    mittee 184; Bordesley Green 188,
    Bournville 189; Calthorpe Estate
    182, 203; Chelmsley Wood 202;
    City Architect 200-201, 202; City
    Surveyor and Engineer 197-8;
    Communist Party 199; controversy

over flat location 198;
    decides to build flats 195-7;
    deputation visits flats in other
    cities 133, 134, 193-4; Duddeston
    198, 199; Edgbaston 182, 198,
    193; Emily Street 195; Estates
    Committee 192, 194, 195; Finance
    Committee 194-5; Garrison Lane
    flats 192, 194; Health Committee
    187; House Building Committee
    200; Housing Committee 188-9;
    Improvement Committee 183, 184,
    185, 186-7; Improvement scheme
    183; Labour Group and Party
    194, 195, 196, 198-9, 200, 202;
    land shortage 160, 192-3, 200;
    Medical Officer of Health 186,
    190; Milk Street 186 -7, model
    dwellings 182, 189; Moseley 193;
    Nechells 198, 199; open space
    provision 143; opposition to flats
    185, 188-91, 201-2; 'patching'
    policy 188, 192; Palmer Street
    tenements 189; population
    densities 181-2; private builders
    182-3; Public Works Committee
    190, 193, 199; St. Martins Flats
    134; slum clearance 182; suburban
    housing 188, 192, 200; Trades
    Council 187-8; Unionist Group
    and Party 194, 199, 200
Birmingham Artisans' Dwellings Co. Ltd.
    183
Birmingham Post 196
block dwellings 107; *see also* tenements
Bolt, Joseph 64
Booth, Lawrence 93
Boston (Mass.) 10
British Constructional Steelwork
    Association 128
Bronx 10
Builder, The 23, 25, 27, 34, 36, 37, 59,
    69-70, 92
builders: and high flats 155, 166-8,
    177; private 80, 88, 114, 208,
    236 *see also* local authorities *and
    specific cities*

244